Charles H.H. Wright

Biblical Essays

Or, exegetical studies on the books of Job and Jonah, Ezekiel's prophecy of Gog and

Magog, St. Peter's

Charles H.H. Wright

Biblical Essays
Or, exegetical studies on the books of Job and Jonah, Ezekiel's prophecy of Gog and Magog, St. Peter's

ISBN/EAN: 9783337114558

Printed in Europe, USA, Canada, Australia, Japan

Cover: Foto ©Lupo / pixelio.de

More available books at **www.hansebooks.com**

BIBLICAL ESSAYS;

OR,

Exegetical Studies

ON

THE BOOKS OF JOB AND JONAH, EZEKIEL'S PROPHECY OF GOG
AND MAGOG, ST. PETER'S "SPIRITS IN PRISON," AND
THE KEY TO THE APOCALYPSE.

BY

CHARLES HENRY HAMILTON WRIGHT, D.D.

*Of Trinity College, Dublin; M.A. of Exeter College, Oxford;
Ph.D. of the University of Leipzig;
Bampton Lecturer for 1878 in the University of Oxford;
Donnellan Lecturer (1880-81) in the University of Dublin;
Incumbent of Bethesda Church, Dublin;
Late of St. Mary's, Belfast.*

EDINBURGH:
T. & T. CLARK, 38 GEORGE STREET.
1886.

PRINTED BY MORRISON AND GIBB

FOR

T. & T. CLARK, EDINBURGH.

LONDON, .	HAMILTON, ADAMS, AND CO.
DUBLIN, .	GEO. HERBERT.
NEW YORK, .	SCRIBNER AND WELFORD.

TO THE

Most Rev. Anton Niklas Sundberg,

DOCTOR OF PHILOSOPHY, LAW, AND THEOLOGY;
ARCHBISHOP OF UPSALA; PRIMATE OF SWEDEN; VICE-CHANCELLOR OF THE
UNIVERSITY OF UPSALA, ETC.,

IN MEMORIAM
OF THE
GREAT UNIVERSITY FESTIVAL AT UPSALA, 1877;

IN RECOGNITION OF
THE ARCHBISHOP'S HIGH PERSONAL QUALITIES AS A SCHOLAR
AND A CHURCHMAN;

IN TOKEN OF ADMIRATION
FOR THE
CHURCH OF SWEDEN, OVER WHICH HE PRESIDES,
ON ACCOUNT OF
ITS RETENTION OF THE ANCIENT EPISCOPAL GOVERNMENT, ITS
PROTESTANT DOCTRINES, AND EVANGELICAL TRUTH;

AND

AS A MARK OF ESTEEM
FOR
THE SWEDISH NATION, TO WHICH THE WRITER IS ALLIED BY
MARRIAGE WITH A DAUGHTER OF ONE OF SWEDEN'S DISTINGUISHED
MEN OF SCIENCE,

THE LATE NILS WILHELM ALMROTH,
KNIGHT OF THE NORTH STAR,
GOVERNOR OF THE ROYAL MINT, STOCKHOLM;

This Volume

IS, BY PERMISSION,

DEDICATED BY THE AUTHOR.

INTRODUCTION.

THE object of this volume of Exegetical Studies is to place before English students of the Bible, in a popular form, certain important questions connected with the interpretation of the Writings of the Old and New Testament. The discussion of critical questions, on which scholars only could be competent to form a correct judgment, has, as far as possible, been avoided, though it has been necessary occasionally to notice such points in the footnotes. The "Studies," therefore, contained in the volume are rather to be regarded in the light of articles written for the general reader, in which only portions of the topics discussed are brought under review, than as scientific monographs, in which greater fulness of detail would justly be required. It is the aim of the writer to stir up earnest inquiry, to stimulate religious thought, to remove difficulties from the path of the intelligent believer in the Sacred Scriptures, and to point out some general principles which may lead to a better understanding of the Hebrew prophets.

The chapter on the Book of Job is a revised and corrected edition of a sermon-essay contained in a volume published in 1864, when the writer was British Chaplain at Dresden.

Its purpose is to point out the meaning of the Book of Job as a whole. It was impossible to do more within the limits within which it was necessary to restrict the volume. It will, therefore, not be considered strange that no notice has been there taken of important contributions to the literature of that book made by the great German critics, such as Delitzsch, Ewald, and Merx, or to the popular English commentary of Cox, or to the more recent and very suggestive work of a namesake, the Rev. G. H. Bateson Wright, M.A., of Queen's College, Oxford (London: Williams & Norgate, 1883). The "study" as now published is, in some respects, indeed, a review of the able commentaries on Job written by Rev. Professor A. B. Davidson, D.D., LL.D., of New College, Edinburgh. The writer differs, however, decidedly from some of the views of that excellent scholar, especially in his conception of Satan as represented in the Book of Job.

The second study in the volume, namely, that on "the Book of Jonah considered from an allegorical point of view," will probably be of more general interest. It is necessary, however, in this Introduction to supplement to a considerable extent the arguments presented in that "study." For as the proof-sheets were passing through the press, a new work on the subject came into the hands of the writer, of which he was unable to avail himself in the body of the work, viz. *Jonah (eine alt-testamentliche Parabel) aus dem Urtext übersetzt und erklärt*, von Prof. Dr. Friedrich Bergmann in Strassburg. Strassburg: Verlag von Treuttel und Würtz, 1885. Moreover the attention of the author was at the same time directed towards another work, with which he had not been previously acquainted, and which requires a more extended notice, namely *Studies in the Book of Jonah; a Defence and an Exposition*, by R. A. Redford, M.A., LL.B., Professor of Systematic Theology and Apologetics, New College, London (Hodder & Stoughton, 1883).

The perusal of the latter work compels the writer to state in plain terms what he would otherwise have preferred his readers to have discovered for themselves, namely that the essay in this volume was designed to be a "defence" of the Book of Jonah. The object which the writer had in view was to point out—without prejudice to the opinion popular in this country, which regards the Book of Jonah as a purely historical narrative—that there was a safer line of defence, which ought not to be neglected by an apologist of Sacred Scripture. The Book of Jonah, whatever is affirmed as to its historical character, is of much more importance regarded as an historico-symbolical prophecy, or, in other words, as a divinely-constructed allegory, in which the past history of Israel is described, the future of Israel depicted, and, as a necessary consequence thereof (see pp. 62–65), the history of Israel's Messiah delineated.

It is generally conceded that a genuine historical narrative may be treated also allegorically, and the sacred writers themselves have actually expounded historical facts in a similar manner.

The essay was originally drawn up with the view of applying this principle to the Book of Jonah. It was thought well to sketch the leading arguments presented by Dr. Pusey in favour of the historical credibility of the book. The writer considered it better to leave the first section of his "study" in the form it was originally drawn up, inasmuch as the statement on p. 39 (though apparently inconsistent with the ultimate conclusion) is, as it stands, perfectly defensible.

It is no fault of the author, that, however inclined a reader may be to endorse the arguments presented by Dr. Pusey (the most learned and able defender of the historical credibility of the narrative), he cannot rise from the perusal of those arguments without feeling, to use the words of Professor Redford, that "the element of the ludicrous and grotesque is to us almost inseparable from the narrative of Jonah." Professor Redford, who is a defender of the historical truth of the story, adds very naïvely: "this we must do our best to overcome." Later on in his work he remarks: "There are wonderful instances of fish swallowing the bodies of men, and in some cases throwing them out alive. But it does not seem of any importance to dwell on such narratives, as Dr. Pusey has done, for they provoke in some minds a feeling of repulsion, which forbids the calm consideration of the text itself" (*Studies in the Book of Jonah*, p. 25, and p. 33).

Prebendary Huxtable, in the *Speaker's Commentary*, also admits the "grotesque" character of the narrative. He observes: "We may in all reverence infer that this most strange and otherwise utterly unaccountable circumstance was ordered by Divine Providence for the very purpose of furnishing a typical prediction in which both the Lord Jesus Himself and His Church, as taught by Him, should recognise the distinct foreshadowing of His preordained death and resurrection. The all-but consummated sacrifice of Isaac by his father is a piece of history which stands in this respect by the side of Jonah's three days' burial in the fish. Either narrative, if regarded by itself, shocks all the sense of probability; either, when regarded as typical, is seen to be in strict accordance with the main purpose of Divine revelation."

Whatever truth may be found in Mr. Huxtable's statement with respect to the narrative contained in the Book of Jonah, we are very far from admitting the justice of his remarks on the story of Abraham's sacrifice of Isaac contained in the Book of Genesis. The historic truthfulness of the latter narrative is quite capable of defence without any recourse being had to the typical interpretation of the event.[1]

As Professor Redford is the latest and most uncompromising champion of the popular view, it is well to note his further remarks on the miraculous preservation of Jonah. He writes (p. 33): "Those who wish to put together the facts and opinions which prove the possibility of a human body being held inside a 'great fish,' have only to read the evidence adduced by Dr. Pusey in his Introduction to Jonah. We desire to lay no special stress on such facts, as relieving the difficulty of faith, because the main point is left untouched by them, how a man could be preserved alive in the body of a fish for three days and three nights. But then, was he alive? The language of the psalm which Jonah offered up as thanksgiving seems to imply that he was either actually dead, or in a state of unconsciousness."[2]

---

[1] We have discussed the subject here referred to in an article on "The Old Testament and Human Sacrifices" in the *British and Foreign Evangelical Review* for July 1884. That article, together with a later one on "Human Sacrifices in the Old Testament," which appeared in the same Review for January 1885, was intended, by a discussion of the Biblical passages, to supplement an article in the *Nineteenth Century* for November 1883 on "The Jews and the Malicious Charge of Human Sacrifice." In the last-named article the writer gave a sketch of the remarkable trial of ten Jews in Hungary, on the charge of having murdered a Christian maiden in order to obtain her blood for purposes connected with the Jewish ritual, and gave an outline of the remarkable controversy in Germany, aroused by the false statement made by Prof. Rohling of Prag that human sacrifices were commended in Rabbinical writings as meritorious in the sight of God.

[2] In a state of coma or unconsciousness a man is generally supposed to require as much, or nearly as much, air as when conscious.

Mr. Redford admits "the poetic hyperbole of the composition," but argues that the language used in the hymn of Jonah "points to the natural fact of death, or insensibility." He maintains that narrative describes either (1) "a maintenance supernaturally of life in circumstances which would naturally involve death, or (2) a miraculous suspension of animation for some forty-eight hours or more; or (3) a revival of an extinguished life, a literal raising of Jonah from the dead" (*Studies*, p. 22). In the commencement of his work Mr. Redford promised to "carefully discuss" this subject, but he has not done so. In several passages towards the close of his book, however, he reaffirms his belief that Jonah was "actually raised from the dead," although he is not certain that such was the "popular belief" of the Jews in the days of our Lord (p. 286).

But the novel theory that Jonah when swallowed up by the fish was soon deprived of life, and that he was afterwards raised from the dead when vomited forth on the dry land, is opposed to the tenor of the whole narrative. The psalm of Jonah may indeed have been composed "entirely *ex post facto*." It may be "a recollection of the rapid thoughts which passed through the mind of the prophet as he sank in the waters." But the expressions in the second part of that psalm are decidedly opposed to the idea that the life of the prophet was taken away even for a season. Mr. Redford, indeed, admits that the words of ver. 1 "if taken literally suppose a state of consciousness." His method of getting over the difficulty, by asserting that the Hebrew phrase can be explained "without forcing" to mean "when Jonah came out of the bowels of the fish," does speak much for his knowledge of Hebrew. The adoption of the theory of an actual resurrection of Jonah from the state of death, would not lessen the difficulties which beset the path of those who maintain the Divine inspiration and authority of the Book of Jonah.

The most formidable difficulties (see pp. 71, 72) in the way of regarding the Book of Jonah to be a record of historical facts, do not arise from the miracles therein recorded, though, according to Professor Redford, they partake of "the element of the ludicrous and grotesque." The greatest difficulty is the absence of the slightest allusion in any other part of the Old Testament to the mission on which Jonah was sent, notwithstanding its marvellous accompaniments, and its wonderful success. For if those be facts of history, the mission of Jonah was the most stupendous event which ever happened to any of the Hebrew prophets. Why should such a mission have been passed over in utter silence in the historical books of the Old Testament, in which matters of far inferior importance are related circumstantially? Is it moreover conceivable that the prophets who prophesied so much concerning Assyria should never have alluded to such a fact, if it were a simple matter of history? But just as the defenders of the credibility of the story, as Mr. Redford has well pointed out, have made no attempt to meet the chief difficulty in it, namely, the preservation of Jonah *alive* for three full days within the interior of the fish (while citing instances enough to prove that a man could be swallowed whole and entire)—so the advocates of the historical view of the book have not honestly faced the difficulty with which that theory has to contend, namely, the silence of Scripture.

If, however, it can be shown satisfactorily that the book was originally intended as an allegory, and that the allegory itself is a prophecy, the sneers so often levelled at the book by sceptics fall harmlessly to the ground. The beauty of its diction, the sublimity of its teachings (which have been pointed out by Ewald), the grandeur of its doctrines, its marvellous anticipations of the events which occurred in the morning of Christianity, all combine to give it a high position among the products of Divine inspiration.

Mr. Huxtable is, indeed, justified in maintaining that there is no need to be startled if no confirmation of the history is found in the Assyrian inscriptions, inasmuch as from the nature of those inscriptions "a merely moral or religious element is not to be looked for" in them. But it is significant that no reference is made to the history of Jonah's mission by any of the successors of that prophet, and that no mention whatever is made in the book itself of the name of the king of Nineveh then upon the throne.

Mr. Redford observes that "the gist of the whole

narrative is the *Divine dealing with Jonah* as the representative of His people. As an incident in the life of an individual, it would be moral history; but as it is, it is a profoundly significant parable, pointing to the solemn responsibilities of Israel as the messenger of Divine mercy to the world" (p. 23). Later on in his work he remarks, "The admission that the whole can be viewed as a parable, does not militate, in the least degree, against the truthfulness of the story, but rather lends it a very special character" (p. 149). He confesses that the moral identification of the prophet and the people is quite a familiar thought in the whole of the prophetic period. Hence the difficulty, sometimes, of exactly distinguishing what is said of the individual in his personal capacity, and what is said representatively." Mr. Redford has in these remarks come very near the recognition of the truth pointed at in pp. 62 ff. as the key which solves the enigma of the work. He confesses "it is easy to recognise in the Book of Jonah a parable which would very powerfully appeal to the whole nation." Israel might, he says, be described as fleeing from their mission. He asks, " were they not in danger of being plunged into the great, heaving '*sea of troubles*,' where the monster of the deep would await them?" But Mr. Redford has failed to notice that the very incidents of the story are really derived from the allegorical language of the prophets. When constrained by Professor Cheyne's remarks (in an article on Jonah in the *Theological*

Review for 1877) to notice that " the belly of a sea-monster is actually used in Jeremiah (li. 34, 44) as a figure for the captivity of Israel," he has not observed the significance of the fact that the captivity of Israel is there described as the swallowing up of the people by a sea-monster, and that the restoration of the Jews is also spoken of under the figure of a fish vomiting forth its prey alive. He simply says: " Jeremiah may have taken it from Jonah, and the presence of the allusions in his writings confirm, so far, the priority of Jonah " (p. 39).

The suggestion that the passage in Jeremiah is borrowed from the Book of Jonah is crude. But it is worth noting that Mr. Redford considers the conclusion of the latter book " also wonderfully significant." From the typical or parabolic point of view he explains the gourd "' the son of a night,' the mere offspring of changing circumstances," to represent the Jewish legal system. But he surely forgets that a system which was in existence from the very childhood (Hos. xi. 1) of the Hebrew nation could not be represented, even in a parable, by a gourd depicted as only springing up to shelter the prophet when grieving at God's mercy in sparing Nineveh from destruction.

The Rev. T. K. Cheyne, D.D., now Oriel Professor of Exegesis in the University of Oxford, in the articles in the *Theological Review* already referred to, has taken the symbolic view advocated by Bloch (see our note 2 on p. 53), although he has supported it by a myth-theory which is not satisfactory, notwithstanding all that has been urged by that scholar in its favour in his great work on the *Prophecies of Isaiah* (in the notes on Isa. xxvii.) as well as in his observations (on *Jeremiah* li.) in the *Pulpit Commentary*. Prof. Cheyne is moreover the author of the article on Jonah in the ninth edition of the *Encyclopædia Britannica* (1881), and has also in his work on Isaiah called attention to the symbolic meaning of the name *Jonah*, on which much more could be said than has been noted in our study.

Redford asserts that "the whole of the modern critical school of Germany is actuated by a fierce hatred of the supernatural." There are, no doubt, some "German" as well as English critics and men of science who display such "hatred." But as a description of "the modern critical school of Germany" the statement is not correct. However opposed a theologian may himself be to the admission of the idea that a mythical element exists in the Old Testament Scriptures (and we freely confess that we are opposed to the idea), he ought to remember that among the critics who maintain that a mythical element can be traced in Biblical phraseology, there are not a few who possess as firm a faith in "the supernatural," and in the truth of "the miraculous," as any of their opponents. Many of these scholars are believers in the reality of Christ's resurrection from the dead, which is the real test-point of Christian faith. A theologian ought to endeavour to comprehend the standpoint of the writers from whom he may feel constrained to differ. The cause of truth is not advanced by a wholesale condemnation of arguments, the drift of which is sometimes imperfectly understood, as "flimsy criticisms," although such statements may evoke the applause of persons ignorant of the questions at stake. It is also inconsistent for Mr. Redford to comment in one place on the absurdity of regarding proper names like that of Jonah as symbolic (p. 41), while in a later passage he draws deductions from an explanation of the proper names of Elijah and Elisha as indications of "a distinct advance in revelation" (p. 196).

Professor Cheyne admits that the Book of Jonah has a prophetico-allegorical aspect, that "Jonah the recalcitrant prophet may well be a type of offending Israel," and that from a post-exilic point of view the calamities of Israel were naturally seen to have arisen from the abnegation of her prophetic mission. But he has not traced out the allegory in its details. If it should be ultimately proved that Isaiah and Jeremiah and the writer of the Book of Jonah were led to make use of the symbol of the dragon or sea-monster because the cloud-dragon, the seven-headed serpent (also termed Tiamtu, *the sea*, like תְּהוֹם in Gen. i. 2) formed "an essential part of Babylonian, Assyrian, and at least at one period popular Jewish mythology," the correctness of our exposition "would not be in the slightest degree imperilled thereby." Nor is there anything whatever in that idea of Cheyne's derogatory to Divine inspiration.

We see, however, no reason to accept the view propounded by Kuenen, and viewed at least with favour by Cheyne, that the painful circumstances connected with the "mixed marriages" and the divorce of their Gentile wives by the Jews of that period, insisted on by Ezra (Ezra ix., x.)—though the righteousness of that act has sometimes been called in question—led to the composition of the Book of Jonah. There is no statement in the book itself to lead one to the conclusion that it claims Jonah as its author. But though it is evident that the book was written after the restoration from Babylon, there is nothing which can be fairly interpreted as an allusion to the episode of the marriage difficulty. The Book of Jonah, however, contains indications of having been composed at a time when the Jews had been expecting an overthrow of the Gentile power, and when their hopes were for a season disappointed. These indications point to its composition at some date shortly after the governorship of Zerubbabel (see pp. 84–89).

Our attempt to trace the allegory in the second part of the book may be regarded as somewhat novel. The allegorical meaning of the first part of the book has often been more or less distinctly explained. In the second part the interpretation of "the gourd" is the main difficulty. But the importance of the position occupied by Zerubbabel on the occasion of the Return from Captivity, the hopes that naturally centred round his person as the representative of the house of David, the disappointment caused by the early removal of that chieftain from the scene, and the consequent chaotic state of the Jewish colony, will all be clear to those who peruse with attention the Books of Ezra and Nehemiah alongside with those of Haggai and Zechariah. These facts, only slightly glanced at in our study, strongly support the interpretation there given of the gourd which sheltered the prophet.

We have briefly called attention to the striking similarity between the closing scene in the narrative of Jonah and the conclusion of our Lord's parable of the Prodigal Son (see pp. 73, 96, 97). If the latter could be distinctly proved to have been derived from the former, the fact would not be without an important bearing on the question as to the sense in which the Book of Jonah was regarded by our Lord. For as Jonah was indignant because Nineveh was spared, so the elder brother is represented by our Lord as angry because his father had received back the prodigal. If it be urged that the prodigal son cannot signify the Gentiles, because the prodigal in the commencement of the story is stated to have received his share of his father's property (Luke xv. 12, 13), it may be well to observe that there is a striking parallel even in that particular between the description as to Israel and the nations, given in the New Testament parable, and the statements of the Old Testament. For according to the Old Testament the Most High gave also to the nations " their inheritance " (Deut. xxxii. 8). Jehovah meted out to each nation the land of its possession, as well as gave over certain peoples into the hands of others. But while "riches"—the "riches of the Gentiles"—were abundantly vouchsafed to other nations, the most valuable "portion" of "the inheritance" which fell to the lot of Israel was that Jehovah was their God (Deut. xxxii. 9, 12, comp. Ps. xv. 5, 6). All nations, according to the Old Testament statements, possess an equal share in the blessings of nature, such as the sun, moon, and stars (Deut. iv. 19; Ps. xix. 1–6). Compare the New Testament statements in Matt. v. 45; Acts xvii. 26. But the law of the Lord was the special inheritance of Israel (Deut. iv. 20; Ps. xix. 7–11). The believing Jews could not endure in the early days of Christianity that the gift of which they chiefly boasted should be communicated on equal terms to the Gentiles.

It has been too often assumed without consideration that our Lord's references to Jonah (Matt. xii. 39 ff.; Luke xi. 29 ff.) prove that He regarded the incidents of that story to be literal facts. The argument has been briefly noticed on p. 69. But it may here be further remarked that the repentance of the Ninevites mentioned at the close of the book has ever been a difficulty in the way of viewing the narrative as historical. It has been attempted to obviate the difficulty in two ways, either by maintaining the conversion in question to have been "superficial and short-lived" (Huxtable); or by asserting that there is "no reason to suppose that every individual, or even the majority, *literally repented;* for, referring to the pleading of Abraham with God for Sodom, we know that even a small number of true penitents would save the city" (Redford, p. 17; the italics are his own).

But our Lord did not consider the repentance of Nineveh "superficial or short-lived." He spoke solemnly of the penitence of the Ninevites as destined in the day of judgment to condemn the impenitence of the Israelites. The repentance of the Ninevites must, therefore, have been in His view more genuine than the repentance of "Jerusalem and all Judea and all the region about Jordan," who went forth to hear John the Baptist, and "were baptized of him in the river Jordan, confessing their sins" (Matt. iii. 5, 6). For "the men of Nineveh shall stand up in the judgment with this generation, and shall condemn it" (Matt. xii. 41), notwithstanding the marvellous work of John the Baptist three years before. The contrast drawn in that passage shows, as Reuss has observed, that our Lord regarded the story in the Book of Jonah as a significant parable, and referred to the incidents of that story as an English preacher might refer to some detail in the allegories of John Bunyan.

Every striking detail in the narrative of Jonah has its counterpart in expressions employed by the prophets of Israel. The allegory seems to have been mainly constructed from the significant passages in Jer. li. 34, 44. We believe firmly in the book as prophetic in its character, and as pointing onward to Christ. But, even apart from all Christology, the story of the book will, we submit, be seen on fair examination to be an outline in allegorical language of the history of Israel down to the later days of Zechariah. If a key can be shown to fit the wards of a lock, it may be presumed that it (or at least a key of a similar construction) was intended to open the lock in question.

It may be well to note here, in passing, that Mr. Redford denies that the words of our Lord necessarily imply that the sign given to the Ninevites in favour of Jonah's mission was the wonderful deliverance vouchsafed to that prophet. In this he seems to agree with Dr. Samuel Davidson, who, in his *Introduction to the Old Testament* (vol. iii. p. 282), maintains that the only sign vouchsafed was the preaching of Jonah itself. That scholar says: "The Saviour willed that men should believe in Him, and receive His doctrine without external sign or miracle, because His life showed Him to be a divinely-sent messenger; just as Jonah was believed without any further sign. Nothing but the *sign of Jonah* was given to the Pharisees, *i.e.* the call to repentance." We cannot, however, believe that this is a correct statement either of the facts of the evangelical history, or of the meaning of our Lord in His reference to the history of Jonah (see p. 68).

We have felt constrained to notice Professor Redford's book at such length, not for its intrinsic importance, but because we are now specially writing for the English religious public who may peruse that work, and be influenced by its arguments.

Some well-intentioned defenders of Scripture who "have a zeal for God but not according to knowledge" (Rom. x. 2), often maintain that nothing in the Sacred Writings ought to be regarded as allegorical unless distinctly set forth as such. Such objectors forget that allegorical narratives were always wont to be related as historical facts, though the meaning might afterwards in some cases (though not in all) be explained by the narrator. The well-known story which Nathan told to David was in form so natural and truthful that it at once aroused the anger of the monarch, who failed at first to recognise his own likeness in the glass held up to his view (2 Sam. xii. 1–7). The narrative of the wise woman of Tekoa, invented at Joab's suggestion, in order to bring about the reconciliation of Absalom with his father, had a similar effect (2 Sam. xiv.). It, too, was an allegory, but that parable had not to be explained. Similar is the case of the allegorical tale of the prisoner let loose, related by an anonymous prophet to Ahab (1 Kings xx. 39–41), and the grander and more sublime parable of Michaiah the son of Imlah (1 Kings xxii. 19–22). There is still a dispute among the most orthodox commentators whether the narrative at the commencement of Hosea is a description of fact, or is simply allegory; whether Jeremiah in his early days actually visited the Euphrates to hide his girdle in the hole of the rock, or whether that work was only performed in vision (Jer. xiii.). Many things were related as facts which were designed only to be understood as allegories. A remarkable instance will be found noticed on pp. 70, 71. Nor is it strange that such allegories should in process of time have been sometimes mistaken for history.

It is not necessary to say much here about the work of Professor Bergmann of Strassburg. As indicated on the title-page, Bergmann maintains the Book of Jonah to be a religious-philosophical parable. He does not, however, view it as an allegory, and evidently does not regard it either as divinely inspired, or prophetical in its character. According to him, the book was intended as a vindication of the righteousness of God, and sets forth the Divine long-suffering of the rebellious, and His merciful dealings with penitent transgressors.

In Bergmann's treatment of the passages in the Gospels which refer to the story of Jonah, he has reverted to the old rationalistic standpoint, and regards the New Testament reference to Jonah in the fish's belly as introduced by the "short-sighted and wonder-stricken Judæo-Christian," who is supposed to have reduced the Gospel of St. Matthew into its present form.

One specimen may here suffice of the strange fancies which Professor Bergmann ventures to put forward as sober exegesis, and is itself deserving of a place in a museum of curiosities of Biblical interpretation.

According to him, when the sailors in the storm

awoke Jonah and bid him call on his God, had Jonah not been a stubborn character, when he had once recognised that the storm was sent forth for his sake, he would have called on Jehovah for pardon, and God mercifully would have saved him and his comrades from destruction. But Jonah was one of these hard-hearted and self-righteous individuals who are indisposed to acknowledge their own sin, though quick to perceive transgression in others. Jonah preferred to die "like a righteous hero" than humble himself before Jehovah. He determined, therefore, in his pride, to offer himself up as a sacrifice, and gave himself up as "a guiltless offering to the wrath of God." The "heroism" of Jonah would have been worthy of admiration had Jonah, indeed, thrown himself into the breach with a better conscience, but Jonah was "an erring stupid zealot," who, like all religious and political zealots, was zealous from very stupidity, and who in his ignorance offered up himself as self-righteous.

It is unnecessary to discuss such wild fancies, or to criticise seriously the alterations which have to be introduced into the text of the book to give countenance to such interpretations. Professor Bergmann is not likely to find many here or in Germany willing to adopt his line of exegesis.

We must, however, here bring our Introduction to a close. The study on Ezekiel's prophecy of Gog and Magog will, we hope, tend to show that the prophecy is no prediction of the future of Russia, but has a grander and more practical object. The chapter on the Key of the Apocalypse presented in Rev. xii. is a re-issue, in a greatly revised and enlarged form, of an article which appeared in 1880 under a different title in the *Homiletic Quarterly*. These two "studies" will, we hope, point out some of the true principles of prophetic interpretation to those desirous of becoming in reality students of the Biblical prophecies.

The study on "the Spirits in Prison" will best tell its own tale. For obvious reasons, it is a more critical essay than any of the others.

The Author earnestly hopes that this little volume may help to a better understanding of the precious word of inspiration, which was intended to be a lamp unto the believers' feet and light unto their path (Ps. cxix. 105).

33 MESPIL ROAD, DUBLIN,
   March 26, 1886.

CONTENTS.

	PAGE
I. THE BOOK OF JOB,	1

The Book based on historical fact—The opening narrative supplies key to its meaning—Attempts to fill up Scripture statements—All afflictions from God—Satan as the adversary—Not a mere instrument of God's providence—Views of Prof. A. B. Davidson—Old Testament passages explaining prologue—Micaiah's vision—Satan under Divine control—"Sons of God" not angels—The intermarriages in Book of Genesis—"Sons of God" in Old Testament—Times of solemn assembly—The great contest—The accuser and the Advocate—Satan's challenge—Satan inflicts evils on Job—Job as victor in first contest—Satan assails his person—Job's wife—Job still victorious in second trial—The third trial one from the hands of men, Job's friends and their opinions—His opening lament—Reproved by Eliphaz—Job's consciousness of integrity—Bildad's insinuations—Job's reply—Zophar's assertions—The patriarch's indignation—Faith in darkness—Storm in deep waters—Replies of the friends—Job's entreaties—Job accused of gross transgression—Victor in debate—Elihu intervenes—New view of afflictions—Appearance of the Almighty—The problem solved, and yet not solved—Job's repentance and restoration, ... 1-33

II. THE BOOK OF JONAH CONSIDERED FROM AN ALLEGORICAL POINT OF VIEW, . . . 34

§ 1. Introduction—History and allegory—Weakness of objections urged against the credibility of the Book of Jonah—No historical confirmation of its narrative—No reference to the story in heathen legends, ... 34-41

§ 2. The prophet Jonah and his era—The prophetic commission—Jonah's flight—Jonah a representative of Israel—His sleep on the vessel—The storm on the sea of nations—The sea-monster swallows up Israel — The allegory founded on descriptions given in the Hebrew prophets, . 42–56

§ 3. The prayer of Jonah a collection of sentences chiefly from the Psalms — Israel's songs in her exile — The allegory expounded first of Israel, and then of Israel's Messiah, ... 56–66

§ 4. Difficulties in the Book of Jonah regarded as an historical narrative — The New Testament references thereto — The book an allegorical description of Israel's past, and a prophecy of Israel's future, ... 66–74

§ 5. The restoration of Jonah to the prophetic office — His renewed commission — The overthrow of the nations — The voices of the Hebrew prophets — Expectations of the Jews at the restoration from Babylon — Penitent Nineveh — Readiness of the Gentiles to learn religious truths from Israel — Conditional character of prophecy — The gourd or palmchrist of Jonah — The Davidic governor, Zerubbabel the son of Shealtiel, . . . 74–89

§ 6. The Book of Jonah essentially a book of prophecy, and not of history — The judgment announced to the world — The conversion of the Gentiles and the jealousy of the Jews — The great controversy in the early days of the Christian Church — The prophetic allegory of the Prodigal Son and his Elder Brother, . . . 90–98

III. EZEKIEL'S PROPHECY OF GOG AND MAGOG, . . 99

Nations disposed to self-laudation — God the God of all — Israel the only elect nation — Jeremiah on judgments decreed against nations — English national pride — England and Russia — Prophecies supposed to refer to Russia — Apparent evidence in favour of that view — The names Rosh and Russia not identical — Gog in Assyrian inscriptions — Great invasion of Scythians — Their auxiliaries, Gimmeri — Tubal and Meshak — Togarmah — Scythian invasion known to Ezekiel — Gog and Magog names of terror — The latter days or years — Ezekiel's prophecy not designed as literal — Palestine not the only scene of conflict — Gog's exploits and destruction the theme of all the prophets — Gog under Divine control — Absurd explanations of text in Ezekiel — Confederacy of Gog and Magog not one against religion — Its aim filthy lucre — Slave traders on the scent — Absurdly transformed into heroes — Imagery of Ezekiel common to all the prophets, the pestilences — The hailstones and fire — The internecine conflict — The earthquakes — Our Lord's painting of the latter days — The feast of the birds and beasts — The

spoils of the foe—The weapons of Gog's army—
Used for firewood—The great burial-place—The
valley of multitude—Ezekiel on the passengers
—The burial described — Ezekiel's descriptions
partly drawn from Book of Exodus—The prophecy an allegory—The conversion of Israel—
The Messianic age—The picture as seen by
Ezekiel—The Jews often oppressed for love of
money—The days of deliverance, . . 99–137

IV. THE SPIRITS IN PRISON. A study on 1 Pet. iii. 18-20
and iv. 6, ... 138

Dean Plumptre's book — Consensus of modern
scholars — Silence of Scripture on the intermediate state—Orthodox divines and "the larger
hope"—Bishop Horsley—Professor Schweizer of
Zürich — Mistakes of Authorized Version—The
Revised Version—Christ quickened in the Spirit
—The context of 1 Pet. iii. 18-20—Exhortation
in preparation for day of trial—No new truth
revealed — No preaching of Christ to departed
spirits elsewhere referred to — Historical tradition on the descent into hell — Statements of
Hermas—Speculations of Clement of Alexandria
—Justin Martyr—Irenæus—Thaddæus' summary
of faith—Abgar correspondence—Gospel of Nicodemus—No allusion of the Fathers to a preaching to antediluvians — Views of Augustine —
Spirits in prison—Isaiah's prophecy—The pit and
prison—Isaiah and St. Peter—Christ as Spirit,
the Pre-incarnate Word — As head of angels—
In angelic form — Preaching to antediluvians—
Augustine on Noah's preaching—Spirit of Christ
in the prophets — The expression "went,"
πορευθείς—" Spirits *who are* in prison " or "spirits
who were in prison " — Character of antediluvians—" Aforetime disobedient "—Summary of
statements in 1 Pet. iii. 19—Context of the
disputed passage in chap. iv.—The same contrast
drawn as in chap. iii. — The preaching only a
past transaction — The gospel preached — Comparison between Christ and His people—Object
of gospel being preached to early believers —
Ways of God and man—" Preached to the dead "
— Believers only referred to—Other theories—
Limbus patrum—Orthodox theologians and "the
larger hope," 138–197

V. THE KEY TO THE APOCALYPSE, PRESENTED IN THE
VISION OF REV. XII., ... 198
General agreement among expositors — Worthless
expositions—New interpretations of Apocalypse—

Apocalypse not a sealed book—Visions a comfort to Church in all ages—Church and Christ's advent—Prophecy not history written in advance—Events in Book not in chronological order—The six seals—Synchronisms of Mede—Opening of chap. xii.—Work of Church—Her double temptation—Depicted as woman—In heaven—The dragon—Clothed with light—With the sun—Moon under her feet—Crown of stars—The man child, Christ—Christ as Son of the Church—Old Testament parallels—The travailing woman—The man-child of Isaiah—The man-child of Revelation—Christ saved from Satan—Caught up to the throne—Conflicting interpretations of the vision, E. B. Elliott—G. S. Faber—Von Hofmann—Ebrard—Author of "The Parousia"—Archdeacon Farrar—Nero and his name—Zahn's "Studies"—Kliefoth—The dragon swaying Pagan Rome—Weakness of Antichrist's kingdom—The ten horns—The two legs of Daniel's image—The dragon's tail—War in heaven—Old Testament parallels—Rev. xii. and Dan. xii. compared—The victory of Messiah—First and second advent—Victory of Michael—The 1260 days—Two periods of a time, times and a half—The times of the Gentiles—Israel and its Messiah, ... 198-252

INDEXES, ... 253

EXEGETICAL STUDIES.

I.

THE BOOK OF JOB.

MANY interesting questions have been raised concerning the patriarch whose trials and sufferings form the basis of the Book of Job. It has often been maintained that the book is allegorical, and that Job, as an individual, had no historical existence. However incorrect this may be, and however little countenance is given to it by the phenomena of the book, the view cannot in itself be fairly regarded as derogatory to the inspired character of the work, or necessarily opposed to the notices of Job in other parts of Scripture. It is, however, more correct to regard the book as based on historical facts, which have been made use of by the sacred writer in order more vividly to point out some of the general causes which tend to explain the affliction of the upright and righteous on earth.

The narrative given in the prologue (chaps. i. and ii.) supplies the key for the comprehension of the poem that succeeds. But in order to understand that narrative more perfectly, it is necessary to have distinct views upon two points, namely, the character of the malignant being termed "the Adversary," or Satan, and the nature of those designated in Job i. 6, ii. 1, "the sons of God."

It is well to be careful against arbitrarily "reading into" the Book of Job ideas which are only found in later books of Holy Scripture. But it must be remembered at the same time that it is not possible, from the fragmentary references which occur in any book, to give a precise account of the opinions held on all points by the particular author. In the case of the Biblical writers, it is safer, and more in accordance with true criticism, to fill up the fragmentary statements found in one book by the fuller statements made in another, than arbitrarily to fill in the outlines of the picture drawn by one writer with details out of harmony with the general spirit of Biblical literature. If it be unscientific to assert without evidence the absolute harmony of the Biblical writers, it is surely equally unscientific to assume without evidence that the opinions of the several writers are different, if not contradictory.

It is certain that the writer of the Book of Job was strongly impressed with the truth expressed in the saying of Amos, "Shall evil befall a city, and the Lord hath not done it?" (Amos iii. 6). In the Book of Exodus, the sin of Pharaoh in refusing to obey the divine command to "let Israel go" is fully recognised and exposed. But the truth is never for a moment concealed that man, even when violently opposed to the will of God, cannot thwart the carrying out of that will unless by the divine permission. The sacred writer does not regard himself as palliating in any degree the guilt of the Egyptian monarch when he ascribes to the workings of Divine Providence even that king's unwillingness to obey: "The Lord hardened Pharaoh's heart, and he did not let the children of Israel go" (Ex. x. 20).

In accordance with a similar principle, the afflictions of Job are throughout the Book of Job recognised as coming from God, in the sense of having been distinctly permitted by the Almighty. But those sufferings are also represented by the author as the work of Satan, or the Adversary. This latter fact ought not, however, to lead us to identify in any way the work of Satan and that of God. Satan is represented as the doer of the evil, while God is represented simply as having permitted the evil to be done for certain purposes not obscurely hinted at in the book.

In examining into the question who or what is designated in the Book of Job as "the Satan," we must not reject the light afforded by the narrative of the Book of Genesis, in which "the Adversary" is depicted as a serpent at "enmity" with man and seeking his ruin (Gen. iii.). Nor can we leave out of sight the statements in the Book of Leviticus, where Azazel, the evil spirit, is contrasted with Jehovah (Lev. xvi. 8), and the goat laden with the sin of Israel was directed to be sent forth into the wilderness, away from the camp, to be sent back by a symbol to him who was the real originator and cause of Israel's transgression,[1] who had been Israel's tempter, and consequently Israel's foe. Similar in spirit, though not in external form, is the remarkable vision of Zechariah, in which Satan is represented as seeking to prevent the Angel of Jehovah from removing the filthy garments from Joshua the high priest (chap. iii. 1–3), who is there the representative of the Jewish Church. For that vision, in which the Evil Angel is represented in his character of Accuser and Adversary, and in which he receives a solemn rebuke from the Angel of Jehovah, who is also Jehovah, stands in a close connection to the prologue of the Book of Job.[2]

It is therefore not a little surprising that Professor A. B. Davidson should maintain that in the Book of Job "there is no antagonism between God

---

[1] That 'Azazel (עֲזָאזֵל) ought not to be rendered "*scape-goat*," but is to be regarded as the evil spirit, the spirit who has *turned himself away* from God (as the word more probably implies), is tolerably clear from ver. 8, in which he is personally contrasted with Jehovah. There may have been good reasons for the general silence of the Pentateuch on the question of the existence of the Evil One, but the story of the temptation in Gen. iii. is quite enough to prove that the idea of such a Tempter was not unknown to the author or authors of the Pentateuch.

[2] See further remarks on p. 13.

and the Satan," that the Satan represented in that book " is the servant of God represented or carrying out His trying, sifting providence, and the opposer of men *because* he is the minister of God," that he " is a mere instrument in the economy of God's providence, and though represented as a person, his personal standing is only of the slightest consequence. Hence he does not appear in the epilogue. His part was, in the service of God, to try Job; that done, he disappears, having no place assigned to him among the *dramatis personæ* of the poem."[1]

This view of Satan appears " altogether at variance with Old Testament conceptions." Any attempt to construct out of the fragmentary sketches of Satan given in the prologue of the Book of Job a picture different from that set forth in the other Scriptures, is doomed to result in failure. Such fragmentary sketches are not sufficient of themselves to give any complete picture. But they harmonize and fall in with the later revelations on the same subject, and they ought, therefore, not to be treated as diverse or opposed. If it could be proved satisfactorily that the writer of the Book of Job held such a view as that expounded by Professor Davidson, it would be tolerably clear that he must have lived long posterior to the exile. For the doctrine of the author

---

[1] *The Cambridge Bible for Schools and Colleges. The Book of Job, with Notes, Introduction, and Appendix.* By Rev. A. B. Davidson, D.D., LL.D., Professor of Hebrew and Old Testament Exegesis in the New College, Edinburgh, 1884, pp. xxxii., xxxiii. See, however, our remarks on p. 25.

would then look like a philosophical attempt to explain away the conflict between God and Satan, which was certainly taught distinctly after the restoration from Babylon.

There are two passages in the Old Testament which cast no small light upon this portion of the prologue of the Book of Job. These are the vision of Micaiah, the son of Imlah, recorded in 1 Kings xxii. 19–23, and the vision of Zechariah already referred to (Zech. iii. 1–3). In the former passage Jehovah is represented as sitting on His throne, and all the host of heaven standing by Him on His right hand and on His left, when the Lord asks, "Who shall entice Ahab that he may go up and fall at Ramoth-Gilead? And one said on this manner, and another said on that manner. And there came forth the spirit [1] and stood before the Lord, and said, I will entice him. And the Lord said unto him, Wherewith? And he said, I will go forth, and will be a lying spirit in the mouth of all his prophets. And He said, Thou shalt entice him, and shall prevail also: go forth and do so."

The doctrine set forth in Micaiah's vision is not peculiar to that prophet. It is that taught in many parts of the Old Testament and repeated in the New

---

[1] The article is expressed in the Hebrew text. Both the Authorized and the Revised Versions have regarded the article here as generic, and hence have left it untranslated. But it is more likely that it has the usual definite sense. The Evil Spirit was no doubt frequently spoken of among the Israelites, even though it is seldom directly mentioned in Old Testament literature.

(2 Thess. ii. 10–12). It is set forth plainly in Ezek. xiv. 9: "If the prophet be deceived and speaketh a word, I, the Lord, have deceived that prophet, and I will stretch out my hand upon him and will destroy him from the midst of my people Israel." But "the spirit," described by Micaiah as "a lying spirit," was there no "mere instrument in the economy of God's providence." The prophets of lies spoke visions out of their own heart, and not out of the mouth of the Lord (Jer. xxii. 16). Though "sent" in one sense as a judicial punishment upon obstinate transgressors, and permitted in judgment to lead astray a people who had wandered wilfully after their own ways, the false prophets were not "sent" by Jehovah in the higher or true sense of that expression (Jer. xiv. 13–15). Satan, whom our Lord describes as having "from the beginning" of the world's history been "a liar" as well as "a murderer" (John viii. 44), was the "lying spirit" in the mouth of the prophets of Ahab, and "the Adversary," "the Satan," and calumniator of Job.

It is not correct, therefore, to regard Satan in the prologue to the Book of Job as presenting himself before God "to report or to receive commissions," as if he were "that one of God's ministers whose part it is to oppose men in their pretensions to a right standing before God." He is figuratively represented as presenting himself before God in the moral character of "the serpent," who having chosen evil as his good is compelled to eat dust all the days of his miserable life (Gen. iii. 14; Isa. lxv. 25); but who, notwithstanding, has to come trembling, like one of "the crawling things of the earth," out of his close places unto the Lord (Micah vii. 16, 17). He acts, indeed, as "the Accuser," but his weakness is shown by his inability without special permission to "hurt" the Lord's people (Isa. xi. 9). Hence, in New Testament times, those who were once enrolled in "the city of God" had to be "cut off" from that "city," and delivered over to Satan, ere they could fall fully under his power (comp. 1 Cor. v. 3-5; 1 Tim. i. 20). For in the higher sense even Satan is compelled to await God's commands, and to do God's will, though he knows it not, like his agent Caiaphas (John xi. 49-52), or like the storm-winds of the heavens, or the four war-chariots, or world-empires, which are also represented as "going forth from standing before the Lord of the whole earth" (Zech. vi. 5).[1]

"The sons of God" spoken of in Job i. 6 and ii. 1, have been generally explained to mean "the angels." But there is grave reason to believe that the popular interpretation is incorrect. The precise expression found in these two passages occurs elsewhere only in Gen. vi. 2, 4. The phrase occurs with a slight variation also in Job xxxviii. 7.[2] In the latter passage

---

[1] See my *Bampton Lectures on Zechariah* on the passage.

[2] The expression בְּנֵי הָאֱלֹהִים, "*sons of the Elohim*" or *God*, occurs only in Gen. vi. 2, 4 and in Job i. 6, ii. 1; בְּנֵי אֱלֹהִים, which may be regarded as identical, is the phrase found in Job xxxviii. 7. Another expression, בְּנֵי אֵלִים, is found in Ps. xxix. 1, lxxxix. 6, and is rendered in both the Authorized and Revised Versions

the usage of Hebrew parallelism leads us to interpret the phrase to mean "the stars."[1] For the stars are represented there as rejoicing in chorus at the creation of a new planet. The sacred writer represents the Almighty as asking Job—

> "Where wast thou when I laid the foundations of the earth?
> Declare, if thou hast understanding.
>
> . . . .
>
> When the morning stars sang together,
> And all the sons of God shouted for joy?'

Similar poetical figures, like this of the stars rejoicing and shouting for joy, are found in other passages, as in Isa. xxxv. 1, 2, where the wilderness is spoken of as rejoicing with joy and singing; or in Isa. lv. 12, where the trees of the field are described as clapping their hands for joy. In Gen. vi. 2, 4, "the sons of God" are described as intermarrying with "the daughters of men," which intermarriages led

(following most of the ancient expositors) by "*the mighty*," and "*the sons of the mighty.*" The Psalmist, however, refers probably to the kings and mighty men of the earth. This view is strongly confirmed by the comparison of Ps. xxix. 1 with Ps. xcvi. 7. Many commentators, however, take an opposite view, and consider the angels to be referred to. The phrase בְּנֵי אֵלִים has been rendered, as in the margin of the Revised Version, *sons of God*, but it is in any case not identical with בני האלהים.

[1] There is no objection whatever to the stars, as created by God, being spoken of as *sons of God*. For in Job xxxviii. 28, God is, by implication, as Creator, referred to as the Father of the rain and dew. *Father* is sometimes used in the sense of *creator*. Hence the prophet remonstrates with the idolatrous Jews on the folly of calling an idol their father (Jer. ii. 27), and repentant Israel speaks of God as their Father (Isa. lxiii. 16, lxiv. 8), as having been their Creator as well as their Redeemer.

to an awful increase of wickedness, and ultimately caused the Lord to destroy the earth with the flood. Angels cannot be signified in that passage. The notion of fleshly intercourse between angels and earthly women is foreign to the sobriety of the Old Testament narratives, though quite in accordance with heathen mythologies. Our Lord's words in reference to the righteous, "in the resurrection they neither marry nor are given in marriage, but are as the angels of God in heaven" (Matt. xxii. 30; Mark xii. 35; Luke xx. 35, 36), are, in our opinion, decisive against the theory. The attempt to explain that declaration as if it referred only to angels in their present or final state, and not to angels in some previous condition, is in itself destructive of the hypothesis.[1] Nor can we fairly interpret our Lord's words as referring merely to what angels do, without giving any indication as to the powers which they may possess in a dormant condition. Our Lord's words, fairly interpreted, necessarily imply that among those higher beings there is no distinction similar to that known as sex in this lower sphere. Hence we cannot conceive under any circumstances that angels could be tempted by the fascinations of earthly beauty.[2]

[1] For in that case the individuals referred to were not angels, but in some lower condition; and yet, according to the hypothesis, the phrase "sons of God" is supposed to indicate the angels as a higher class of beings than men. It will, moreover, scarcely be maintained that a class of beings, not elsewhere mentioned in Scripture, is referred to in Gen. vi.

[2] The ablest book written on this subject in English is from the pen of an Irish clergyman. Though the conclusions Mr. Fleming

If, then, "the sons of God" in Gen. vi. are not angels, they must needs have been the professors of religion in that early day, who, generally speaking, must have belonged to the family of Seth; while "the daughters of men" alluded to must have been fascinating women belonging to the family of Cain. The two families, who had been divided, owing to the crime of Cain, were in the days of Enos again united before one common family altar. This appears to be the meaning of the obscure text, "then they began to call on the name of Jehovah" (Gen. iv. 26). The Israelites, as the professors of the true religion, are similarly termed in Hos. i. 10, " the sons of the living God," and were called by Moses, " the sons of the Lord your God" (Deut. xiv. 1). Asaph in his psalm, in his address to God, alludes to "the generation of thy sons" (Ps. lxxiii. 15), and Solomon also speaks of the Lord's "sons" (Prov. xiv. 26). The prophet Isaiah represents God as thus remonstrating with Israel: "I have nourished and brought up sons, and they have rebelled against me" (Isa. i. 2).[1] See also Isa. xliii. 6; Jer. iii. 19. We are justified, in face of

---

has arrived at on the subject are very different from our own, his book exhibits much reading, and is worthy of careful perusal. Its title is, *The Fallen Angels and the Heroes of Mythology, the same with "the sons of God" and "the mighty men" of the Sixth Chapter of the First Book of Moses.* By the Rev. John Fleming, A.B., Incumbent of Ventry and Kildrum, Diocese of Ardfert; Rural Dean; and Irish Society's Missionary. Dublin: Hodges, Foster, & Figgis, Booksellers to the University, 1879.

[1] In order that the general reader may not be misled by the use of *children* in some cases and *sons* in others, we have translated in these passages the Hebrew word throughout by *sons*.

such passages, and of the usage of the New Testament in which the expression "sons of God" is used exclusively of men, and not of angels, in insisting that the expression "sons of God" ought, if possible, to be interpreted both in Gen. vi. and in Job of men and not of angels.[1]

Though it would be quite in accordance with the vision of Micaiah, already alluded to (pp. 6, 7), to explain the passages in Job which speak of the meeting together of the sons of God to present themselves before the Lord as an assembly of the angels before the divine throne, assembled there to receive the divine commands, like the angel-riders in the first of Zechariah's visions (chap. i. 8–11), it is, nevertheless, more in harmony with the usage of Scripture (and more consonant with the epilogue of the Book of Job, in which all mention both of "the sons of God" and of the Adversary is dropped out of sight) to explain "the sons of God" in the prologue as simply meaning the professors of religion in the time of Job. Even in those early patriarchal days in which Job is supposed to have lived, there appear to have been special places where persons assembled for divine worship, and also set times appointed by mutual consent, if not by divine direction, for the solemn worship of God.

---

[1] Dr. Samuel Lee of Cambridge, in his *Commentary on Job*, approximates to this view. For he notes that "sons of God" in the passage in Job may mean *men*, but men transferred to the higher sphere. The latter suggestion is, however, utterly unnecessary.

At such a time of solemn assembly, when God's professing people were gathered together for holy worship, the sacred writer represents two great spiritual beings as also present. He draws aside the curtain which hides the invisible from the visible, the spiritual from the material world, and exhibits to the reader, in the midst of the congregation of worshippers, the Great Accuser of the brethren and the Great Advocate of the people of God.

In two other passages of Scripture the same realities are presented. In Zechariah (chap. iii. 1-5) the Angel of the Lord is represented as contending with the Adversary, the subject of dispute there being the Jewish Church, or the body mystical of Moses, clad with filthy garments.[1] In Rev. xii. 7-11 a warfare is depicted as carried on in heaven between the great archangel Michael, or Christ, with His angels or servants, against Satan, under the figure of the great dragon, with his angels or servants, which results in the victory of the former and the defeat of the latter. In the latter passage, too, the Evil One is referred to in the words: "the accuser of our brethren is cast down, which accused them before our God day and night."

In such an assembly, where the good and evil angels met face to face, each on his peculiar business, the Angel of the Covenant (who in Zechariah is also called by the sacred name of Jehovah, the pre-incarnate

---

[1] See the *Bampton Lectures on Zechariah*, pp. 53-59, in which this question is discussed at length.

Word) demanded of Satan: "Whence comest thou?" —from doing what deeds of evil hast thou come, even here, to pervert the right ways of the Lord? With unabashed countenance the Adversary replied: "From going to and fro in the earth, and from walking up and down in it;"—from a busy prosecution of my work, seeking whom I may devour, have I come hither, even here to ply my work and to help on evil.

"Hast thou considered my servant Job," rejoined the Lord, "that there is none like him in the earth, a perfect and an upright man, one that feareth God and escheweth evil?" hast thou marked how he has withstood temptations, and, amid corruption on every side, has remained firm and uncontaminated?

The Accuser of the brethren daringly replied: "Doth Job serve God for nought? Hast Thou not made an hedge about him, and about his house, and about all that he hath on every side? Thou hast blessed the work of his hands, and his substance is increased in the land. But put forth Thine hand now, and touch all that he hath, and he will renounce Thee to Thy face."

Thus was the gauntlet thrown down. God's trusty servant was accused of selfishness, and a slight was cast upon the knowledge of Him "who searcheth the reins and the heart." The challenge was at once accepted. In order that the disinterested piety of His servant might be made manifest to the universe, the Lord gave Satan permission to put Job to the test.

"Behold, all that he hath is in thy power; only upon himself put not forth thine hand."

Armed with this fearful permission, Satan went forth from the presence of the Lord to execute all the evil that his malice could devise. Job was at the time the greatest of all the men of the East, his substance was immense, and in the number of oxen, asses, sheep, camels, and servants, he surpassed all the men of the country; he was likewise blessed in his family, for he had seven sons and three daughters.

It was a day of festivity in the family of the patriarch, but Job was himself not present at the festive circle, when a messenger, entering in hot haste, brought the startling news that the oxen were ploughing and the asses feeding beside them, when the Sabeans fell upon them, slew the servants with the edge of the sword, and carried off all the cattle. Scarce had he ceased his narration, when another messenger appeared on the scene with still more evil tidings. The lightning of God had fallen upon the flocks of the sheep and upon their shepherds, and sheep and shepherds together had perished in the fell conflagration, the messenger alone having escaped to bring the heavy tidings. Scarcely is this tale told when another messenger arrives bringing further dismal intelligence. The Chaldeans had fallen upon the camels, and had carried them off; the servants that watched over the animals were also overmastered and slain. Worse than all, a fourth messenger came running in with the terrible news that the seven children of Job who had met together in harmless festivity, and for whose spiritual welfare the patriarch was so concerned that he was wont to offer sacrifices for them continually, had met with a fearful fate: a great wind from the wilderness smote upon the house in which they were assembled, and sons and daughters were alike buried under one melancholy pile.

Thus, as it appeared, had both God and man combined to bring ruin and desolation upon the patriarch. A heavy cloud of mystery hung over this sad dispensation. Job was not conscious of having committed any enormous sin, and yet he had suffered terrible calamities. He knew not the hidden reason of those ills. Overwhelmed with grief and reduced to utter destitution, Job gave utterance to the words of lofty resignation: " The Lord gave, and the Lord hath taken away; blessed be the name of the Lord." Job's religion was thus unmistakeably proved to be a religion of love and reverential fear, and not the offspring of mere selfishness.

Time rolled on; again the sacred day arrived when the sons of God went to present themselves before the Lord at His altar; and the poor afflicted patriarch was doubtless not absent from that assembly. There were also present, — invisible, however, to human eye,—the Great Advocate, the Captain of the Lord's host, and the wicked Accuser who sought to devour the people of the Lord. Again the Lord triumphantly interrogated Satan, and pointed out to him the victorious result of the trial. With more bitter malignity than before, Satan now assailed the character of Job's religion, and insinuated that the reason of Job's continued stedfastness was the selfishness of his nature, and his insensibility to all evils that did not affect his own person. The challenge thus for the second time thrown down was again accepted, and Satan received permission to afflict the person of Job, provided only that he did not take his life. Satan accordingly smote the patriarch with a plague of burning ulcers, which covered his entire body, causing excruciating agony, rendered his appearance horrible and his breath offensive, so that the poor afflicted man became loathsome to behold.

Fearful as was this affliction, mysterious as was its cause, and unable as Job was to reconcile it with the justice of the Almighty, he yet maintained his integrity, and held fast his grasp of Heaven. In the first temptation he recognised God's right to deal as He thought fit with the things He had freely bestowed on him. He now recognised God's right to deal as He saw fit with his person. "Dost thou still hold fast thine integrity?" said his wife; "curse God and die," for death will soon put an end to thy miserable existence. Beautifully resigned was the reply of the patriarch: "Thou speakest as one of the foolish women speaketh. What! shall we receive good at the hand of God, and shall we not receive evil?"

The second trial was thus met with submission by the afflicted child of God; in the terrible contest Job remained the victor. His religion was proved to be a reality, and manifested as not merely outward show. Satan now vanished from the scene, no more to reappear.

A further trial, however, still awaited the patriarch, a trial at the hands of man. Far from receiving relief from sympathizing friends, Job's misery was unwittingly to be aggravated by well-meaning comforters. The trial was, perhaps, designed by divine wisdom, as a necessary preparation to be undergone before Job could be restored again to his former position. He required to learn many lessons before he was again prepared for prosperity, before he could understand the dealings of God with him. The dark trials which had come upon him had shaken, although they had not overthrown, his faith. From the trial to which he was now to be subjected, Job was to come forth like gold.

Three friends who had heard of the patriarch's downfall came to express their deep sympathy with him. They were probably men of exalted station,—according to the Greek translators, they were kings,—but whatever rank they belonged to, they were narrow-minded men, and were led by the mistaken religious views they had adopted to ascribe the calamity of their friend to an erroneous cause.

According to their theory, afflictions were sent by God as punishments for the sins of men. They looked to the punitive side of affliction and saw no other. Their views were grounded on truth, but not on the whole truth. They saw part of a large question, and thought they saw it all. Affliction is caused by sin, Job is afflicted, therefore he must have sinned; afflicted, too, in an unexampled degree, and, therefore, Job must have committed some extraordinary sin.

To persons with such convictions deeply rooted in their minds, the patriarch, after the first few days of sorrow had been spent in silence, poured out his bitter complaint. With such a heavy load of sorrow crushing him to the ground, life was far from a blessing, and in striking terms he cursed the night in which he was conceived, and the day in which he was born. To his circumscribed vision it appeared best that he should descend as soon as possible to that grave, where the wicked cease from troubling, and where the weary are at rest.

Eliphaz, probably the oldest and certainly the ablest of the three friends, began the discussion with the patriarch (iv. 15). In mild and soothing tones, Eliphaz apologized for the intrusion of himself and his friends on Job in the midst of such sorrow. Strong, however, in the conviction that such miseries as Job suffered could only be caused by some terrible iniquity, he expressed his surprise that a man like Job, who had often been the support of others, should be so overwhelmed with sorrow as to give vent to passionate exclamations. He reminded Job firmly of the supposed truth (which Job, in other circumstances, might himself have been ready to admit) that no one who was innocent ever perished, and that the righteous were never cut off, thus plainly leaving the deduction to be drawn that Job must have been guilty of secret sin. In language dictated by a desire to be faithful, he hinted at the conclusion at which he and his friends had arrived on the patriarch's case, and after pointing out the consequent impiety and sin of complaining against God, and the uses to which affliction might be turned, concluded with the exhortation to Job to hear what was spoken, and to ponder on it for his good.

Eliphaz in this speech touched the poor patriarch to the very quick. Like a heartless bystander, who looks callously upon some sufferer in agony, Eliphaz treated the exclamations uttered in Job's anguish as criminal. He imagined that by demonstrating the sin of complaining against God, he could close for ever the patriarch's mouth. Job was not, however, to be thus easily silenced; he felt conscious of his integrity, notwithstanding the dark insinuations of his friends, and though conscious of sin in general (vii. 19, 21), was certain that the fearful afflictions he suffered were not deserved. In piteous language he described the loathsome state of his poor body (vii. 4, 5), and turned towards heaven to beg in agonizing strains for relief. In touching terms he expressed his bitter disappointment at such language coming from men who had been his friends. Like noisy brooks, swollen by winter's rains, they had at one time been loud in their professions of attachment; they were also but too like those brooks when dried up by the summer's heat, fatally disappointing the parched traveller's hopes in the day of distress. No word of sympathy had fallen from their lips, no balm of Gilead had been poured upon his bleeding wounds.

Bildad in his rejoinder added little to the arguments adduced by Eliphaz. God must ever be true, and what He does must be right; He rewards the righteous, and punishes the wicked. Job's sufferings were, in Bildad's view, a sad confirmation of this truth. The calamity which had befallen Job's children must necessarily have been the result of their transgression (viii. 4). The Almighty could not act unjustly. If Job had been pure and upright his prosperity would have continued. His misfortunes must be traced to some acts of transgression. As the rush by the river's side does not grow without mire to nourish it, so misery must have its cause in some sin lying at the root (viii. 11–13). Such, Bildad informs Job, was the unanimous belief of his friends, and not only their creed, but that of the wise of former times, whom Bildad is ever fond of quoting in defence of his views. Job was but too plainly proved to have been a hypocrite; had he been upright, God would have upheld his cause. Yet if Job were willing to return to God, He would return to him, and grant him joy and peace in his latter end.

Job's reply to Bildad contains some fine passages. He ironically assents to his statement that God deals with man strictly according to retributive justice. But how can a man in such a case prove himself just before God? If he were to dare to contend with God, he could not answer Him one of a thousand questions. It were hopeless to think of reasoning with such an adversary; better, says Job, to fall down humbly before Him, and make supplication to "my opponent" (A. V. "my judge").[1] But, as the patriarch points out, God's retributive justice is not always so clearly exhibited as his friends had ventured to assert. God had afflicted him though innocent; God destroys alike often the guiltless and the guilty (ix. 22). Having thus replied to Bildad, Job burst forth in a strain of

---

[1] So the word in ix. 15 should perhaps rather be rendered, and not *my judge*, as the Authorized Version has it. The Revised Version has more correctly "*mine adversary.*" The Hebrew שֹׁפֵט is a *judge*, while מְשֹׁפֵט is *one who goes to law with another, an opponent*. Exactly the same distinction exists between the Arabic حَاكِم and مُحَاكِم. *Vid.* Gesenius' *Thesaurus*, p. 1464. In the *Lexicon Manuale*, Gesenius viewed the two participles as identical in meaning, and so they are viewed even in the latest editions of his work by Mühlau and Volck (8th ed. 1878; 9th ed. 1883). Böttcher, however, regards the form in question as a collective (a broken plural form), simply more expressive than the ordinary Kal participle used for *judge*. See his *Neue Aehrenlese*, 1406. The matter cannot be fully discussed here.

remonstrance with God, and besought Him to clear away the darkness which surrounded the mysterious visitation, and to explain why He had so inexplicably changed His mode of dealing with His servant. In these burning remonstrances the patriarch gives vent to his intense longing for some mediator, some daysman, between himself and the Almighty.

Zophar now took up the argument against Job (xi.). He accused Job of ignorance, and pointed out God's wisdom. He accused Job of mockery and impiety, and expressed a wish that God would indeed speak and open His lips against Job, when the wickedness of Job would be manifested, and his guilt be brought to light. He adduced no arguments, but warned the patriarch to put away iniquity, and his misery would soon be forgotten.

Zophar, indeed, adduced no arguments in proof of his assertions, but he exhibited considerable irritation against Job for the persistence with which he had maintained his innocence, and charged the patriarch with being an empty talker and full of boastings.[1]

Job's indignation was now fully aroused. Unable any longer to endure the dark insinuations of his friends, and their want of sympathy with his calamity, he no longer stood upon the defensive, but assumed the offensive. In reference to the proud assumption of his friends, he remarked with bitter irony: "No doubt

---

[1] *Lies*, which is the Authorized Version rendering of xi. 2, is somewhat too strong. The Revised Version has correctly rendered "thy boastings."

ye are the people, and wisdom shall die with you. But I have understanding as well as you; I am not inferior to you; yea, who knoweth not such things as these?" (xii. 2, 3). His friends had brought forward nothing new, but had only given utterance to what he knew as well as they. They had not even been honest in the expression of their opinions, for they had upheld what was neither in unison with the convictions of their hearts or with their own experience. "Ye are forgers of lies, ye are all physicians of no value," ignorant quacks incompetent to understand the disease they proposed to cure. "Will ye speak unrighteously for God, and talk deceitfully for Him? Will ye accept His person? will ye contend for God?" "He will surely reprove you if ye do secretly accept persons" (xiii. 7, 8, 10). Though you vainly imagine that He will approve of your feigned words in His defence, you will find at last that you shall receive rebuke and shame at His hands.

Amid the wail of woe that proceeded so oft from the patriarch, and the fearful darkness that gathered around his path, there still lingered in his bosom the hope and conviction that God was after all his friend. To Him, therefore, he appealed to explain His strange dealings, and to Him he turned when condemned by his friends. Like the Psalmist he could say: "My soul waiteth only upon God, from Him cometh my salvation" (Ps. lxii. 1). The descriptions of the natural misery of man, and of the sin of which the entire race is guilty, the utter destruction of man and the bright hope of another life, presented in the fourteenth chapter, form one of the most striking parts of this wonderful poem.

"It is easily seen," beautifully remarks Prof. Davidson,[1] "that this storm of passion and doubt into which Job has been worked is one that rages, like all storms in deep waters, merely on the surface,—deep down (always when he forgets himself) his faith and fundamental conceptions of God are calm and undisturbed. The very deeps of darkness into which he sinks but give him clearer glimpses of heavenly light —as when one descends between engulfing waves, he sees the stars invisible to those on calmer waters. And out of the extremity of human woe, Job rises to the extremity of human hope. Because the perfect conception of misery—concentrated sin and wrath and speedy dissolution—overbalances itself, the mind, from its nature and inherent conceptions of man and God, immediately swings itself aloft, and from the shortness and the miserable abandonment by God of this life, finds and utters the necessity of an endless and blessed life with Him anew (xiv. 13 ff.). A man with such firm foothold on the past, and such

---

[1] *A Commentary, Grammatical and Exegetical, on the Book of Job:* with a Translation. By Rev. A. B. Davidson. Vol. i. p. 178 (Williams & Norgate, 1862). A work, the second volume of which, alas! never appeared, owing mainly to the sad want of appreciation shown for such books in this country. There is some compensation for the loss, indeed, in the fact that Prof. A. B. Davidson is the author of the Commentary on the Book of Job in the *Cambridge Bible for Schools and Colleges* (Cambridge, 1884), already referred to. But the non-appearance of the larger work is still much to be regretted.

occasional convulsive grasps of the future, is not one readily to fall into Atheism."

The rejoinder of Eliphaz (xv.) was fierce and cutting. The patriarch had now shown himself in his true colours as one who had no fear of God, who restrained prayer before the Most High, who condemned himself by his own foolish and daring words, and ventured to set himself against the Almighty, and madly to rush upon God with the thick bosses of his bucklers.

Broken down with sorrow upon sorrow, Job replied: "I have heard many such things: miserable comforters are ye all." "I also could speak as ye do: if your soul were in my soul's stead, I could join together words against you, and shake mine head at you." But if you were in such circumstances, "I would strengthen you with my mouth, and the solace of my lips should assuage your grief" (xvi. 2, 4, 5). "My face is foul with weeping, and on my eyelids is the shadow of death; although there is no violence in mine hands, and my prayer is pure. O earth, cover not thou my blood, and let my cry have no resting place. Even now, behold, my witness is in heaven, and He that voucheth for me (my sponsor) is on high. My friends scorn me, but my eye poureth out tears unto God, that He would maintain the right of a man with God, and of a son of man with his neighbour!" (xvi. 16–21).

Bildad was not overcome by Job's tears and entreaties. With the intense earnestness of a bigot, convinced that his opinions are true, even though he cannot prove his points, Bildad spoke out still more bitterly. Job's hypocrisy was, in his opinion, most awful to behold; he was a wicked man, the light of whose tent had been blown out by the Most High, and his lamp and fire extinguished. His fate should prove a solemn warning to others, and men as they passed by might well exclaim: "Surely such are the dwellings of the unrighteous, and this is the place of him that knoweth not God" (xviii. 21).

Again the patriarch entreated his friends at least to be silent. He had replied to their arguments, they had nothing left but invective. "Have pity upon me, have pity upon me, O ye my friends; for the hand of God hath touched me. Oh that my words were now written! oh that they were inscribed in a book! That with an iron pen and lead they were graven in the rock for ever! But I know that my Redeemer liveth,[1] and that He shall stand up at the last upon the earth: and after my skin hath been thus destroyed, yet from my flesh" (or, "apart from my flesh," in the disembodied state,[2]) "shall I see God" (xix. 21, 23–26).

[1] Or, "And a Later One (an after-one, he that cometh after me) shall stand upon the earth." Ewald renders אַחֲרוֹן by *Nachmann*. Davidson in his earlier work maintained that "undoubtedly אַחֲרוֹן (the Later One) is He who inaugurates the אַחֲרִית הַיָּמִים (the latter days), or Messianic era, *i.e.* the Messiah." He explains it in his later work as an epithet of God, as "The first and the last" (Isa. xliv. 6, xlviii. 12); and as a parallel to "My God" in the first clause, and therefore as nearly equivalent in sense to "in aftertime He shall stand."

[2] This is the sense which is most in harmony with the context; the reference to the resurrection does not so well agree with the context.

Notwithstanding this pathetic appeal, the discussion between Job and his friends waxed fiercer and fiercer. Eliphaz in his third speech no longer sought to conceal his impressions. Drawing now upon his imagination for the facts required, he declared Job's wickedness to be great. It was his cruelty towards his own flesh and blood, his shameless disregard of the poor, his neglect of the widow, and his unfeeling conduct towards the orphan, which had all by a righteous retribution brought upon him a well-merited affliction (xxi. 5–10).

In his closing speech Job triumphantly defends himself against such fearful charges; he feelingly contrasts his former with his present state (xxix., xxx.). He enlarges on the wisdom of God, but declares the workings of His providence as inscrutable, and once more, having solemnly protested his innocence of the charges adduced against him, appeals to heaven for an explanation of his woes (xxxi.).

Thus far had Job come off victorious; his three friends had been worsted in the debate. Their theory, that affliction was always the consequence of sin, was too narrow, it did not accord with even ordinary experience, it did not explain the sufferings of Job. Those friends had also been convicted of partiality and injustice. In upholding what they believed to be the cause of God, they in the heat of argument went beyond their conscientious convictions, and in charging the patriarch with crimes of which they had no evidence, they had been convicted themselves as transgressors.

On the other hand, Job, goaded on by their accusations, had been guilty of uttering impious words against God, and had called in question the divine justice. Scripture paints men as they are, and does not hesitate to put into the mouth of Job the dark thoughts that often suggest themselves to the minds of even pious men in the depth of sorrow and distress. "The utterances of anguish," as Prof. Davidson has remarked, "are not to be rigidly measured by the square of dogmatic truth; and we cannot attach to Job the same blame as we should were his sentiments given out calmly, nor can we attach to the sentiments the same weight as if they were the deliberate convictions of the understanding."

Another speaker is now represented as appearing on the scene. Elihu belonged to the family from whence Abraham had sprung, and, young as he was in years, modesty had kept him from taking any part in the discussion, which he is supposed to have listened to as a casual bystander. It is unnecessary for our present purpose to discuss the genuineness of this portion of the book. Whether it was an insertion tacked on by the author himself to the original work, or added thereto by a later hand, it forms a very important addition to the argument of the book.

Elihu was indignant at the result of the controversy. He was indignant at the inability shown by the three disputants, and was pained at the words

Job had uttered. He could not any longer, therefore, remain silent. He began by apologizing as a young man for venturing to take part in the debate. He pointed out to Job that affliction was often sent by God as chastisement, and was employed to teach man humility. God is a God of justice, and cannot treat man unjustly. Nor does God keep silence. He speaks to man in various ways. He is a God of goodness and truth, while sin in man is sufficient in itself to account for any trials that man may have to endure. "Surely it is meet to be said unto God, I have borne chastisement, I will not offend any more. That which I see not, teach Thou me: if I have done iniquity, I will do it no more" (xxxiv. 31, 32); for after all, "Who is a Teacher like God?" (xxxvi. 22). He teaches man by suffering, He educates His own children. Thus sufferings are loving stripes from a Father's hand: "Whom the Lord loveth He chasteneth, and scourgeth every son whom He receiveth" (Heb. xii. 5, 11; Prov. iii. 11, 12). Afflictions are sent as punishments, but they are also sent as corrections. They are purgative. Elihu's argument might well be summed up in the remarkable words of Habakkuk in reference to the cruel and insulting Chaldeans: "Art not Thou from everlasting, Jehovah my God, mine Holy One? we shall not die. O Jehovah, Thou hast ordained him for judgment; and Thou, O Rock, hast established him for correction" (Hab. i. 12).

Interrupting Elihu in his speech, the Almighty

Himself is next introduced as speaking out of the storm-cloud. The speech of God is the more remarkable, because at first sight it appears to ignore altogether the question at issue. The Almighty did not condescend to reply to Job's charges, nor did He even upbraid him with impiety. He did not unravel the mystery of evil, He did not speak about the afflictions of Job. He made His glory in creation to pass before the patriarch, He showed His own wondrous dealings in the natural world which man is unable to understand, and left Job to draw from thence the conclusion that if he could not comprehend the mere natural world, he could not expect to understand God's moral government and the deep mysteries connected with it.

Davidson well observes in his later work, p. 260: "The solution to Job's problem given in God's answer from the storm is a religious solution, not a speculative one. It is a solution to the heart, not to the intellect. It is such a solution as only God could give; a solution which does not solve the perplexity, but buries it under the tide of a fuller life and joy in God. It is a solution as broad as Job's life and not merely the measure of his understanding; the same solution as was given to the doubting apostle, making him to exclaim, 'My Lord and my God!' and teaching him that not through his sense of touch or his eyesight, but through a broader sense, God makes Himself felt by man."

The sight of the Almighty and of His glory were quite enough for Job. The few words of rebuke addressed to Job by God in the conclusion of this speech (xl. 7 ff.) prostrated him in the dust. The riddle for the solution of which he had longed was no more thought of, Job was content resignedly to await God's time for its explanation. He asked no longer the cause of the stripes he had received; it was sufficient that they came from a Father's hand. In the sanctuary of God he learned the lesson, not to be learned outside its walls—a lesson of patience. The patient one was shown his impatience, the just man beheld his own injustice. With the cry, as it were, of "Father, I have sinned," the patriarch prostrated himself before Him who was indeed his Father. He had in heart wandered far from his home, but his wanderings were now over; he would fain return. The Father's pardon was not long delayed, the kiss of love was imprinted on the son's lips, and the order to bring forth the best robe, to clothe withal the poor penitent, was almost immediately given.

Job was restored to health and prosperity, his wealth was doubled. His friends were condemned for their sin against God whom they had misrepresented, and for their sins against Job whom they had falsely accused. They were bidden to ask Job to intercede for them, and to offer up, at the same time, a sacrifice to God. They were then pardoned and forgiven, and the storm-cloud which seemed big with vengeance burst thus in blessings on the heads of all.

Thus does the Book of Job at least partially explain God's designs in affliction. The story told at the beginning of the book solves, as far as is possible on earth, the dark problem of human suffering. Trials are not only punitive and purgative, but sometimes also probative. The main object for Job's heavy trial was his probation—his sufferings were designed to test his faith. But they were also useful in other ways. Job learned in his affliction more of God's dealings than he had known before. He acquired a deeper knowledge of sin, and his own words received a striking fulfilment: "When He hath tried me, I shall come forth like gold" (xxiii. 10).

"Count it all joy," writes St. James, "when ye fall into manifold temptations (or trials); knowing that the proof of your faith worketh patience. And let patience have its perfect work, that ye may be perfect and entire, lacking in nothing" (Jas. i. 2–4).

II.

THE BOOK OF JONAH CONSIDERED FROM AN ALLEGORICAL POINT OF VIEW.

§ 1. *Introduction—History and allegory—Weakness of objections urged against the credibility of the Book of Jonah—No historical confirmation of its narrative—No reference to the story in heathen legends.*

F there be in the early writings of the Old Testament a narrative which must be regarded as historically true, it is the account given in the Book of Genesis of Abraham and his family. Its truth is assumed by the writers of the New Testament, and its smallest details are commented on as fraught with important theological consequences.

And yet the great Apostle of the Gentiles does not hesitate to treat the most striking portions of that story as allegorical, and to use language in reference to that narrative which, if it stood alone, might be interpreted as a denial of its historical character.

His words are: " Tell me, ye that desire to be under

the law, do ye not hear the law? For it is written, that Abraham had two sons, one by the handmaid (namely, Ishmael), and one by the freewoman (namely, Isaac). . . . Which things contain an allegory (or, as in the old version, *which things are an allegory*): for these women (Hagar and Sarai) are two covenants; one from Mount Sinai, bearing children unto bondage, which is Hagar. Now this Hagar is Mount Sinai in Arabia, and answereth to the Jerusalem that now is: for she is in bondage with her children. But the Jerusalem that is above is free, which is our mother. . . . Now we, brethren, as Isaac was, are children of promise. But as then he that was born after the flesh persecuted him that was born after the spirit, even so it is now. Howbeit what saith the Scripture? Cast out the handmaid and her son: for the son of the handmaid shall not inherit with the son of the freewoman. Wherefore, brethren, we are not children of a handmaid, but of the freewoman" (Gal. iv. 21–26, 28–31).

An examination of the Book of Jonah from an allegorical point of view does not involve any denial of its inspiration, or necessarily show any disposition to question its credibility. If it can be shown that, regarded from such a standpoint, the very details of the story, which have always presented peculiar difficulties, have a deeper meaning than generally imagined, the examination may prove helpful to those whose minds have been harassed with doubts, and may lead them to derive profit and instruction from a book which has hitherto only been a source of perplexity. The consideration of the book from such a standpoint cannot shake the faith of any real believer in the sacred records, to whom the book will be alike precious in whatever way it be regarded, whether as a simple historical narrative; or, like the story of Abraham, an historical narrative typical of great spiritual realities; or even as pure allegory, like the story told to Ahab by Micaiah the son of Imlah, in order to arouse that king to a sense of his impending danger, and to instruct the Israelites of that day as to the cause of their calamities (1 Kings xxii. 19–23). Of the latter kind were most of the parables of our Lord, although they sometimes have the appearance of anecdotes drawn from real life (as, for instance, the parables of the Prodigal Son, and of the Rich Man and Lazarus). Allegories of this type, however true they may be in all their spiritual reality, were never designed to be accepted as historical facts.

Some of the objections commonly urged against the credibility of the Book of Jonah have long ago lost much of their force. Popular champions of infidelity have often laughed to scorn the story of Jonah having been three days and three nights in "the whale's belly," and sought to demonstrate the inherent absurdity of the narrative by pointing out the small size of the whale's gullet. It was easy to reply to such an objection, that the Book of Jonah speaks only of "a great fish;" and to point out that in the

New Testament (Matt. xii. 40), the absurdity, if any, was the creation of the translators, for the Greek word rendered "whale" does not necessarily signify that fish.

In order to point out the inherent credibility of the story of the fish swallowing up Jonah and afterwards vomiting him forth alive, Dr. Pusey refers to the statement of Otto Fabricius in his *Fauna Grönlandica*, p. 129, in which that writer states that the shark—which is supposed to have been "the great fish" referred to—is wont to swallow down whole and entire, "dead and sometimes living men, which it finds in the sea." The following is quoted by Dr. Pusey and others from a German naturalist of some note:[1]—"In 1758, in stormy weather, a sailor fell overboard from a frigate in the Mediterranean. A shark was close by, which, as he was swimming and crying for help, took him in his wide throat, so that he forthwith disappeared. Other sailors had leapt into the sloop to help their comrade, while yet swimming; the captain had a gun which stood on the deck discharged at the fish, which struck it so that it cast out the sailor which it had in its throat, who was taken up alive and little injured, by the sloop which had now come up. The fish was harpooned, taken up on the frigate, and dried. The captain made a present of the fish to the sailor who, by God's providence, had been so wonderfully preserved. The sailor went round Europe exhibiting it. He came to Franconia, and it was publicly exhibited here in

---

[1] Müller, *Natursystem von Linné*, iii. p. 268.

Erlangen, as also at Nurnberg and other places. The dried fish was delineated. It was 20 feet long, and, with expanded fins, 9 feet wide, and weighed 3924 lbs. From all this, it is probable that this was the fish of Jonah."

Pusey adds: "This is by no means an isolated account of the size of this fish. Blumenbach states, 'The white shark, or *canis carcharias*, is found of the size of 10,000 lbs., and horses have been found whole in its stomach.' A writer of the sixteenth century on 'the fish of Marseilles' says, 'They of Nice attested to me that they had taken a fish of this sort, approaching to 4000 lbs. weight, in whose body they had found a man whole. Those of Marseilles told something similar, that they had once taken a lamia (so they still popularly call the *carcharias*), and found in it a man in a coat of mail [*loricatus*].' Rondelet says, 'Sometimes it grows to such size that, placed on a carriage, it can hardly be drawn by two horses. I have seen one of moderate size, which weighed 1000 lbs., and when disembowelled and cut in pieces, it had to be put on two carriages.' 'I have seen on the shore of Saintonge a lamia, whose mouth and throat were of such vast size that it would easily swallow a large man.'"

Dr. Kalisch calls attention to the fact that young sharks, which sometimes on occasions of danger take refuge within their parents' mouths, have been occasionally found alive in the stomachs of large sharks. He also quotes a further case noted by

Friedrichsen,[1] namely, that a Danish missionary relates that an Indian swallowed by a shark was found alive in its stomach when the animal was captured, although in this instance the man died shortly after his deliverance from the fish.

Such facts, if properly vouched for, would go far to establish the credibility of the narrative of the Book of Jonah, and show that the statements of the book deserve closer attention than has often been bestowed upon them by superficial objectors.

Up to comparatively recent times, sceptical writers have been wont to regard the description of the size and greatness of Nineveh given in the Book of Jonah as utterly incredible. But the name Nineveh was sometimes employed in a narrower, sometimes in a wider signification. In the former sense, Nineveh, though a great city, was by no means so large as described in our book. In the larger signification, Nineveh included three other cities, which ultimately became portions of Nineveh, that "exceeding great city of three days' journey." It should, however, in common honesty be observed that one of these quarters of the city, namely, that lying to the north, and known as Khorsābād, was, according to the Assyrian inscriptions, built by Sargon in the last decade of the eighth century before Christ, one hundred years later than the time of Jonah. Therefore, although the infidels' sneer at the incredibility of the narrative has long

---

[1] Friedrichsen, P., *Kritische Uebersicht der verschiedenen Ansichten von dem Buche Jonas*, Leipzig 1817.

since been refuted, the absolute correctness of the statement made at the close of the Book of Jonah cannot be demonstrated.¹

No confirmation of the history contained in the Book of Jonah has as yet been discovered in the Assyrian inscriptions hitherto brought to light. What surprises may yet await the investigators in that field it would be rash to assert. It is, however, worthy of notice that the writer of the Book of Jonah does not mention the name of the king of Nineveh referred to in his narrative.

Nor is there any reference to the story of Jonah in the fables of the ancient heathen. It was once, indeed, the fashion to seek to illustrate Bible narratives by comparisons with heathen legends. This was not unfrequently done in such a manner as might lead a reader to imagine that the commentator considered the narratives of Holy Writ were in need of support from other sources. Dr. Pusey notes that the Fathers were more cautious in this particular than Christian divines of more modern times, and he quotes among others an observation on the point by S. Cyril of Alexandria: "We do not use their fables to confirm things divine; but we mention them to a good end, in answer to unbelievers, that *their* received histories too do not reject such relations."

There are several heathen myths in which stories

---

¹ See Schrader, *Die Keilinschriften u. das Alte Test.* 2te Ausg. p. 448. See also Kalisch's remarks on the subject in his *Bible Studies on Jonah*, pp. 223-26.

are told of persons exposed to sea-monsters and wonderfully rescued. But not one of these narratives, however, when fairly examined, is similar to that of Jonah, or can with any degree of plausibility be regarded as either the original of our story, or as derived therefrom. Numerous attempts have been made by critics of former days to connect such legends with the Book of Jonah, but the failure of all those attempts is now generally acknowledged. The myth of Perseus and his rescue of the beautiful Andromeda from the jaws of a sea-monster has nothing in common with the history of Jonah, except the circumstance that a sea-monster is spoken of in both narratives. The story of Hercules and his rescue of Hesione, also from a sea-monster, is probably an allegory descriptive of the efforts of the sea to sweep away the land. The latter legend is somewhat more akin to our narrative in the form it assumes in a poem of Lycophron, a grammarian and poet of the second century before Christ, who lived at the court of Ptolemy Philadelphus, and was employed in the great Alexandrian Library. But even in the latter case the connection is very doubtful, and seems rather to have been created by the comments of Christian writers than to have formed any part of the original myth.[1]

---

[1] See Kalisch's *Bible Studies*, Part ii. "The Book of Jonah," pp. 177 ff., whose remarks on this head are far more satisfactory than those of Dr. Pusey.

§ 2. *The prophet Jonah and his era — The prophetic commission — Jonah's flight — Jonah a representative of Israel — His sleep on the vessel — The storm on the sea of nations — The sea-monster swallows up Israel — The allegory founded on descriptions given in the Hebrew prophets.*

If the Book of Jonah was written by the prophet Jonah himself, it would be the earliest of the books of the prophets contained in the Old Testament. In 2 Kings xiv. 25, Jeroboam II. king of Israel (*circa* 800 B.C.) is said to have "restored the border of Israel from the entering in of Hamath (in the north, not far from Damascus) unto the sea of the Arabah (or the Dead Sea in the south), according to the word of the Lord, the God of Israel, which He spake by the hand of His servant Jonah, the son of Amittai, the prophet, which was of Gath-hepher." The town here mentioned was in the eastern border of Zebulon (Josh. xix. 13), in the district afterwards known as Galilee. Jonah, therefore, lived prior to 800 B.C., and may have been a contemporary of Elisha. It is possible he may even have seen the great Elijah, although the tradition that he was the son of the widow of Zarephath whom Elijah raised to life, seems to have arisen simply from the correspondence in Hebrew between the last word which occurs in the widow's remark, recorded in 1 Kings xvii. 24 : "I know . . . that the word of the Lord in thy mouth is *truth* (אֱמֶת)," and the name of Jonah's father, Amittai (אֲמִתַּי), which signifies *truthful*.

In the lifetime of the prophet spoken of in the First Book of Kings the Assyrian empire had already come into connection with Israel. Jehu, who reigned from about B.C. 883 to 855, was, according to the Assyrian inscriptions, a vassal of the great king of Assyria. The king of Assyria also received tribute from the king of Israel in B.C. 800, and it was probably owing to the fact of this alliance between Israel and Assyria that Jeroboam II. was so successful in his wars with Syria.[1] Jonah, who lived in, or previous to, the reign of Jeroboam II., was consequently the first prophet raised up after the shadow of Assyria fell across the path of Israel. This, as will be seen, is a fact of no little significance.

According to the narrative of the book before us, Jonah was commanded by God to arise and go to Nineveh and cry against that city, because its wickedness was come up before the Most High. Instead, however, of obeying the divine direction and setting out on the journey to the east, Jonah rose up to flee to Tarshish in Spain, the farthest bounds of the maritime commerce of Phœnicia. By acting in this manner he was flying from the presence of Jehovah, that is, from standing in the Lord's presence as His servant and prophet. In simple words, Jonah, on account of a repugnance to perform the special work

---

[1] See Schrader, *Die Keilinschriften u. das A. T.* pp. 208, 216, 217.

allotted to him, sought to lay down and abandon the prophetic office to which he had been called by God.

This is the real meaning of the expression made use of in Jonah i. 3. The narrative does not represent Jonah so ignorant and simple as to imagine that he could escape from the all-searching eye of Jehovah. He was well acquainted with the truth expressed by David in Ps. cxxxix. 7,—

> "Whither shall I go from Thy Spirit?
> Or whither shall I flee from Thy presence?"

The phrase, "fled from the presence of the Lord," is figurative, and is contrasted with the "standing before the Lord of hosts" as His prophet.[1] The latter phrase was repeatedly used by Elisha, Jonah's probable predecessor in the prophetic office (2 Kings iii. 14, v. 16; comp. 2 Sam. xvi. 19). As Cain, when convicted of murder, separated himself from the family altar in front of Eden, and went out from the presence of the Lord to the land of Nod (comp. Ps. li. 11), so Jonah sought to escape from the irksome commission imposed on him by fleeing from the land where Jehovah specially manifested His presence, and by abandoning the work he had been commanded

---

[1] See the remarks of Kalisch in his *Bible Studies on the Book of Jonah*, pp. 135 ff., and his philological remarks on p. 145. The Targum correctly states that Jonah fled "in order not to prophesy in the name of the Lord." As Kalisch observes, Jonah, when an obedient prophet and in the Holy Land, was "before the Lord" (לִפְנֵי יהוה); when he abandoned his prophetic office, left the Holy Land, and fled, he escaped (מִלִּפְנֵי יהוה) "from before the Lord."

to perform. Jonah thus cut himself off from the inheritance of the Lord, from the land where the divine blessing might be expected. He sought to take up his abode "away from the presence of the Lord" (comp. 1 Sam. xxvi. 19, 20), in the lands of nations where no Israelite had a right to expect aught but a curse.

Jonah, the first prophet raised up after the Israelites came in contact with the world-power by which they were soon to be so heavily scourged, was a remarkable type and symbol of the nation of Israel. That nation was separated to be a holy people unto Jehovah, to keep alive the lamp of truth, to be a light in the darkness of the world. There was not only judgment but mercy, even towards the Gentile nations, in this selection of Israel. That people were to be the depositories of divine truth, the recipients of divine revelation. Their prosperity was to be a lesson to the nations around, who should exclaim: "Happy is the people that is in such a case: happy is the people whose God is Jehovah" (Ps. cxliv. 15).

The name Jonah signifies "a dove." Ephraim, the northern kingdom, the kingdom of Israel as distinguished from that of Judah, is termed by Hosea, the only other prophetic writer who belonged to that kingdom, "a silly dove" (Hos. vii. 11); and when that prophet predicts the return from captivity, he speaks of Ephraim as returning as "a dove out of the land of Assyria" (Hos. xi. 11). Among the Rabbis the dove was regarded as a symbol of the congregation of

Israel; and the dove sent forth from the ark of Noah, who returned in the evening with an olive branch in her beak, was viewed as a symbol of Israel who was to bring light at eventide to poor storm-tossed humanity, in accordance with the prophecy: "Arise, shine, for thy light is come" (Isa. lx. 1–3). According to the Jewish legend, the olive branch was plucked off by the dove from a tree of Paradise. As it is said in Genesis that the dove returned to the ark because she found "no rest for the sole of her foot" (Gen. viii. 9), a Midrash beautifully compares the same expression which is used by Moses in Deut. xxviii. 65 in reference to Israel scattered among the nations, who is destined to find no rest for the sole of her foot until she, too, returns to the ark from whence she came forth. Amittai, the name of Jonah's father, which signifies *truthful*, lends itself also easily to the purposes of allegory. For Israel is represented as the son, the first-born of the living and true God (Ex. iv. 22; Deut. xiv. 1, xxxii. 6; Hos. xi. 1).

Israel, although intended to be a witness and upholder of divine truth (Isa. xliii. 10), often apostatized from her God. Her repeated fallings-away into idolatry are recorded in the sacred books. The people desired to be like the nations; they followed their customs, they were led astray by their idolatries. Instead of standing in the presence of the Lord, and doing service as His prophets and ministers, "they mocked the messengers of God, and despised His words, and scoffed at His prophets, until the wrath of Jehovah arose against His people, till there was no remedy" (2 Chron. xxxvi. 16).

Hence the mighty storm sent forth upon the sea of nations; judgment had to commence at the house of God (1 Pet. iv. 17). Hence "there is sorrow on the sea, it cannot be quiet" (Jer. xlix. 23). The words of Ezekiel in reference to Tyre might be used of Israel: "Thy rowers have brought thee into great waters: the east wind hath broken thee in the heart of the seas" (Ezek. xxvii. 26). When the Assyrian and Babylonian powers swept over the waters like a mighty storm, the mariners on the sea of nations cried every man unto his god, and cast forth the wares that they carried (tribute-money in abundance) to lighten the ship in the storm. But none of the gods of the nations were able to deliver their lands out of the hand of the kings of Assyria or of Babylon. "Where were the gods of Hamath and Arpad? Where were the gods of Sepharvaim? Did they deliver Samaria out of the hand of the destroyer?" (Isa. xxxvi. 18, 19). Nor would even Jehovah deliver Jerusalem the holy city out of the hand of the enemy. For her transgressions Jerusalem was delivered up to the foe. Hence the exclamation of the prophet in the name of the Lord: "Ho! Assyria, the rod of mine anger, the staff in whose hand is my indignation. I will send him against a profane nation, against the people of my wrath will I give him a charge to take the spoil, and to take the prey," etc. (Isa. x. 5, 6). Assyria at first, and Babylon afterwards, were instruments of vengeance in the hands of Jehovah wherewith to chastise His rebellious people, they were the Lord's "battle-axe and weapons of war" (Jer. li. 20), wherewith He smote them to the ground in the day of His fury.

The storm arose around the ship that carried Jonah. But while the mariners toiled and struggled with the tempest, Jonah went down into the innermost parts of the ship and fell asleep. It is unnecessary curiously to investigate whether the heavy sleep of the prophet was brought on by sorrow and anxiety, or whether it was the sleep of unconcern and forgetfulness.[1] The description in the Book of Jonah admirably describes the state of Israel previous to the Babylonian captivity. Isaiah gives vent to the following striking exclamation when seeking to arouse his people from their slumbers: "The Lord hath poured out upon you the spirit of deep sleep, and hath closed your eyes, the prophets; and your heads, the seers, hath He covered" (Isa. xxix. 10). For Israel had been led astray by those who were "blind leaders of the blind," by false prophets, and by seers who prophesied lies in God's name, saying, "I have dreamed, and have dreamed" (Jer. xxiii. 25), who cried "Peace, peace, when there was no peace" (Jer. vi. 14), who were "all dumb

---

[1] The former, however, seems rather to be designed by the use of the verb in the original (וַיֵּרָדַם), as Kalisch has well pointed out in his philological remarks. Bergmann unnecessarily explains it as "sought to sleep."

dogs, who could not bark, dreaming, lying down, loving to slumber" (Isa. lvi. 10).

Jonah, ere he embarked in their vessel, informed the mariners that he was flying from the presence of Jehovah (i. 10), and that by casting in his lot with them he was forsaking the service of his God. They, however, took him in gladly, for he paid the fare which they demanded. Their thoughts were probably similar to those of Pharaoh when he exclaimed, "Who is Jehovah, that I should hearken unto His voice?" (Ex. v. 2); or like those of the chief priests and elders of Jews, who on a more awful occasion callously exclaimed, on hearing the confession of guilt from the lips of the despairing Judas, "What is that to us? see thou to it" (Matt. xxvii. 4). But when the "ship was like to be broken," the mariners in their distress aroused the sleeping prophet, and bid him also cry aloud to his God for deliverance. One of the greatest French statesmen, though an unbeliever, asked for the rites of the Church when dying, on the ground that he would not be such a fool as to despise any chance, however small, in such a trying hour. So the mariners in the storm were not disposed to quarrel with any prayer in the day of their sore distress. It was but natural, however, that the thought should soon arise in the hearts of the superstitious sailors that the tempest raging around them was no ordinary storm, but one aroused by the wrath of Heaven. They accordingly cast lots in order to discover for whose sake the storm had been sent forth, and the lot fell upon Jonah. Eagerly interrogated respecting his country, his people, and his crime, the prophet calmly and proudly replied: "I am a Hebrew, and I fear Jehovah, the God of heaven, who made the sea and the dry land." The God whose service Jonah so strangely relinquished was now to him a dread reality, the religion once apparently despised was a cause of boasting. In the hour of danger, with Heaven frowning on him, and with men scowling at him, Jonah suddenly stood forth as a bold confessor, exclaiming almost in the language of Job: "Though He slay me, yet will I wait for Him" (Job xiii. 15). The reply to his questioners was the simple recital of his creed. It was not a penitential confession of personal guilt, it was a summary of the creed of the Psalmist:—

> "The sea is His, and He made it:
> And His hands formed the dry land.
> O come, let us worship and bow down:
> Let us kneel before Jehovah our Maker."—Ps. xcv. 5, 6.

It was a protest against idolatry delivered in the very face of idolaters, and is strangely illustrative of the truth expressed by a great Rabbi of later days: "The heathen, when evil befalls them, curse their gods; but we praise our God in prosperity and in adversity, and cry, Praise be to the Judge of Truth!"[1]

It is highly significant that the prophet did not

[1] R. Akiba, see Dr. J. Hamburger, *Real-Encyclopädie für Bibel und Talmud*, Abth. ii. p. 38.

condescend—whatever he may have felt in his soul—to express any regret for his notorious sin. But when the mariners further asked him what they should do, Jonah immediately directed them to cast him overboard into the sea. It must not be forgotten that if there were false prophets in Israel who were among the causes which brought about Israel's ruin, there were also genuine prophets of Jehovah who were enlightened by divine wisdom to comprehend that the way to a national amelioration lay through a national death, and such a calamity alone could bring about the nation's resurrection to a higher life. But those prophets were accused, and that very naturally, of weakening the hands of their countrymen in the last campaign against Babylon (Jer. xxxviii. 4), and even of inviting in the invader and destroyer of the land. As messengers of Jehovah, the prophets of Israel had to perform the sad duty of denouncing Jehovah's wrath against their own country. They were even commanded in their prophecies to summon the Chaldæan invaders against Jerusalem: "Prepare ye war against her. . . . Thus hath the Lord of hosts said, Hew ye down trees, and cast up a mount against Jerusalem: this is the city to be visited" (Jer. vi. 4, 6).

Thus in the Book of Jonah, in accordance with the command pronounced with his own lips, Jonah, as Israel's representative, was cast forth into the yawning billows which threatened immediate death. The prophet was instantly swallowed up by a great fish prepared by Divine Providence specially for the purpose; and Jonah was in the belly of the fish three days and three nights, after which period the Lord spoke unto the fish, and it vomited Jonah out upon the dry land.

In Isa. xxvii. it is predicted that "Jehovah with His sword—the hard, and the great, and the strong (sword)—shall punish leviathan the swift serpent, and leviathan the crooked serpent; and He shall slay the sea-monster (הַתַּנִּין) which is in the sea." The world-power is there described under its three great heads: Leviathan the swift serpent signified Assyria, with its capital Nineveh on the swiftly-flowing Tigris; leviathan the crooked serpent indicated Babylon, which lay on the crooked and labyrinth-like Euphrates; while "the sea-monster which is in the sea" indicated Egypt, of which that was a common emblem. Though the world-power was thus represented under three heads, it was in all its forms essentially the same, and was to be overturned by one weapon, the sword of Jehovah, which is described as "hard," *i.e.* well-tempered, so that it cannot be broken; "great," for it hath executed judgment in heaven upon the rebellious host on high (Isa. xxxiv. 5), and therefore may well be feared when it descends to earth; and it is "strong" and able to smite the nations (Rev. xix. 15) with its sharp two-edged blade (Rev. i. 16, ii. 13).

Under two of these terrible forms the world-power is depicted by Jeremiah as working its will on Israel:

"Israel is a scattered sheep; the lions have driven him away: first the king of Assyria hath devoured him; and last this Nebuchadrezzar king of Babylon hath broken his bones" (Jer. l. 17). The more complete picture which is pourtrayed in the Book of Jonah, if that book be considered as an allegory, is presented to view in Jer. li. 34: "Nebuchadrezzar the king of Babylon hath devoured me, he hath crushed me, he hath made me an empty vessel, he hath swallowed me[1] up like the sea-monster (כַּתַּנִּין), he hath filled his maw (his belly) with my delicates, he hath cast me out."

Thus plainly does Jeremiah present a picture of the sea-monster, the great fish swallowing up Israel, and filling its belly therewith.[2] Hosea further fills up the allegorical representation when he says:

[1] The word used here is בָּלַע, which is also employed in Jonah i. 17, or, according to the Hebrew division of the book, in chap. ii. 1.

[2] Our attention was first directed specially to this fact by the suggestive remarks of Rabbi J. S. Bloch on the Book of Jonah in his *Studien zur Geschichte der Sammlung der alt-hebräischen Literatur* (Leipzig 1875), pp. 72–96. Though in the explanation of the details of the allegory we differ in many particulars from that scholar, even in the explanation of the early chapters, and Bloch gives no suggestions as to his mode of explaining the second portion of the book, yet it was his remarks which first put us upon the right track leading to the solution of the curious difficulties of the book. Kleinert (in Lange's *Bibelwerk*) adopts substantially the same view as we do, but he has not gone sufficiently into the details, nor pointed out that the very details of the allegory are all borrowed from the language of the prophets. The previous attempts to explain the book as an allegory must be regarded as failures, such as, for instance, that of von der Hardt. The Roman Catholic scholar Kaulen (see note on p. 67) is sometimes referred to as a defender of

"Come, and let us return unto the Lord: for He hath torn, and He will heal us; He hath smitten, and He will bind us up. After two days will He revive us: on the third[1] day He will raise us up, and we shall live before Him" (Hos. vi. 1, 2). In the latter description distinct reference is made to the three days spent in the interior of the sea-monster, the short period of the Babylonish captivity being thus signified.

The picture of the Book of Jonah would not be complete if no instance could be quoted from the prophets of the significant detail of the sea-monster disgorging its prey. But this actually occurs in another passage of Jeremiah (li. 44), where Jehovah says: "I will do judgment upon Bel in Babylon, and I will bring forth out of his mouth that which he hath swallowed up." Thus distinctly do the prophets of Israel represent the captivity of the chosen people as the swallowing up of Israel by a sea-monster; thus

the allegorical sense. But Kaulen maintains the truth of the historical narrative, although he also expounds the book allegorically, morally (*moraliter*), and mystically. Kalisch's work gives such a complete sketch of the literature on the Book of Jonah, that it is somewhat surprising to find that he has nowhere noticed Bloch's contribution to its exegesis. The notices of the allegorical interpretation given by Pusey in his *Minor Prophets* are very defective, and it is strange that Archdeacon Perowne, in his small volume in the *Cambridge Series of Commentaries*, shows no acquaintance with Kleinert's important work. Nor indeed does the *Speaker's Commentary* treat the allegorists much better.

[1] *Two* and *three* is no doubt occasionally used as an indefinite number, as in Isa. xvii. 6; Amos i. 3; Prov. xxx. 15, 18; Sir. l. 27. But the use of that phrase here is somewhat more precise, more in accordance with 2 Kings xx. 5; Luke xiii. 32. See p. 65.

do they further describe Israel in captivity as in the great fish's belly, and speak of Israel remaining almost in a state of death in the maw of the sea-monster for three mystical days, and even further predict that the monster would be ultimately compelled to disgorge its prey alive. While other nations deported from their lands were absorbed into the body of the conquering nation, Israel was not thus absorbed, but was kept nationally distinct as a people (Num. xxiii. 9), and the prophets foresaw that it alone of the nations should be restored and brought back to the land of promise, once granted to them by the Most High.[1]

No violence would therefore be put upon the narrative of the Book of Jonah (so far as yet considered), if the story of that book were regarded as pure allegory. The language employed lends itself readily to such a treatment. The selection of the prophet Jonah as the representative of Israel is peculiarly suitable. Israel owed all her pre-eminence to her prophets: "By a prophet Jehovah brought

---

[1] It must not, however, be forgotten that Jeremiah predicts the carrying away of Moab into captivity, and its restoration from captivity "in the latter days" (Jer. xlviii. 46, 47). A similar prophecy was uttered with respect to the Ammonites, who were also to be brought back from captivity (Jer. xlix. 6). The same statement occurs in reference to Elam "in the latter days" (Jer. xlix. 39). These prophecies, however, cannot be proved to have been literally fulfilled, and it is a serious question whether they were ever intended to be so understood, or whether by the return of the captivities thus specified the prophet did not refer to the universal blessing which was ultimately to be bestowed upon all nations through the instrumentality of Israel and its Messiah.

Israel out of Egypt, and by a prophet was he preserved" (Hos. xii. 13). Jonah belonged to the northern kingdom, the portion of Israel which was most steeped in Gentilism and idolatry. Consequently he was peculiarly fitted to represent Abraham, the ancestor of Israel, who had been called out of a land and people of idolaters. Jonah lived at a time when the Gentile power had begun to gird up its loins for the work of destroying Israel. Moreover, Israel as the prophetic nation of humanity, the nation through whom the knowledge of the true God was to be imparted to the world, could only be properly represented in an allegory by a prophet, and only by a prophet who (owing to the incidents of his personal history being unknown) might without any violence to actual history form a leading character in such a divinely-constructed parable.

§ 3. *The prayer of Jonah a collection of sentences chiefly from the Psalms—Israel's songs in her exile—The allegory expounded first of Israel, and then of Israel's Messiah.*

The prayer of Jonah in the fish's belly must now be examined paragraph by paragraph.

It begins thus: "I called by reason of mine distress unto the Lord, and He answered me. Out of the belly of Sheol cried I; Thou heardest my voice." David's expression concerning his deliverance from Saul must here been noted: "In my distress

I called upon the Lord, and cried unto my God" (Ps. xviii. 6). There is even a more close parallel to be found in Ps. cxx., a psalm composed after the captivity: "In my distress I cried unto the Lord, and He answered me." On the reference to Sheol, observe David's words in Ps. xviii. 5: "The cords of Sheol were round about me, the snares of death came upon me."

Jonah continues, ver. 3: "For Thou didst cast me into the depth, in the heart of the seas, and the flood was round about me; all Thy waves and Thy billows passed over me." The words of David (in Ps. xviii. 4) must be borne in mind: "The cords of death compassed me, and the floods of ungodliness made me afraid." But even a closer parallel may be discovered in one of the psalms belonging the exile (Ps. xlii. 7): "Deep calleth unto deep; all Thy waves and Thy billows are gone over me." The latter clause is identical with that of Jonah. The phrase, "the heart of the sea," occurs in Miriam's song of triumph sung beside the waters of the Red Sea (Ex. xv. 8). Compare also on the whole passage, Ps. lxxxviii. 6, 7.

Ver. 4: "And I said, I am cast out from before Thine eyes; yet will I look again toward Thy holy temple." Jonah's words in this verse are partly borrowed from Ps. xxxi. 22: "I said in my haste, I am cut off from before Thine eyes: nevertheless Thou heardest the voice of my supplications;" and from Ps. xviii. 6: "He heard my voice out of His temple, and my cry before Him came into His ears."

But Jonah proceeds (vers. 5 and 6): "The waters compassed me about, even to the soul: the deep was round about me, the weeds were wrapped about my head. I went down to the bottoms of the mountains; the earth with her bars *closed* upon me for ever: yet hast Thou brought up my life from corruption, O Lord my God." The language of Ps. lxix. 1, 2, which was probably written during the captivity, is very similar: "Save me, O God; for the waters are come in unto my soul. I sink in deep mire, where there is no standing: I am come into deep waters, where the floods overflow me;" and in ver. 15: "Let not the waterflood overwhelm me. Neither let the deep swallow me up; and let not the pit shut her mouth upon me." Compare also the language of the Book of Lamentations, iii. 54: "Waters flowed over mine head; I said I am cut off." The language of David in Ps. xxx. 3 must also be noted: "O Lord, Thou hast brought up my soul from Sheol: Thou hast kept me alive, that I should not go down to the pit." Observe also Ps. xvi. 10: "For Thou wilt not leave my soul to Sheol; neither wilt Thou suffer thine Holy One to see corruption."

Vers. 5 and 6 are the only portions of the prayer of Jonah in which expressions really original are to be discovered. The reference to the sea "weeds" is probably a reminiscence of the deliverance at the Red Sea, "the weedy sea" as it is termed in the Hebrew.[1]

---

[1] Dr. Kalisch observes: "The Targum, in rendering ימא דסוף תלי עיל מרישי, 'the sea-weed Sea was suspended over my head,' points to a

Job speaks of "the bars and doors of the sea" (xxxviii. 10). Jonah alone alludes to "the bars of the earth." It must also not be left out of sight that Zechariah, the great prophet of the Restoration, similarly refers to the great deliverance from Egypt in former days, the circumstances connected therewith being employed in his book as types of the future deliverance (Zech. x. 10–12). "Under the symbol of an exodus from Egypt and from under its power, and of a march through a sea and a river, such as occurred in the days of the first triumphal march of Israel, the great truth is set forth, that amid all trials and afflictions the covenant people would be delivered by the protecting hand of God."[1]

The closing verses of Jonah's prayer (vers. 7–9) are as follows: "When my soul fainted within me, I remembered the Lord: and my prayer came in unto Thee, into Thine holy temple. They that regard lying vanities forsake their own mercy. But I will sacrifice unto Thee with the voice of thanksgiving; I will pay that which I have vowed. Salvation is of the Lord."

Jewish tradition explicitly stated by the Rabbins, contending that God showed Jonah the Red Sea, and, for his comfort and encouragement, allowed him to behold how the Israelites passed over the dry bed in safety; for the fish's eyes were like windows through which the prophet was able to see all that happened in the waters, while the monster had in its interior a large jewel luminous like the sun (*Yalkut, Jon.* § 550)." "According to the tenor of the book, the sea-weed did not cling round the head of Jonah, but of the fish; which discrepancy, however, the author could hardly deem of much importance in a poetical composition."—Kalisch's *Bible Studies on Jonah*, p. 214.

[1] See *Bampton Lectures on Zechariah*, p. 296.

All these clauses are borrowed from the Psalms. In Ps. cxlii. 3 the identical phrase occurs, "When my spirit fainted within me;" while "I remembered Jehovah" is met with in Ps. cxix. 55, "I have remembered Thy name, Jehovah, in the night." "My prayer came in unto Thee into Thy holy temple," is a slight variation of Ps. xviii. 6. The phrase "they that observe lying vanities" is taken from Ps. xxxi. 6, where idolaters are thus described. Idols are termed "lying vanities" in contrast with "the God of truth," 2 Chron. xv. 3, one of whose attributes is mercy.[1] Ver. 9 is almost a quotation of Ps. cxvi. 17; while the closing expression, "Salvation is of Jehovah," is taken from Ps. iii. 8.

Few persons, after such a comparison of all the clauses of Jonah's psalm of thanksgiving, will, we think, be found willing to endorse Dr. Pusey's startling assertion, that no one could have written that hymn who had not himself been delivered from some such peril as that depicted in the story of the book. Dr. Pusey admits "that no image so well expresses the overwhelmedness under affliction or temptation as the pressure of a storm by land, or being overflooded by the waves of the sea. . . . Of this sort," he notes, "are those images which Jonah took from the Psalms. But" he adds, "a description so minute as

---

[1] הַסְדָּם, compare חַסְדִּי, "my mercy," applied to God, Ps. cxliv. 2. In Jonah the expression "*their mercy*" evidently signifies "the mercy shown to them" (compare "the mercies of David," *i.e.* the kindness bestowed upon David, Isa. lv. 3), which men soon forget and drive out of their thoughts. See Kalisch, p. 217.

the whole of Jonah's would be allegory, not metaphor." The possibility of the language used being allegorical thus suggested itself to Dr. Pusey's mind, but he was not led to examine whether that might not be the true explanation of the phenomena of the so-called prayer. It is highly significant that almost every sentence of the song of Jonah is either directly borrowed from, or can be illustrated by, the songs sung either in anticipation of the captivity, or during the dark days of Israel's exile from her land.

It is also worthy of notice that not a single note of repentance is struck in the hymn from first to last. It contains no lamentation for sin, though it is replete with the voice of thanksgiving for deliverance. The only sin alluded to in the psalm is the sin of idolatry, alluded to in ver. 8, which sin was not committed by Jonah, but by the Gentiles who knew not the God of Israel and yet cast His prophet into the sea. Something like the same phenomenon is exhibited in some of the psalms composed in the days of exile, such as Ps. xlii., xliii., xliv. Swallowed up by an idolatrous nation, the noble protest the Israelites made against idolatry in the land of idols was one of the grandest characteristics of the faithful remnant in the days of the Babylonish captivity. Jonah's hymn fits in admirably into an allegory of which the exile of Israel is the theme. It is not such a hymn as could have been naturally composed under the circumstances narrated in the book, if those circumstances be regarded as literal facts. Nor is it such a hymn as one would have expected a man rescued from the stomach of an actual sea-monster to have composed as a memorial of his deliverance.

The key to open this and many a difficult lock in the Old Testament is the right comprehension of the name and position of "the servant of Jehovah." Israel as a nation, "Israel according to the flesh," is called by that high appellation. But the nation was deaf to the call of God, deaf to the appeals of His prophets, and so blind that it did not behold the real glory of its position. Jehovah therefore expostulates with them in the following words: "Who is blind, but my servant? or deaf, as my messenger that I send? who is blind as he who is given up to me (*i.e.* devoted professedly to my service), and blind as the servant of Jehovah?" (Isa. xlii. 19). Thus was the nation of Israel condemned for its blindness. But, as Delitzsch well observes, "Israel according to the flesh" is only the outer circle. There is an inner circle, composed of the faithful in Israel. This is the "Israel according to the spirit," which in a higher sense is also termed "the servant of Jehovah," is spoken of with approval, and promised divine grace to perform the work and service befitting such a position. The centre-point of the inner circle is the great Messiah, the Christ of God, He concerning whom Jehovah says: "Behold my servant, whom I uphold; my chosen, in whom my soul delighteth: I have put my spirit upon Him: He shall bring forth judgment to the nations" (Isa. xlii. 1). This is the servant whose work and ultimate victory is depicted in the afterpart of that chapter, and whose strange travail with its blessed result is so marvellously depicted in the glorious passional of Isaiah lii., liii. The unfaithfulness of "Israel according to the flesh," in discharging the performance of the duty imposed on it as Jehovah's servant, led to the selection of "Israel according to the spirit." And "the weakness of the flesh" even in the latter case ultimately led to the setting apart to the office of "servant of Jehovah" in the highest sense, Him who in very deed was holy, sinless, undefiled, separated from sinners (Heb. vii. 26), able to speak in righteousness, mighty to save (Isa. lxiii. 1).

The history of Israel shadows forth, more or less distinctly, the history of Messiah. Israel was punished for their sins; they knew their Lord's will and they did it not, and so they received many stripes (Luke xii. 47). Israel therefore, as a nation, was cast forth to be swallowed up by the sea-monster. In the interior of that monster the nation had to abide in a state of national death, or suspended animation, during the mystical "three days and three nights," singing strangely, however, "the Lord's songs in a strange land," and testifying in the very heart of the dragon to the vanity and folly of idolatry. What then occurred had never previously happened. The monster voluntarily disgorged its prey; and the exiles returned and came singing unto Zion, singing as they went along,—

> "When the Lord turned again the captivity of Zion,
> We were like unto them that dream.
> Then was our mouth filled with laughter,
> And our tongue with singing:
> Then said they among the nations,
> The Lord hath done great things for them.
> The Lord hath done great things for us;
> Whereof we are glad."—Ps. cxxvi. 1-3.

The returning exiles of Israel were "a sign and a wonder" unto "the men of that generation," to the men of Nineveh, to the inhabitants of Babylon. The nations had never before seen such a national resurrection. It was a new birth, the nation was born in a day (Isa. lxvi. 8). That march from Babylon to Jerusalem, though unaccompanied by any miraculous portent, was as marvellous an event as the march from Egypt, commenced on the night of the first Passover, which led the nation ultimately to Canaan.

But a greater than Jonah is pointed out in the allegory. Jonah, the dove, was regarded by the men of old as a symbol of Israel. Jonah, the dove, was also employed by the Rabbis as a symbol of the Messiah. An allegory which depicts the one must necessarily point out the other. Messiah was punished for sin, but for sin which was not His own: "He was wounded for our transgressions, He was bruised for our iniquities: the chastisement of our peace was upon Him; and with His stripes we are healed. . . . The Lord hath laid on Him the iniquity of us all" (Isa. liii. 5, 6). He, too, was swallowed up, not, indeed by the sea-monster or world-power,—

the dragon of Rev. xii. which sought in vain to devour Him. For His kingdom was not of this world (John xix. 36), and therefore it could not be destroyed by any earthly power. He overcame the world (John xvi. 33). But He was for a season swallowed up by a still greater monster, Death, which has swallowed up, and swallows up still unceasingly, the sons of men. The lot fell upon Him (John xi. 49, 50), and by the directions of His own people, but by the hands of the Gentiles, He was cast forth into the abyss. He went down, "descended into the lower parts of the earth" (Eph. iv. 10). He tarried within the gates of Sheol (the Under-world) or Hades (the Unseen) three literal days,—the days to which the mystical three of Hosea ultimately pointed. He "went down to the pit," having "in the days of His flesh offered up prayers and supplications, with strong crying and tears, unto Him that was able to save Him from death, and having been heard for His godly fear, though He was a Son, yet learned obedience by the things which He suffered" (Heb. v. 7, 8), and "through death He brought to nought him that had the power of death, that is, the devil" (Heb. ii. 14). For "now hath Christ been raised from the dead, the first-fruits of them that are asleep. For since by man came death, by man came also the resurrection of the dead. For as in Adam all die, so also in Christ shall all be made alive" (1 Cor. xv. 20–22). The Son of man was a sign to the men of His generation (Luke x. 30). He was "saved" first

Himself, and thus fitted to become the saviour of others (comp. Zech. ix. 9;[1] Heb. v. 7–10). He could close His thanksgiving psalm, like Jonah, or Israel of old, with a "salvation to Jehovah." For, "being by the right hand of God exalted, and having received of the Father the promise of the Holy Ghost," He poured forth on the day of Pentecost precious rain upon His inheritance (Acts ii. 33). The allegory concerning Jonah, if an allegory, is fully and beautifully realized in the history of Israel and its return from captivity. Like all those prophecies which treat of Israel, it has also received its highest and most glorious accomplishment in the history of Israel's Messiah, the Son of man of the New Testament, and in His resurrection from the dead.

§ 4. *Difficulties in the Book of Jonah regarded as an historical narrative—The New Testament references thereto—The book an allegorical description of Israel's past, and a prophecy of Israel's future.*

The real difficulties which lie in the way of regarding the Book of Jonah as historical, do not arise from the fact that wonders and miracles are related therein. Some objections, indeed, brought against the narrative can be easily answered. There is, for example, no necessity to suppose that Jonah actually composed the "prayer" or hymn of the second chapter while in the belly of the fish. The

---
[1] See *Bampton Lectures on Zechariah*, p. 234 ff.

historical truth of the book would not be endangered were it to be maintained that the song was composed by Jonah in later days in memory of his wonderful deliverance.[1]

But more serious difficulties present themselves when the narrative is carefully examined. The storm is said to have taken place in the eastern part of the Mediterranean. But in that case the story of the deliverance of Jonah could not have become known at Nineveh until long after the event and, since the Assyrian territory did not extend to the Mediterranean, the miracle could scarcely have become known to Ninevites except through Jonah's own report.

The Old Testament narrative does not, perhaps, necessarily imply that the Ninevites heard any-

---

[1] Kaulen, the pious Roman Catholic expositor (*Librum Jonæ prophetæ, exposuit Franciscus Kaulen*, Mogunt. 1862), has considered it necessary to caution his readers against imagining that the second chapter of the book contains all the prayers which Jonah poured out to God during those three consecutive days. He maintains that only those sayings are mentioned which comprise, as it were, the beginning and the end of that supplication (sed ea tantum commemorantur dicta, quæ orandi quasi epilogum and conclusionem efficiunt). He argues, in a footnote, that this is shown in the Hebrew text, because Hebrew forms are made use of which are used in narrating past events. He notices that S. Jerome similarly understood the text: "Non dixit *clamo* sed *clamavi*: nec de futuro precatur, sed de præterito gratias agit." Pusey takes a similar view, observing in chap. ii. 1: "When the three days and nights were passed, he uttered this devotion." The idea that such slavish punctiliousness to accuracy in the smallest details ought to be looked for in the sacred writings, far from promoting the interests of faith, tends in the very opposite direction. Such minute accuracy does not characterize sacred Scripture.

thing of the matter; and if the story were mentioned only in the Old Testament, it would be quite appropriate to quote as parallels to the consternation caused in Nineveh by the preaching of Jonah, such incidents as the alarm created in Jerusalem by the piercing cry of Jesus the son of Anan,[1] or the terror once occasioned at Constantinople by the prediction of a soldier that the city was to perish by fire from heaven;[2] or even to adduce the statement of Layard, that he has "known a Christian priest frighten a whole Mussulman town to repentance by proclaiming that he had a divine mission to announce a coming earthquake or plague."[3] Such cases are amply sufficient to prove the possibility of the king and people of Nineveh being alarmed by the unwonted spectacle of "an unknown Hebrew in a prophet's austere and homely attire passing through the splendid streets of the proudest town of the Eastern world, uttering words of rebuke and menace" (Kalisch).

But the New Testament goes further. In one of our Lord's discourses it is stated that there should no sign be given to the men of that generation "but the sign of Jonah. For even as Jonah became a sign unto the Ninevites, so shall also the Son of man be to this generation." "The men of Nineveh shall stand up in the judgment with this generation, and shall

---

[1] Josephus, *De Bello Jud.* vi. 5. 3.

[2] See Augustine's account of this incident, quoted in Pusey's *Minor Prophets*, p. 278.

[3] Layard's *Babylon and Nineveh*, p. 632; and Pusey in his *Introduction to Jonah*, p. 255.

condemn it: for they repented at the preaching of Jonah; and behold a greater than Jonah is here" (Luke xi. 29, 30, 32).[1] The words used plainly imply that the Ninevites had a knowledge of Jonah's deliverance from the fish's belly, and that that deliverance was a "sign" to them. It was, then, not the weird and strange appearance of the Hebrew prophet as he uttered his predictions in the streets of Nineveh which led the people to give credence to the denunciations of the prophet as the utterances of one who spoke with the authority of Heaven, but the fact that the man who uttered such threatenings had been marvellously delivered from the belly of a fish in order that he might perform that special work.

It must be admitted that the New Testament has thus considerably increased the difficulties which beset the apologist of the Book of Jonah, if the book is to be viewed as a historical narrative. But if it can be shown that the book is a prophetico-allegorical history of the people of Israel, our Lord's words create, as we shall see, no difficulty whatever. For His references to the narrative of Jonah do not necessarily imply the historical truth of the event in the precise form in which it is presented in the Book of Jonah. The reference of our Lord would be fully justified even if it could be shown that the Book of Jonah was an allegory or symbolical prophecy like

---

[1] See the parallel passage in Matt. xii. 38-41, in which, however, it is not exactly stated that Jonah's deliverance was made known to the people of Nineveh.

Ezekiel's description (chap. xxiii.) of Oholah and Oholibah, or like our Lord's own story of the prodigal son and his elder brother (Luke xv.).

For Messiah and the people of Israel are so closely connected together that the prophecies which relate to the one refer more or less directly to the other. It has been noticed that Messiah and Israel are both termed "the servant of Jehovah," the one in the higher, the other in a lower sense of the phrase. The events which happened to the people of Israel in the infancy of that nation, find in some respects a counterpart in the history of Israel's King. The world-power sought to destroy both in infancy (Ex. i. 15–22; Matt. ii.); they were both driven into Egypt for temporary deliverance from danger (Gen. xlv. 7–11; Matt. ii. 13–15), and after a season were called forth out of that land (comp. Hos. xi. 1 with Matt. ii. 15). A prophetical allegory, depicting the temporary death of the nation and its resurrection anew to a national existence, might therefore very properly be referred to as containing a prophecy of the death and resurrection of Israel's Lord and King.[1]

For it ought not to be forgotten that the description in Ezekiel of the national resurrection of Israel (Ezek. xxxvii. 1–14) is related with so much fulness of detail that that prophecy has frequently been

---

[1] The language used of the nation in Isa. xxvi. 19 must not be forgotten, nor should the significant reference of S. Paul to the resurrection of Christ on the third day as "according to the Scriptures (1 Cor. xv. 4) be overlooked (comp. Luke xxiv. 46). See our remarks on Hos. vi. 1, 2, on pp. 54, 65.

misunderstood to be a prediction of the resurrection of the dead at the last day. Deductions have even been drawn from that prophecy of Israel's restoration which have seriously affected the correct comprehension of the scriptural doctrine of the resurrection of the body.[1] It need not therefore surprise us to find that the symbolical allegory of the Book of Jonah in process of time came to be regarded as literal history.[2]

Had the collectors of the canon of the Old Testament viewed the Book of Jonah as historical, they would scarcely have inserted it in its present position among the prophetical, instead of with the historical books. If the incidents mentioned in the book were historical, it is more than strange that no allusion is made to any one of them in the Books of the Kings and the Chronicles. Although the writer of 2 Kings mentions Jonah the prophet, and one of his predictions (2 Kings xiv. 25), he never alludes to the wonderful mission on which that prophet was sent.

---

[1] In mediæval times it was generally believed that the Scripture taught the resurrection of every portion of the original body. Hence the frequent allusion made to the collecting together of all the particles of each human body from all quarters in the day of resurrection. The supposed truth was often set forth to the eye in paintings. But the apostle's words in 1 Cor. xv. 35–42 distinctly negative any such idea. The body of the resurrection is regarded by him as no more identical in all its component particles with that committed to the grave, than the plant which springs from the seed is identical in its particles with the seed originally deposited in the soil. There is a close connection between the seed and the plant which grows from it, but there is no identity in their component particles.

[2] It is referred to as historical truth in Tob. xiv. 4, 8 ; 3 Macc. vi. 8 ; Joseph. *Antiq.* ix. 10. 2.

No prophet was ever despatched on a grander and more important mission; and the outcome of Jonah's preaching, if the narrative be regarded as history, was the most wonderful success ever experienced. When compared with the result of Jonah's preaching, Elijah's controversy with Israel on Mount Carmel (1 Kings xviii.) sinks into utter insignificance. Why then should the latter incident have been recorded in the Books of the Kings (1 Kings xviii.), while the most extraordinary fact connected with a prophet is passed over in silence by the Hebrew historians? No reference is made to the mission of Jonah in the prophecies of the later prophets, although they delivered many predictions against Assyria. Is it not strange that in those numerous denunciations not the slightest allusion was ever made to the wonderful warning which Assyria received, and which the capital city of that empire is said to have taken so deeply to heart?

It is not, then, the miracles recorded in the book which constitute the real difficulties in the way of regarding the book as actual history. The formidable difficulties are those just mentioned. There is, moreover, much omitted in the Book of Jonah which, if it were a historical narrative, ought properly to have been mentioned. Nothing is said in the book concerning the special sins of which Nineveh has been guilty, and of which the king and people repented at the preaching of Jonah. Kaulen and others suppose that the sins then repented of were lust and luxury. But was not the sin of idolatry one of the very chief of Nineveh's transgressions? (Nah. i. 14, iii. 4). Are we to suppose that the Ninevites abandoned for a season their sins of lust and luxury? Would such a repentance have been acceptable, if they had not also turned from idols to serve the living and true God? But where, as Kalisch well inquires, is there the slightest trace in history of the Ninevites ever having done homage to the God of Israel? Where is there the slightest trace of their having, even for a season, renounced their ancestral worship?

If the book be regarded as an historical narrative, it is a serious defect in it that no mention is made therein of the name of the king of Nineveh who was seated then upon the throne. The history of Jonah prior to this great mission, his journey to Nineveh (no easy journey in that day), and his subsequent fortunes, are all passed over in silence. Regarded from a historical standpoint, the story closes abruptly with God's rebuke of Jonah's discontent. The result of that rebuke upon the prophet (a gap in the story, too often filled up by the fancy of commentators) is not recorded in the book. There is, indeed, a remarkable New Testament parallel to this,—a parallel, too, which was probably not undesigned. In our Lord's parable of the Prodigal Son, the result of the father's entreaty with the elder son is also left out. That parable closes abruptly, just like the Book of Jonah. There is, we maintain, a deep reason for the omission. Both narratives are, as shall be shown hereafter, allegorical representations of one and the same fact, of Israel, the people of God, the people of Messiah, strangely discontented with results which ought to have been to them causes of the highest exultation.

§ 5. *The restoration of Jonah to the prophetic office—His renewed commission—The overthrow of the nations—The voices of the Hebrew prophets—Expectations of the Jews at the restoration from Babylon—Penitent Nineveh—Readiness of the Gentiles to learn religious truths from Israel—Conditional character of prophecy—The gourd or palmchrist of Jonah—The Davidic governor, Zerubbabel the son of Shealtiel.*

When restored once more to his country and to his work by the marvellous deliverance from the belly of the sea-monster, Jonah received a second commission from God to arise and go to Nineveh, and to preach to that city the preaching which he had been commanded. Jonah was not a second time disobedient to the divine command, although, as shown in the sequel of the story, the commission he was entrusted with was still far from agreeable to him. He set out, however, upon the journey, and, on entering the great city Nineveh, commenced his preaching with the awful announcement, "Yet forty days, and Nineveh shall be overthrown!"

The voices of the prophets of Israel were not specially directed against the great nations of the world until Israel and Judah were threatened with attack by the great world-empires. The earlier Hebrew prophets, from Samuel to Jonah, occupied themselves mainly with pointing out the low state of religion in their own land, and with calling Israel to repentance. They seldom spoke of the nations of the outside world, with the exception of those whose territories bordered on the Holy Land. The prophetical books contained in the canon of the Old Testament all belong to the period in which the attention of the prophets was by degrees turned, under divine direction, towards the great world which lay outside of the land of Israel. It was not intended that Israel should be for ever isolated and cut off from the great nations of the earth. A considerable portion of the prophecies of Isaiah and the other prophets are occupied with matters which concern "the regions beyond." This is a characteristic, however, especially of the writings of Jeremiah, Ezekiel, Daniel, and Zechariah, many of whose prophecies seem to have been, directly or indirectly, designed for foreign peoples. Israel, the prophet of humanity, began to discharge her mission to the world at the very time when she began to be shorn of her national independence. Her peculiar greatness was exhibited most brightly in the time of trouble and distress.

The prophets of Israel often dilate on the approaching destruction of the nations because of their sins, and on the subsequent deliverance of Israel. They foresaw the sorrows which afterwards fell upon their own nation on account of sin. Israel was to be punished but not destroyed, while Assyria, the world-power—like that depicted in the Book of the Revelation (xvii. 11)—"was to go into perdition" (Num. xxiv. 24). Against the great city of the nations, Israel's prophets proclaimed: "Yet forty days and Nineveh shall be destroyed." They announced the latter fact to their own nation in such words as "Hide thyself for a little moment, until the indignation be overpast. For, behold, Jehovah cometh forth out of His place to punish the inhabitants of the earth for their iniquity: the earth also shall disclose her blood, and shall no more cover her slain" (Isa. xxvi. 20, 21).

This truth is remarkably illustrated in the vision in which Jeremiah represents himself as taking "the cup of the wine of fury" at the hand of Jehovah, and giving all the nations a drink thereof, beginning with Jerusalem and the cities of Judah, and ending with the king of Babylon: "All the kings of the north, far and near, one with another, and all the kingdoms of the world, which are upon the face of the earth, and the king of Sheshach shall drink after them" (Jer. xxv. 15–31). The same subject of prediction was taken up by Ezekiel and continued by Daniel.[1] Many passages in the Psalms and the

---

[1] The other prophets speak in general of the destruction of particular nations, but all the prophets touch more or less upon the same theme, *e.g.* Joel iii. 2; Obad. 15; Micah vii. 15; Zeph. iii. 8, etc.

prophets, especially in Isaiah, speak of the conversion of the nations, and foreshadow the time when "the earth shall be full of the knowledge of the Lord, as the waters cover the sea" (Isa. xi. 9). But the general drift of Hebrew prophecy is that the nations are to be brought low by judgment, destroyed as "nations," and after that, the remnant are to be affrighted, and to give glory to the God of heaven (Rev. xi. 13).

When, therefore, the people of Israel[1] were restored after the Babylonish captivity, and the first bands of the returning exiles trod again the sacred soil of Palestine, there was a general expectation that the divine judgments would speedily be poured out upon all the adversaries of Jehovah and His people, and that the great city of the nations would be visited for its sins. Considerable disappointment prevailed among the Jews who had returned when these expected judgments did not at once take place, and when they saw that the cities of the nations were not overwhelmed by the wrath of the Almighty. The state of feeling prevalent at the time of the Restoration can easily be perceived by those who read with attention the books of the Old Testament which

---

[1] We have designedly spoken of the restoration of Israel after the Babylonish captivity as a protest against the misunderstanding which confines that restoration to the tribes of Judah and Benjamin. See the remarks on this subject in the *Bampton Lectures on Zechariah*, pp. 278-285. The name "Israel" is frequently employed in the prophets and elsewhere to designate Judah, which had an equal right with Ephraim to that honourable appellation.

treat of that special period. Haggai and Zechariah were raised up to cheer the returned exiles in that time of gloom and depression. Haggai predicted the shaking of the nations, and Zechariah in his opening vision described the Angel of Jehovah as pouring forth intercessory prayer in order that the longed-for breaking up of the Gentile power might speedily take place.

Shortly after the overthrow of the Jewish kingdom by Nebuchadnezzar, signs were displayed by the Gentiles of a disposition to learn in matters of religion from the people of Israel. Faith in idolatry was somewhat shaken, and Israel in its low estate began to act as an instructor to the nations. The Book of Daniel narrates that Nebuchadnezzar, the proud monarch of the Gentile world, though "mad upon idols" (Jer. l. 38), was on several occasions forced to acknowledge that the God of Israel was the God of gods and the Lord of kings (Dan. ii. 47). Despite the contempt he had once felt for the Deity worshipped by the nation which had been trodden under foot by his armies, Nebuchadnezzar decreed that no one should speak amiss against the God of Israel (Dan. iii. 29). On a later occasion that monarch humbled himself in penitence before the King of Heaven for his pride and transgressions (Dan. iv. 34–37), and confessed that he had been taught by experience that the Most High ruleth in the kingdom of heaven, and setteth up over it whomsoever He will (Dan. v. 21).

Such a disposition was not confined to the great king of Babylon. At an earlier period the nations planted in the northern parts of Palestine, in the room of the Israelites carried away captive by the king of Assyria, displayed anxiety to learn the manner in which they ought to worship Jehovah (2 Kings xvii. 24–41). Those colonists had, no doubt, a very imperfect conception of Jehovah as "the God of the land," and hence they continued for some time the worship of their own gods. In process of time the Gentile colonists, however, intermarried with the poor Israelites who were left by the Assyrians behind in the land.[1] For a time they were not disposed to forget their Gentile origin, which was originally a matter for boasting. In later times they also laid stress when convenient upon their Gentile origin (Ezra iv. 7–16); but the influence of the religion of Israel (which they finally adopted in a purer form than they did at first (2 Kings xvii. 32–41)), induced the Samaritans at last to lay claim in the most unqualified manner to an Israelitish origin (John iv. 12). Their request in the days of Zerubbabel to be permitted to share in the work of rebuilding the temple was not received in a friendly spirit by the Jews who had then returned from Babylon. The latter looked upon the Samaritans as "adversaries," and probably had good

---

[1] See *Bampton Lectures on Zechariah*, pp. 244 ff. and 284 ff. That many of the poor Israelites were left behind when the Assyrians carried Israel away captive, as in the later deportation of Judah to Babylon (2 Kings xxv. 12, 22), is evident from the narrative in 2 Chron. xxx. 1, 5–11, xxxiv. 9.

grounds for their suspicions (Ezra iv. 1-6). But the very fact of such an overture having been made to the Jews by the Samaritans—a proposal distinctly based on the declaration that they also worshipped the God of Israel, and did sacrifice unto Him (Ezra iv. 2)—proves at least the extension among the Gentiles of faith in Jehovah. Many, too, of the Gentiles who dwelt in that portion of the Holy Land which was taken possession of by the Jews who returned from Babylon, voluntarily attached themselves to the Jewish religion (Ezra vi. 21); and mention is also incidentally made in the Book of Esther (Esth. viii. 17) of a considerable spread of faith in the God of Israel among the nations of the Persian empire. Moreover, not a few of the hereditary foes of Israel, such as the Philistines, in the period after the Return, by degrees became incorporated into the nation of Israel (Zech. ix. 6, 7).[1]

It did not fall within the scope of the authors of the Old Testament books which belong to the period referred to, to give any account of the spread of the spirit of penitence and religion among the Gentiles. The incidental notices of the fact already alluded to suffice, however, to prove that the sojourn of Israel in captivity had a beneficial effect upon the heathen world. The idea of the conversion of the nations, and of their repentance towards God, is often met with in the Hebrew prophets. It is not a little significant that the King of Zion is depicted by

[1] See *Bampton Lectures on Zechariah*, pp. 218-220.

Zechariah as destined to destroy the military power of Ephraim and Judah prior to the great period of the conversion of the Gentiles (Zech. ix. 9, 10). The same writer, in his closing chapter,—while he predicts a gathering together of the nations against Jerusalem and Judah, and describes the utter overthrow of that confederacy,—proceeds to speak afterwards of the nations being converted to the God of Israel, and pourtrays them as keeping the feast of Tabernacles and worshipping the King, Jehovah of hosts, in Jerusalem (Zech. xiv. 16, 17).[1]

In the same spirit, and with the same object in view, the Book of Jonah describes penitent Nineveh as mercifully spared by a God that delights in mercy. Notwithstanding the solemn prediction, "Yet forty days and Nineveh shall be overthrown," when the people of Nineveh repented in sackcloth and ashes, the sword that was stretched out against them (as against Israel in a former day) was put up again into its sheath. The prediction of Jonah, ushered in though it was by wondrous prodigies, was not accomplished. The transgressions of Nineveh were forgiven, her sins were covered (Ps. xxxii. 1).

Jeremiah, whose writings peculiarly abound with prophecies of the ruin and downfall of the various

---

[1] Inasmuch as a great deal of popular misconception exists as to the meaning of these prophecies, and the crudest views have been put forth concerning them in pamphlets and tracts professing to sketch out what is to happen in the future, I may be permitted to refer to the last chapter of the *Bampton Lectures on Zechariah*, entitled "The Eschatology of Zechariah, or 'the Last Things,' as seen in the light of the Old Dispensation."

Gentile nations, was commissioned to lay down in express terms the following great principle which influences God's dealings with the nations: "At what instant I shall speak concerning a nation, and concerning a kingdom, to pluck up and to break down and to destroy it; if that nation, concerning which I have spoken, turn from their evil, I will repent of the evil that I thought to do unto them" (Jer. xviii. 7, 8). In other words, the Divine denunciations of wrath against any nation are conditional on the continuance in evil of the nation specially threatened. The ruin of kingdoms announced by any prophet might be averted by their repentance. If God visits the iniquity of the fathers upon the children, upon the third and fourth generation of them that hate Him, He will as assuredly show mercy even to the people of the third or fourth generation, if their hatred be transformed into love, and if they keep His commandments (Ex. xx. 5, 6). Jeremiah was directed to collect together and make a digest of his most terrible prophecies against Israel and Judah, in the hope, however slight it might be, that the people concerned would give heed to the evil which God purposed to do unto them, and repent and obtain forgiveness (Jer. xxxvi. 3, 7). The principle laid down by Jeremiah in reference to nations is further expounded by Ezekiel as applicable to the case of individuals (Ezek. xxxiii. 8, 13–16). The principle itself had long before been laid down virtually in the Second Commandment of the Law. Daniel's exhortation of Nebuchadnezzar to repentance (Dan. iv. 27) was founded on the hope that Nebuchadnezzar's calamities, though distinctly predicted, might be averted (as in the case of Ahab, 1 Kings xxi. 29); and the recognition in the most distinct manner of the truth in its bearing upon judgments threatened to the nations is one of the leading principles which underlie the Book of Jonah.

For the Book of Jonah states in the most precise terms that the unwillingness exhibited at first by the prophet to execute the great commission with which he was entrusted was in reality due to the conviction in his innermost soul that God was "gracious and full of compassion, slow to anger and plenteous in mercy" (Jonah iv. 2). However much he longed for the overthrow of the great city, in order that his own nation might escape the danger impending from that quarter, Jonah considered it was quite possible that God might repent of the evil which He designed to do to Nineveh (Jonah iv. 2, 3). Consequently he feared that the predictions, which he, as the prophet of Jehovah, might utter, were not likely after all to be accomplished, but that in the very discharge of the mission he himself might come under the charge of having been a deceiver and a false prophet.

The difficulty suggested was no mere imaginary conception of the prophet. But it is remarkable that no solution of it is vouchsafed in the Book of Jonah. The difficulty is not concealed; on the contrary, it is even brought into bold relief in the book. But there is no attempt made by the writer to solve the problem, or to explain and justify the divine method of procedure. The mission of the Hebrew prophet is described as so successful that the king and people of Nineveh, stricken with terror at the idea of the coming destruction, repented in dust and ashes. The consequence of this exhibition of penitence was that Nineveh was spared by the long-suffering of God.

It is not therefore surprising to read that Jonah was greatly displeased at the result. His prophecy was apparently a failure. The forty days expired, and Nineveh was not overthrown. He could not adapt himself to the altered circumstances of the position. He could not bring himself to rejoice in the exhibition of Divine mercy and long-suffering. He hoped in some way or other that the threatened judgment might yet be executed. He went out of the city, "made him a booth, and sat sullenly under it in the shadow, till he might see what would become of the city."

It has been already noticed that the exiles who returned from Babylon to Jerusalem murmured at the non-fulfilment of the prophecies concerning the destruction of Babylon, and the breaking up of the Gentile power. Though restored to their country, the Jews were still servants under the Gentile yoke. Their bodies, their cattle, and their goods were in the power of their enemies, and they were consequently in great distress (Neh. ix. 36, 37). Dissatisfied at this state of things, it was quite natural for the Jews in Jerusalem in their ruined city to scan eagerly the horizon in order to discover any one who would bring them from that distant land the wished-for news of the great overthrow. Under their poor shelter in their desolated country, the Jews watched and waited to see what would become of the great city of the nations.

The discontented and murmuring prophet was not forgotten by his God. In mercy and in love Jehovah did not grant his angry petition and take away his life. He was not left without some refreshment in his day of sorrow and gloom. In his evil case Divine Providence caused a gourd or palmchrist to shoot up over Jonah's booth, which overshadowed it and sheltered the head of the prophet from the burning rays of the Eastern sun. The booth in itself was, indeed, but a slight protection from the scorching heat of the sun, which, combined with the sultry east wind, was certain very soon to burn up the twigs and leafy foliage with which it was covered.[1] The palmchrist or gourd was no small advantage, and Jonah was exceeding glad because of it.

The Jewish exiles who, after the seventy years'

---

[1] There is, however, no need whatever to suppose that Jonah's booth or tabernacle (סֻכָּה) was constructed according to the directions given in the Talmud for the construction of the booths used at the feast of Tabernacles. It is impossible to prove, as Dr. Pusey asserts, that it was such a booth as did not "exclude the sun." The heat of the sun, no doubt, was able to shrivel up the foliage of the branches which formed its covering; and that foliage was, no doubt, damaged by the spreading out of the tendrils of the palmchrist, so that

captivity in Babylon, returned to their own land, were not a little comforted and cheered by the fact that Sheshbazzar the prince of Judah (Ezra i. 8), or, according to his proper Israelite designation, Zerubbabel the son of Shealtiel, of the royal house of David (1 Chron. iii. 17-19), had been placed by Cyrus at the head of the infant State. As their forefathers in the days of Zedekiah hoped that the day of calamity was over when that prince was placed upon the throne of Judah, and said among themselves, "Under his shadow we shall live among the nations" (Lam. iv. 20)—so the restored exiles imagined that now, at length, the day of blessing had begun to dawn upon them, and that the morning of the day had come whose sun was not to go down in darkness. Nurtured as they were on Messianic hopes, it was quite natural that they should now anticipate that the "shoot" would "come forth out of the stock of Jesse, and a branch out of his roots would bear fruit" (Isa. xi. 1).

Such hopes had also been directly fostered by the words of Haggai the prophet in reference to Zerubbabel. The prophet Jeremiah said of Zerubbabel's grandfather, Coniah (Jeconiah, 1 Chron. iii. 16, or

---

the original shady character of the booth was materially injured both by the rapid decay of the palmchrist and by the insects (the worm or worms), which consumed not only the leaves of the palmchrist, but also the leaves which were on the branches of the trees with which Jonah covered the booth. Compare the expressions: "in the shadow" (בְּצֵל), in ver. 5, "that it might be a shadow (צֵל) over his head," in ver. 6, with the statement in ver. 8.

Jehoiachin, 2 Kings xxiv. 6, 8), that though he were the signet upon Jehovah's right hand, yet he would be plucked off from thence (Jer. xxii. 24). But the prophet Haggai was directed, at a time when the whole earth was sitting still and at rest (Zech. i. 11), to predict a great shaking of the heavens and the earth, and to speak and say to Zerubbabel that "in that day, saith Jehovah of hosts, will I take thee, O Zerubbabel, my servant, the son of Shealtiel, saith Jehovah, and will make thee as the signet:[1] for I have chosen thee, saith Jehovah of hosts" (Hag. ii. 23). The sequel, indeed, made it abundantly manifest that the promise made to Zerubbabel, like that first made to Abraham (Gen. xii. 1–3), was intended to be fulfilled not to Zerubbabel himself, but in the person of his great descendant; but as Haggai had prophesied that Zerubbabel was to be replaced as the signet upon the Lord's right hand, it is not surprising that the Jews should have expected that he would soon be manifested, not as a mere Persian viceroy, but as the Anointed of Jehovah (Lam. iv. 20); that the government would be upon the shoulder (Isa. ix. 6) of him who had the signet-ring (comp. Gen. xl. 41, 42); and that the Israelites would indeed sit down under his shadow with great delight, and his fruit be sweet to their taste (Cant. ii. 3).

---

[1] The Hebrew has the article (כַּחוֹתָם), and though it is quite lawful to regard it as the generic article, and render it, as in the Revised Version, "as a signet," yet it appears preferable to give here the full force owing to the reference to the חוֹתָם עַל־יַד יְמִינִי of Jer. xxii. 24.

Zechariah was soon commissioned to check such illusory imaginations, and he did so by the significant action recorded in Zech. vi. 9–15, which probably took place in the temple of the Lord. There by divine direction he came forward in the presence of Israel, and placed the twisted fillet of silver and gold, formed out of the gold and silver brought by the Jewish deputation from Babylon, upon the head of Joshua the high priest, instead of upon the head of Zerubbabel. But even that significant action appears to have failed to direct the hopes of the Jews into a higher channel. Had Zerubbabel been crowned instead of Joshua the high priest, the people might have imagined that Zerubbabel was the man referred to in the words of Zechariah: "Behold the man whose name is the Branch!" "Hence in all probability it was that the crown was not placed upon the head of Zerubbabel, but upon that of the high priest. Neither Zechariah the priest-prophet, nor Joshua the high priest, could well have been ignorant of the fact that in Ps. cx. the Messiah was predicted in the character of both king and priest. And inasmuch as the high-priestly office was a typical one, the high priest and the people saw something remarkable in the prophetic words, addressed, indeed, to the high priest, but evidently referring to the Messiah, accompanied as they were by the symbolical act of crowning the high priest with the mark of royal dignity. The whole transaction was a symbolico-prophetical act. In the crowned high priest addressed by the prophet of

Jehovah in those solemn words, a striking picture was exhibited before the people of the long-expected Branch of David."[1]

It was expedient that the prince of David's line should be taken away from the head of the nation in order that the Israelites might set their affections on a coming One greater than Zerubbabel. The palm-christ, therefore, on which the Jews had fixed their hopes, and which for a time shadowed and sheltered them, was destroyed. Zerubbabel soon passed away. Whether his last days were spent in the city of his fathers, or whether he returned to breathe out his last breath in the land of exile, we know not. But his viceroyalty was short. The palmchrist perished as it were in a night. The worm did the work of destruction. The governor of the royal house of David was not permitted by Divine Providence to sit upon David's throne; the holy anointing oil was not poured upon his head. Long before even the days of Israel's partial independence dawned, that noble had been borne to his grave, men had watched sadly over his tomb, the worms covered him (Job xxi. 26; Isa. xiv. 11), the clods of the valley were sweet unto him (Job xxi. 32, 33). By the death of Zerubbabel the hopes of a restoration of the Davidic throne in Jerusalem came to an end, and the house of David sank for centuries into utter insignificance.

[1] *Bampton Lectures on Zechariah*, p. 118.

§ 6. *The Book of Jonah essentially a book of prophecy, not of history—The judgment announced to the world—The conversion of the Gentiles and the jealousy of the Jews—The great controversy in the early days of the Christian Church—The prophetic allegory of the Prodigal Son and his Elder Brother.*

The Book of Jonah was no doubt inserted among the prophets by the wise men who collected the canon of the Old Testament, not so much because the book had been written by a prophet, for most of the sacred writings were supposed to have had prophets for their authors, but because the book was itself essentially prophetical.[1] Whether there be any basis of historical truth at the bottom of the narrative itself or not—and time only can finally resolve that problem—the Book of Jonah seems to have been mainly intended to be a historico-symbolical prophecy. If it alluded to the past, and described the present, it also pointed forward to the future. "That which hath been is that which shall be; and that which hath been done is that which shall be done" (Eccles. i. 9). The history of Israel repeated itself substantially more than once; and the repetition of Israelitish history, which forms, as we maintain, the main sum and substance of the prophecy of the book, took place in the early Christian era.

[1] See my Excursus I. on *The Talmud and the Old Testament Canon*, especially at p. 452 ff., and p. 463, of *The Book of Koheleth considered in relation to Modern Criticism and Modern Pessimism.*

It has frequently been noticed in this essay that the history of Messiah is foreshadowed in the history of Israel. The Book of Jonah is expressly referred to by our Lord as containing a prophecy of His death by the hands of the Gentiles, and of His resurrection after three days (see p. 64 ff.). The work of preaching the gospel to the world after Christ's resurrection was carried on, indeed, by Christ's disciples. Christ after He rose from the dead did not in person exhibit Himself again in the character of the Prophet of the World. But it is distinctly stated that the Lord worked with His people and confirmed the word by the signs that followed (Mark xvi. 20). St. Peter laid stress upon the fact that the gift poured out on the day of Pentecost came directly from the risen Lord: "Being therefore by the right hand of God exalted, and having received of the Father the promise of the Holy Ghost, He hath poured forth this, which ye see and hear" (Acts ii. 33).

The preaching of the gospel to the world, whether Jewish or Gentile, contained in it a declaration of "judgment to come," and a denunciation of a destruction impending over the heads of the ungodly. The point is referred to not only in St. Peter's sermon on the day of Pentecost (Acts ii. 40), but also at the close of St. Paul's great discourse in the synagogue of Antioch in Pisidia (Acts xiii. 40, 41), in his speech on Mars Hill (Acts xvii. 30, 31), in his private discussions with Felix (Acts xxiv. 25), and on other occasions. The cry was raised "in the street of the great city where also the Lord was crucified " (Rev. xi. 8), a cry similar to that spoken of by the prophet, " Yet forty days and Nineveh shall be overthrown : " " The world passeth away and the lust thereof, but he that doeth the will of God abideth for ever " (1 John ii. 17). The voice of warning, " Flee from the wrath to come " (Matt. iii. 7), first lifted up on the banks of the Jordan, was caught up and re-echoed more or less distinctly in all the apostolic letters. It was " sounded forth " not merely by the Apostle of the Circumcision (2 Pet. iii. 10), but also by the Apostle of the Gentiles (2 Thess. i. 7–10). And within a period, in round numbers, of some forty years, the first fury of the tempest fell upon the city of Jerusalem (1 Thess. ii. 16).

The efforts made by our Lord in His lifetime to raise the degraded classes of the Jews were not looked upon with favour by the Pharisees and scribes (Luke xv. 1, 2). It would have been meet for them to have made merry and to have been glad when they saw the " publicans and sinners," who had previously been " dead " to any love of God, awakening to spiritual life under the teaching of Jesus; when those who had been regarded as " lost " were " found again," and seen sitting at the feet of the great Teacher.

But even a stranger phenomenon was exhibited when the very disciples of Jesus, explicitly directed by the Master to go into all the world and make disciples of all nations (Matt. xxviii. 19), showed a deep-seated and decided reluctance to believe that God was " no respecter of persons, but in every nation he that feareth Him, and worketh righteousness, is acceptable to Him" (Acts x. 35). Yet the early Christians were amazed when the Holy Spirit was bestowed upon the Gentiles (Acts x. 45), and were astonished because God granted "to the Gentiles also repentance unto life" (Acts xi. 18). There is little reason to be surprised at the picture of Jonah sitting over against Nineveh, angry and sullen because God had granted repentance and life from the dead to that city after it had been doomed to destruction, when the disciples of Jesus, in the full enjoyment of a Pentecostal effusion of grace, found it so hard to believe in the loving-kindness of God.

It is no doubt true that when the Jewish Christians heard the tidings of the marvellous grace bestowed upon the Gentiles, they "glorified God." The record of the Acts of the Apostles, however, proves that those disciples were not at once emancipated from their prejudices. Even from the standpoint of the Old Dispensation, they ought to have rejoiced at the Gentiles becoming proselytes. But such a small amount of liberality was not exhibited at the outset. And when the Gentiles were "admitted into the fellowship of Christ's communion," and the true consequences of the doctrine that "God hath made of one blood all nations upon the earth" (Acts xvii. 26) began to be perceived, the Jewish Christians strove to force the necks of the Gentiles to stoop under the yoke of the old law of carnal ordinances.

They no doubt argued that if the Gentiles were to be partakers of grace they ought also to become Jews (Esth. viii. 17), and like the servants and slaves of Abraham, they ought to receive on their bodies the sign of circumcision, as did "the father of the faithful" (Gen. xvii. 27).

Notwithstanding, therefore, the "great grace" bestowed upon the Jewish Christians, there was a hard struggle ere uncircumcised Gentiles came to be looked upon by them as Christians equal in position to circumcised Jews. The Council held at Jerusalem decided after much discussion in favour of liberty being granted to the Gentiles (Acts xv. 19–21, 28, 29). But the liberty then formally conceded had again and again to be contended for. In order to gain popularity among their Jewish adherents, Peter and Barnabas were at a later date guilty of dissembling the broad and liberal views they once held on this question (Gal. ii. 11–14). It was long before the old prejudice was really overcome. The men accustomed to drink the "old wine" of the Law did not relish the "new wine" of gospel liberty, and for a considerable period they were wont to maintain that their old wine was "better" (Luke vi. 39). Men who held the faith of Christ did not conform at once to the "canons and decrees" even of an Apostolic Council. Before the contest within the Church of Christ was finally laid to rest, the Jewish temple was destroyed, Jerusalem was trodden down of the Gentiles, and, owing to the success which attended missionary work outside of the limits of Palestine, the Gentile element in the Church had become in a majority.

The attitude which the Christian Church, under apostolic leading, finally took up on this question was no doubt one of the reasons why the Jews showed themselves so unwilling to recognise the claims of Christianity. The "great company" of the Jewish priests who became obedient to the faith (Acts vi. 7) may have continued stedfastly in the apostles' teaching and fellowship (Acts ii. 42). But the number of such adherents does not appear to have increased as time rolled on; while the general reception (however unwilling at first) of the decrees of the first Christian Council had the effect of stopping to a considerable extent conversions among the Jewish people. The Jews were inveterately hostile to the idea that the Gentiles ought to be admitted to an equal position with themselves. They listened attentively to the arguments drawn from the Law and the Prophets in favour of the Messiahship of Jesus; they seemed often ready to admit their full force. But the doctrine of "Christ crucified" and that of the equality of the Gentiles were their real stumbling-blocks. The Jews at Jerusalem listened earnestly to Paul while he related in Hebrew the story of his conversion, and the vision which he had beheld of the glory of the Lord Jesus. They seem, therefore, at that period to have been somewhat better disposed towards Christianity than in the days when Stephen was martyred. But when the apostle proceeded to state that Christ had sent him to the Gentiles, the Jews could abide his speech no longer, but lifting up their voices with one accord, they cried out, "Away with such a fellow from the earth: for it is not fit that he should live" (Acts xxii. 21, 22).

Thus did the Jews, the prophets of humanity, intended by Divine Providence to be the teachers of religion to the world, act when the very mission they had been commissioned to discharge met with its grandest success. When, as foreseen by the prophets (Isa. ii. 3; Micah iv. 2), the law began to go forth from Zion, and the word of Jehovah was being spread from Jerusalem among the nations who had hitherto sat in darkness,—the very people, who ought to have burst forth into shouts of exultation, sat sullen and angry under the miserable Herodian tabernacle, longing for the destruction of the Gentiles, cherishing all sorts of delusory expectations, and meanwhile refusing to enter the hall of feasting, within which was to be heard the sound of "music and dancing," where "the fatted calf," the blessings of the New Dispensation, was being served up for their enjoyment, as well as for the lost prodigals of the Gentiles. "What advantage hath the Jew? or what is the profit of circumcision?" (Rom. iii. 1), was the question they sullenly asked. "Thou never gavest me a kid that I might make merry with my friends; but when this thy son came which hath devoured thy living with harlots, thou killest for him the fatted calf" (Luke xv. 29, 30).

The answer to the murmuring inquiry is thus presented by the great Apostle of the Gentiles. The Jew hath much advantage over the Gentile, there is verily a profit in circumcision: "Much every way: first of all, that they (the Jews) were entrusted with the oracles of God" (Rom. iii. 1, 2). The answer corresponds to the voice of the father: "Son, thou art ever with me, and that which is mine is thine." "Whose is the adoption, and the glory, and the covenants, and the giving of the Law, and the service of God, and the promises; whose are the fathers, and of whom is Christ as concerning the flesh, who is over all, God blessed for ever" (Rom. ix. 4, 5).

The parable of the Prodigal Son—known rightly under that designation, because it was the miserable prodigal who most needed the father's compassion and love—closes with the scene of the father stepping forth from the banqueting-house, the banner over which was love (Cant. ii. 4), to entreat the elder son, proud and indignant at the glad reception of the younger, to enter the hall of feasting. The Book of Jonah closes, too, with the remonstrance of Jehovah with Jonah on account of his unrighteous anger. The abrupt close of the parable and of the prophecy is by no means accidental; it was in both cases specially designed. The Book of Jonah as a symbolico-historical prophecy is most appropriately closed with the divine expostulation.

The voice of the Father of Israel, pleading still with the nation whom He had once chosen as His peculiar people, is a voice distinctly audible all through the books of the New Testament. The parable of our Lord is a prophecy as well as a parable. It is not merely the Jewish tax-gatherers and sinners who are therein represented. The Good Shepherd speaks there, too, of the " other sheep " which were not of the Jewish fold, which also He had to bring back to God, that Jews and Gentiles united in true faith and love might be one flock under one Shepherd (John x. 16). The pleading voice of Messiah, pleading with " His own " people, is still to be heard in the writings of the prophets and apostles. That voice will one day be listened to with gladness by the " backsliding children " of Israel, and the glorious answer to Messiah's entreaty will be that prophesied by Jeremiah: "Behold, we are come unto Thee, for Thou art Jehovah our God " (Jer. iii. 22).

III.

EZEKIEL'S PROPHECY OF GOG AND MAGOG.

"WHAT hast thou which thou didst not receive? but if thou didst receive it, why then dost thou glory, as if thou hadst not received it?" So Paul chode the Corinthian converts (1 Cor. iv. 7), who were disposed to boast of the teachers whom they followed, and the gifts of grace of which they had been made partakers; the most remarkable of which, the wonderful gift of tongues, they were delighted to display, in order to draw forth the admiration of beholders, rather than to promote their edification. The reproof of the apostle is, however, applicable to many other Churches than that of Corinth, and to many other nationalities than the boastful Greeks.

Every nation is more or less disposed to think well of itself, and to glory in the great men which have belonged to it in former days, or the able men belonging to it in the present time. It is quite natural for a people to know its own history better than that of others, and to understand its own good qualities, while it is ignorant of those of others. But it is well to look abroad as well as at home, to observe excellencies in others as well as in ourselves, to become acquainted with our own defects as well as to be able to comment on the shortcomings of other nations. It may be useful to remember the apostolic precept: " Look not every man on his own things, but every man also on the things of others " (Phil. ii. 4). For it lays down a principle which is applicable not only to individuals but also to nationalities—God is the God of the whole earth, and He " hath made of one every nation of men for to dwell on all the face of the earth, having determined their appointed seasons and the bounds of their habitation " (Acts xvii. 26).

The only nation specially selected by God as His own was the people of Israel. That choice and selection was also made for the benefit of the world at large (see p. 45). It is mere folly to speak of any other people as specially " chosen of God." All nations have their appointed places and their special missions. But we cannot always understand what the special mission of each may be. No nation is hated by the Father of all men, " who willeth that all men should be saved, and come to the knowledge of the truth " (1 Tim. ii. 4). No nation is to be regarded as of necessity foredoomed to fall under the divine judgments. The distinct utterance of Jeremiah on this very subject (xviii. 7–10) must never be forgotten; which is the more remarkable as having proceeded from a prophet who uttered, perhaps, more predictions in reference to the ruin and downfall of different nations than any other prophet of Israel. He was emphatically "a prophet unto the nations" (Jer. i. 5). As such he was set by God "over the nations and over the kingdoms, to pluck up and to break down, and to destroy and to overthrow; to build, and to plant" (Jer. i. 10). And yet the teaching of the eighteenth chapter is in substance that no nation is punished but for their own sin voluntarily committed, and that true repentance, as taught in the Book of Jonah, may at any moment stave off the threatened judgment; yea, even though the destroying angel sent forth from Jehovah were standing, as in the case of Jerusalem of old, with the drawn sword in his hand stretched out over the nation (1 Chron. xxi. 15, 16).

English exponents of Scripture have often—in a manner which (were it not for the sacredness of the subject) would be positively amusing—shown a spirit akin to that which gave utterance to the sentiment expressed by the Pharisee of old: "Lord, I thank Thee I am not as other men are." In popular interpretations of the prophecies of the Book of the Revelation, considerable ingenuity has been exerted in order to prove that the English nation is to be exempted from the horrors of "the great tribulation," which these commentators have depicted as destined to come upon all the other nations of the world.[1]

---

[1] See, for example, the remarks in *The National Restoration and Conversion of the Twelve Tribes of Israel*, by the Rev. Walter Chamberlain, M.A. (London: Wertheim & Macintosh, 1854), p. 384,

Some few more ingenious individuals have, under the influence of similar national bigotry, endeavoured to make out that the English nation is derived from the sacred stock of Israel; or, if not actually belonging to the House of Israel, is at least destined to be the people through whom the Israelites are to be brought back to the Land of Promise. It has been seriously urged by some of these would-be interpreters, that the English race must needs be connected with the tribes of Zebulon or Issachar, for the English people "suck of the abundance of the seas and of treasures hid in the sand" (Deut. xxxiii. 18, 19). It was, however, reserved for our own age to witness the culmination of such absurdities, in the recent and widespread attempt of some well-designing but ill-informed English Christians, on the basis of false history, false philology, and false Biblical exegesis, to demonstrate that the Anglo-Saxon race as a whole is to be identified with "the lost tribes" of Israel,

which it will be sufficient to cite as a sample out of many similar. Mr. Chamberlain maintains that while Germany, France, and Russia, with Italy and Greece, shall all be found among the enemies of the Lord in the final struggle, "England, that modern Tarshish, will be found in the Lord, and her mighty armaments waiting to do His will. God be praised, the efforts of our faithful ministers of Christ and the Protestant energies of her people, blessed of God, will be crowned with honour and success"!! Mr. Chamberlain's work exhibits more reading than the most of such publications, though the learning is sadly misapplied. The above is a fair specimen of the spirit which too often characterizes our popular theology. England is viewed as *par excellence* the holy nation, God is spoken of as peculiarly her God, and the salvation of the nations is not unfrequently spoken of as if it depended upon their adoption of the religious opinions peculiar to the English people.

supposed by many to have been swallowed up in the quicksands of history.

Far-seeing politicians have often spoken of the possibility of another struggle between the East and the West, the might of the former directed by the Russian Empire. It was quite natural that the great Napoleon, whose downfall was mainly brought about by the gigantic losses suffered in his Russian campaign, should, on his solitary rock at St. Helena, point to Russia as the danger of the future. But it is only in the last fifty years that Russia, whose assistance was so welcome in England's mortal struggle with France in the early part of this century, has been generally recognised as likely to become in the future England's most dangerous adversary.

We have no intention whatever of indulging here in any speculations as to the future. But it is important to call attention to the fact that no inconsiderable number of our Bible-reading and Bible-loving people have, without inquiry into its correctness, admitted the principle that the Sacred Scriptures contain prophecies of all the great events which are destined to influence human history up to the end of time. Hence, ever since a collision between the empires of England and Russia has become a probability, not a few popular writers—many of them persons who have never studied the first principles of Biblical interpretation—have turned to the writings of the prophets in order to discover where such an event is predicted.

It is not at all strange that persons so predisposed should accept without hesitation the remarkable prophecy of Ezekiel respecting Gog and Magog as clearly predicting "the Coming Struggle." Thousands and tens of thousands of copies of a pamphlet, with that sensational title, were eagerly purchased and discussed in numerous quarters during the struggle between England and Russia, generally known as the Crimean War. The outcome, indeed, of that campaign by no means corresponded with the expectations excited by the popular prophetical expositions of the day; but a considerable portion of the English religious public, little trained to careful examination of first principles, has ever shown itself disposed to listen with eagerness to new predictions of a similar kind, vainly imagining that the former exponents of prophecy have only mistaken "the times and the seasons," but convinced that the prophecy is destined to be accomplished in some similar manner.

The proper names mentioned in Ezekiel's prophecy appear at first sight to afford some basis for such an interpretation as that to which we refer. Gog and Magog, since the time of Josephus, have been interpreted to mean the Scythian tribes living in the Caucasus and the districts between the Caspian Sea and the Sea of Asof, and the Arabic writers use almost the same designation, speaking of Yagug and Magug. Meshech has been supposed to point to Moscow, Tubal to Tobolsk, on the Tobol, the capital of Western Siberia, and it is quite possible to translate the words of Ezek. xxxviii. 2 as in the Revised Version: "Set thy face against Gog, the land of Magog, the prince of Rosh, Meshech, and Tubal." The name Rosh has therefore been easily identified with Russia, and to the untrained mind the correspondence in all these particulars appears marvellous and striking.

It must be acknowledged that no less a scholar than Gesenius was led astray by the similarity of the names Rosh and Russia, and was induced by the authority of Byzantine Greek writers of the tenth century to affirm that the Rosh of Ezekiel—which word the old Greek version (the LXX.) retains in the text—was a Scythian nation belonging to those living near the Taurus range of mountains. Gesenius, after Bochart, fancied that a trace of the name in earlier times might be discovered in the name of a Scythian tribe Rhoxalani, compounded of Rhos and Alani. It has, however, since been shown by scholars that the name of Russian is of Scandinavian origin, that it was borne by the Swedish founders of the Russian State who migrated there in the ninth century, and that through those emigrants into Russia it gradually became the name accepted generally by the Eastern Slavs. Hence there is no real connection between the names *Rosh* and *Russia*.[1] Nor is it absolutely certain that

---

[1] The Slavonic word *Rus*, or *Russ*, originated, it would appear, through the Finnish appellation given to Sweden (*Ruotsi*). The Old Swedish rōþer (*rother*; Old Norse, *rōdhr*), *rowing, navigation*, rōþs-menn, or rōþs-karlar, *rowers, seafarers*, is connected with the same. In Northern Norway, *Rössfolk* (*Rörs-* or *Röds-folk*) still

the translation "Prince of Rosh" is the most correct rendering, although the balance of critical opinion is decidedly in its favour. It is to be noted that Smend, one of the latest critical interpreters of Ezekiel, maintains that the correct translation is that found in the Authorized Version, "the chief prince of Meshek and Tubal."[1] If the word be a proper name it may mean the people of Rash, inhabiting "the land of Rash" on the borders of ancient Elam on the Tigris, although there is some difficulty in the fact that a people dwelling so far to the east should be mentioned

means *fishers* that assemble near the shore during the fishing season. In process of time the signification of the term was lost, and it was treated as a proper name. The name *Ros* ('Ρως) properly belonged to the Swedish settlers in Russia, who, though originally rulers, were ultimately overwhelmed by the Slavonic element. For centuries the influence of the Scandinavians in Russia can be distinctly traced. The Scandinavian designation *Ros* was naturally transliterated into Greek by the Byzantine writers as 'Ρως. But the latter fact cannot be regarded as establishing any connection between that word and that found in Ezekiel. Between the *Russ* of the ninth century after Christ and the *Rosh* (LXX. 'Ρως) of Ezekiel, there intervenes at least some 1400 years. The whole question of the Scandinavian origin of the name has been ably discussed from a linguistic and historical standpoint in the lectures delivered in 1876, in Oxford, by Dr. Vilhelm Thomsen, Professor of Comparative Philology in the University of Copenhagen, published in English under the title, *The Relations between Ancient Russia and Scandinavia, and the Origin of the Russian State*, Parker & Co., Oxford and London, 1877. See especially pp. 92-97.

[1] The LXX., Symm., Theod. regard the word as a proper name. But the pointed Hebrew text, the Targum, Aquila, Jerome, are authorities on the other side. Smend appeals to 2 Kings xxv. 18, 1 Chron. xxvii. 5, and to Ewald's *Gr.* 287. 1. The latter can be examined in Mr. Kennedy's excellent English edition of Ewald's *Syntax of the Hebrew Language* (T. & T. Clark, 1879). See Dr. Rudolf Smend, *Der Prophet Ezechiel erklärt* (Leipzig 1880), in the *Kurzgefasstes Exegetisch. Handbuch zum A. T.*

in connection with peoples of Asia Minor such as were the nations of Meshek and Tubal.[1]

According to the opinions of the best critics, the name Gog is either to be identified with Gugu, Gyges, the name borne by a remarkable king of Lydia, or, perhaps better, with the name Gagi, which also occurs as the name of a king in the Assyrian inscriptions.[2] There is a close connection between the names Gog and Magog. Whether the prefix *ma* in the latter word denotes *land* or *country*, or is a mere preformative, has not yet been distinctly ascertained.[3] Assurbanipal, the great king of Assyria, who lived nearly a century prior to the time of Ezekiel, thus describes his victory over the formidable Scythian tribes who inhabited the mountainous country north of Assyria. "Sarati and Pariza, sons of Gagi (Gog), a chief of the Saka (שחי, Sa-hi, *Scythians*), who had thrown off the yoke of my dominion, seventy-five of their strong cities I took. I carried off their spoil. Themselves alive in hand I took, and brought them to Nineveh, the city of my dominion."[4]

---

[1] The English reader may need to be informed that *Rosh* and *Rash* are identical words, the vowel difference here being of no importance. The Hebrew word *Rosh*, which signifies *a head*, has its plural *Rashim*.

[2] See Schrader, *Keilinschriften und das Alte Test.*, 2nd ed. p. 427; Friedrich Delitzsch, *Wo lag das Paradies?* pp. 246, 247.

[3] See Delitzsch, *Paradies*, as before.

[4] See George Smith's *History of Assurbanipal translated from the Cuneiform Inscriptions* (Williams & Norgate, 1871), pp. 97, 98. Also Delitzsch, p. 247.

Some years afterwards, when Assurbanipal was no more, those Scythian tribes burst forth from their mountain homes, and when the Medes had gained decisive victories over the Assyrians, those northern peoples swooped down upon the victors, beat them in turn in bloody engagements, and became for a time masters of Asia, extending their conquests to the very borders of the Holy Land, and threatening even Egypt in the south. For more than a quarter of a century those savage people rode roughshod over Asia, "during which time their insolence and oppression," as the great Greek historian tells us, "spread ruin on every side" (Herod. i. 103–6). They were devastators, not merely conquerors; their main object was to carry over the wealth of others, their "cattle and goods." Their countless hordes of horsemen traversed the country, with the numerous scalps of their slain foes, which were used as napkins, hanging from their bridle reins. Their archers were the terror of the land, and their quivers were usually covered with human skins, while they sometimes bore aloft as standards flayed bodies of their enemies stretched upon frames. Their drinking cups were human skulls.

Cappadocia, in Asia Minor, known to us in the New Testament as one of the regions of the Apostle Paul's missionary labours, was called by the ancient Armenians Gamir, and the people thereof were known as Gimmeri, the Kimmerians, or Cimmerians of Homer. This is the district known as Gomer in the Bible. In the wars of Asarhaddon and Assurbanipal the people of Gimir are mentioned as common enemies of the Assyrian monarchs at the same time as the Scythians.[1] The Scythian tribes invaded Asia sometimes by the route of the Caucasus, and at other times by the way of Thrace, crossing over the narrow straits known then as the Hellespont, and now as the Dardanelles. Some time previous to the great raid of the Scythians into Asia, war seems to have broken out between them and the Gimmeri; and, according to Herodotus, it was in pursuit of the latter tribes, who were expelled from Europe, that the Scythians crossed over into Asia Minor. In their further raid into Central Asia the Gimmeri probably swelled the Scythian ranks. The warlike nations also of the Mosci and the Tibareni living in the countries north-west of Armenia, often vanquished by the Assyrians, and mentioned in the Assyrian inscriptions as the peoples inhabiting the land of the Mush-ki or Muski, and the land of Tabali or Tabal, adjoining Cilicia, shook off about the same time the Assyrian yoke, and joined with the Scythians, who

---

[1] See Smith's *Assurbanipal*, p. 65 ff., and many other places; *Records of the Past*, vol. ix. p. 46 ff. Friedrich Delitzsch in his *Paradies*, p. 245, refers to Asarh. ii. 6, in which inscription mention is made of *Te-ush-pa-a* and the land of *Gi-mir-ra-a*, and the statement is made by Asarhaddon that Teushpa, the ruler of that distant land, was annihilated with his whole army. The same inscription gives an account of that Assyrian monarch's expeditions against Cilicia (*Hi-lak-ki*) near the land of Tabal. Meshek and Tubal are certainly to be identified with the Muski and Tabali so often spoken of in Assyrian inscriptions. See Delitzsch, p. 250.

traversed their country in their march towards Central Asia.

Among the various nationalities represented by the prophet Ezekiel as trading in the markets of Tyre, along with the merchants of Tarshish in distant Spain, and with the traders of Javan (the Greeks), Tubal and Meshek are spoken of as bringing slaves and copper to Tyre for sale. The people of Togarmah are also mentioned along with the Phœnicians, as offering for sale in the same mart horses and mules in abundance. These people were not improbably tribes inhabiting South-Western Armenia, and possibly were represented among the wild tribes, who, either by persuasion or force, were swept along with the Scythian hordes in their terrific descent upon the rich and civilised cities which belonged to the empires of Assyria and Media.

The name, indeed, of Togarmah has not yet been satisfactorily explained. Christian Armenian writers, on the ground of these passages of Ezekiel, have spoken of their nation as the house of Thorgom, but no satisfactory evidence in support of this identification has been yet afforded.[1] The identification of the name with that of Turk or Turcoman is to be classed among the chimeras of prophetical enthusi-

---

[1] Delitzsch (*Paradies*, p. 246) considers that Togarmah may be connected with the city *Til-ga-rim-ma*, a fortress of Melitene on the borders of Tabal. He observes that Kiepert and Dillmann believe Togarmah to be South-Western Armenia. But Schrader (*Die Keilinschriften und das Alte Test.*, 2nd ed. p. 85) is not satisfied with the identification.

asts or Jewish speculators,[1] on a par with the identification of Rosh as Russia, Meshek as Moscow, Tubal as Tobolski, Gomer as Germany, and Javan as pointing through Ivan, the founder of the Russian Empire, to the connection between the Russian and the Greek Churches.[2]

Ezekiel and his fellow-exiles were carried away captives to Babylonia, and located on the banks of the great canal, termed by him the River Chebar,[3] not many years after the expulsion of the Scythian hordes from that country. The exiles must have often heard of the story how, when the Scythian warriors were weakened by luxury, the Median monarch, after an awful massacre of their chieftains at a banquet of wine, brought the remnant of those savage hordes into subjection, and re-established order and civilisation in those vast territories. Their final massacre and overthrow is alluded to by Ezekiel in his denunciations against Egypt, in recalling to mind the previous downfall of Assyria and Elam. The prophet warns Pharaoh that a similar fate is reserved for his kingdom :—

"There (in the pit of Sheol, or Hades) is Meshek and Tubal, and all her multitude, round about her

---

[1] *E.g.* the distinguished missionary, Rev. Joseph Wolff, LL.D., in his *Researches and Missionary Labours*, 2nd ed., London, Nisbet, 1835, see p. 159, etc.

[2] Chamberlain, *National Restoration of Israel*, pp. 333, 349.

[3] The Chebar, or Kebar, was in Babylonia. See Delitzsch's *Paradies*, p. 48; Schrader, *Keilinschriften*, p. 424, and my article on "The Site of Paradise" in the *Nineteenth Century* for Oct. 1882.

grave, all of them uncircumcised, slain by the sword, though they caused their terror in the land of the living" (Ezek. xxxii. 26).

The very mention of Russians and Frenchmen has in modern days often awakened dread and horror in the lands once overrun by their armies. The names of Tartar and Turk were similarly wont to arouse terror in earlier days. It is therefore only natural to suppose that in the lands of Babylonia the Jewish captives soon learned to pronounce in their own tongue the names of Gog and Magog, of Muski and Tabal, as words suggestive of the wildest and most ferocious cruelties and barbarism, and as names inspiring the utmost fear and terror. The Scythian hordes had, in very deed, in the days of Josiah, approached the confines of the Holy Land, but they were not permitted to traverse its plains or to molest its valleys or hills. There was, however, in the days of Ezekiel reason to fear another Scythian invasion. Ruthless as had been the armies of the Assyrians and those of the Chaldæans, those civilised soldiers were far less to be dreaded than the warriors of the Scythians. The Jews, in their captivity among civilised nations, first learned what a scourge they had escaped, in having been protected by Providence from the horrors of a Scythian invasion, and were led to note that Jehovah might have employed even a more terrible "rod" and "staff" than that of the Chaldæans, with which to have chastised His guilty people.

The prophecy concerning Gog and Magog was to be fulfilled in "the latter years" (xxxviii. 8) or in "the latter days" (xxxviii. 16). Ezekiel is the only prophet who makes use of the former expression. But this fact is of little significance, inasmuch as the prophet himself explains the expression as identical with the latter and more common phrase. The expression "the latter days" is indefinite, and is often employed in cases where no reference is specifically designed to the times immediately preceding the final close of the world's history. The phrase occurs in many prophecies long since accomplished, such as those of Jacob (Gen. xlix. 1), the predictions of Balaam (Num. xxiv. 14), the prophecy of Daniel concerning the wars of the kings of the north and the south (Dan. x. 14), as well as in others partly fulfilled, but yet to be accomplished more fully (such as Isa. ii. 2; Micah iv. 1; Hosea iii. 5; Jer. xxiii. 20, xxx. 24, xlviii. 47, xlix. 39). These prophecies are spoken of as to be accomplished "in the latter days;" while the same expression is used indefinitely for "in after days" in other passages of Scripture (Deut. iv. 30, xxxi. 29).

Ezekiel's prophecy concerning Gog and Magog (xxxviii. 39) contains distinct indications, which are quite sufficient to prove to the intelligent reader that it was never intended to be understood literally. The prophecy is couched in metaphorical language. The awful events, then fresh in the memory of many of his hearers, are employed in it as figures, in order to depict in more vivid colours the vain attacks of the nations of the world on the people whom Jehovah specially had chosen to be His inheritance. The people of Israel, though they were to be chastised for their sins, were not to be cast away, or delivered up entirely to the mercy of their cruel foes. "For the gifts and the calling of God are without repentance," or "not repented of" (Rom. xi. 29).

Though, in the prophecy of Ezekiel the scene of the final catastrophe described is ideally laid in Palestine, the conflict is not necessarily or exclusively thought of as waged in that land. See Ezek. xxxix. 6, and comp. xxxviii. 20, xxxix. 21. Consequently as the struggle itself does not admit of actual localization, save for the purposes of allegory, the enemies alluded to are not to be viewed as persons necessarily belonging to any particular nationalities.

In the opening of the prophecy, Ezekiel introduces the Most High as thus addressing Gog the adversary: "Art thou not he of whom I have spoken in old time by my servants the prophets of Israel, which prophesied in those days for years that I would bring thee against them?"[1] (xxxviii.

---

[1] The Authorized Version inserts a "*not*" in the interrogation, and thus makes the answer expected a distinct affirmative. The Revised Version omits the "not," and renders: "Art thou he of whom I spake?" In the latter case the language is that of wonder and astonishment. The Hebrew has the simple interrogative, which may be rendered in either way. See note on p. 119.

17). Similarly, when the overthrow of Magog is spoken of, it is added: " Behold it is come, and it is done, saith the Lord God, this is the day whereof I have spoken" (xxxix. 8).

While, however, Ezekiel in the name of God thus emphatically states that the invasion of Gog and Magog and the final overthrow of those adversaries were repeatedly spoken of by the prophets of Israel, not a single verse is to be found in any of the books of the prophets, prior to the days of Ezekiel, which depicts by name such an irruption of Gog and Magog.

Are we then to conclude with some critics that the predictions alluded to, though well known in the prophet's days, have been lost, and that the ruthless exploits of Gog and his dire destruction, were actually the theme for years and years of the prophets of Israel, although not a vestige of such prophecies has survived the ravages of time? Or ought we not to regard the prophecies pronounced against Assyria (such as Isa. x. 6), against Edom (Isa. xxxiv.), against Babylon (Isa. xxiv.–xxvii.; Jer. l., li.), against Egypt, Tyre, Moab, Ammon, and the other enemies of Israel, as being in reality the prophecies to which the Lord refers? For those prophecies speak of an irruption of enemies from all quarters of the world against the people of the Lord, in order to devour their persons, and to plunder their goods, and speak at the same time of the overthrow of the adversaries by the putting forth of the right hand of the Lord, which is glorious in power, and has repeatedly dashed to pieces the enemy (Ex. xv. 6). Zephaniah, when prophesying the destruction of Nineveh, speaks of the gathering of the nations (Zeph. iii. 8); and the same phenomenon may be noticed in the other prophecies referred to.

The overthrow of the adversaries of the Lord and His people is, indeed, the great theme of all inspired prophets. When the spirit of prophecy rested for a while even upon a feeble woman like Hannah, her mouth was opened in thanksgiving, not simply to thank God for the blessing of which she was individually made a partaker, but to exalt the majesty of Him "who will keep the feet of His saints, and the wicked shall be silent in darkness; for by strength shall no man prevail. The adversaries of the Lord will be broken to pieces; out of heaven will He thunder upon them; the Lord shall judge the ends of the earth, and He shall give strength unto His king, and exalt the horn of His Messiah" (1 Sam. ii. 9, 10).

Gog, the wild and savage chieftain, was informed by the prophet at the very outset (as Moses and Aaron told the proud king of Egypt) that he was in the hands of one stronger than he, and was, though he knew it not, actually being turned about like a wild and savage animal,—turned round hither and thither by hooks fastened in its jaws (comp. Isa. xxx. 28, xxxvii. 29). This is the meaning of the expression translated in our version (xxxviii. 4): "And I will turn thee back."

It was amusing to note how many English "students of prophecy" availed themselves of this sentence to modify their previous predictions about Russia, when, after the opening battles of the Crimean war, the great northern power appeared, contrary to their original expectations, likely to be worsted in its struggle with the allied forces of Turkey, England, and France. Those would-be expositors then turned back to their "prophetical studies," and endeavoured to twist the sentence of Ezekiel into a prophecy of the defeat of Russia at the first onset, though they held fast to their notion that the prophet spoke of a great victory to be achieved by Gog in a second campaign. But the words of the prophet convey no such meaning. The idea conveyed in the passage is that the adversaries of Jehovah, though they know it not (Isa. x. 7), are directed by a higher power, and that Divine Providence will infallibly guide those who obstinately disobey the commands of God, as it guided Pharaoh of old, into the abyss of destruction, over the precipice into the roaring waves beneath.

The prophet does not represent the object of the confederacy of Gog and Magog as any attempt to extirpate the worship of Jehovah. That confederacy is not pourtrayed as an infidel and God-defying combination. The object of the enemy is simply stated to be the taking of spoil, the capture of prey. The Israelites are described as restored to their land, but the prophet in his allegory does not represent the land of Israel (as in xxxvi. 35) as full of cities duly fenced and inhabited,—but pictures the country as a land of unwalled villages, in which the people dwell confidently and at ease, without walls, or gates, or bars. Hence a golden opportunity was presented to the ruthless invader of taking away cattle and goods, and deriving great spoil. That which Gog and Magog desired was filthy lucre; the love of money and gain was the root of their iniquity. Covetousness was their sin, the greed of things not their own hurried them on to attempt to plunder the people of God.

When the sacred historians, or the books of the prophets, describe armies of Syrians, Assyrians or Chaldæans, going up against the Israelites, bands of merchant traders are also spoken of as hovering in the rear of those armies, ready to purchase the captives taken in war as slaves, and to offer a price for the spoils of war. Joel thus speaks of the Syrians and Zidonians as receiving the sacred spoils, and selling Israelite captives as slaves to the distant Greeks (Joel iii. 4–6). Amos states that the crowning sin of the Philistines and of the Syrians was that they sold their Israelite captives wholesale to the Edomite merchants (i. 6–9). Similar acts are described by the historian in 1 Macc. iii. 41.

The same custom is alluded to in Ezekiel's prophecy. "Sheba, Dedan, and the merchants of Tarshish (the Phœnicians from distant Spain), with all the young lions thereof"—the merchants of the world and not merely traders from the nations round about Israel—the cruel, covetous, rapacious traffickers in human flesh being described as devouring lions (comp. xix. 2, xxxii. 2), are represented as collecting together from all quarters, in order to discover the intentions of the invaders of the Holy Land, and to offer their assistance in the due disposal of the spoil (xxxviii. 13). It ought to be noted that the second word in the phrase, "cattle and goods," employed in the verse, is used of the purchase of slaves (Lev. xxii. 11).[1]

Ezekiel had previously predicted the total overthrow of Tyre. Consequently it would not have been proper, even in an allegory, to have represented the merchants of Tyre as the persons seeking to profit by the results of the invasion of Gog. Hence he introduces into the sacred picture slave-dealers and merchants from Sheba (the Sabeans), from Arabia, and those of Dedan on the Persian Gulf, along with the merchants of far-distant Tarshish. The attempt first to trans-

---

[1] Chamberlain, in his *Restoration of Israel*, p. 234, etc., tries to make out that the interrogative used in the Hebrew "conveys the force of indignant disapproval," and seeks to uphold his views by references to Glassius, *Philologia Sacra*, and to Noldius' *Concord. Particularum*. It is quite true that the simple interrogative here used in the text may be so employed. But, the "*indignant disapproval*" is in every case conveyed in the context, and does not lie in the use of the interrogative. Noldius' *Concordantia* points out that the particle in question is frequently used to denote the simple question in cases where a questioner is uncertain what answer he may receive. The same particle is used both when a negative answer, and also when an affirmative answer is expected. It is useless to cite passages, as they are given in sufficient numbers in every Hebrew Lexicon of value.

form a company of money-loving slave-dealers, who are represented in Ezekiel's picture as desirous to make unholy merchandize of the bodies of men, into heroes, ready to draw the sword in defence of poor oppressed Israel, and then further to explain "the merchants of Tarshish" to mean the mercantile and maritime power of England, is one of the most extraordinary misrepresentations of prophecy that can well be conceived. Russia, Germany, France, and other nations, are doomed, according to this interpretation, to be swept away with "the besom of destruction," while England with its Eastern allies are to be the only Gentile nations who are to choose the better part!! Such pretended "expositions" of the Bible are sad exhibitions, on the part of "evangelical" interpreters, of egotism and national Pharisaism. Such interpretations might well be left to fall by their innate absurdity, were it not that they are again and again cooked up anew, and eagerly devoured as wholesome spiritual food by many who pride themselves on their diligent study of the prophetic word.

The overthrow of Gog and Magog and their rapacious allies, maddened with covetousness and drawn on by the bait of gold to their own destruction, is represented by Ezekiel in strict accordance with the imagery common to the prophets of Israel. Jehovah pleads against the foe with pestilence and blood (xxxviii. 22). It was by a pestilence the great Assyrian army of Sennacherib was overthrown in the very sight of Jerusalem. This is the ordinary way in which the Lord deals with rebel man. "For behold," says Isaiah (lxvi. 15, 16), "Jehovah will come with fire and with His chariots like a whirlwind, to render His anger with fury, and His rebuke with flames of fire. For by fire and by His sword will Jehovah plead with all flesh: and the slain of Jehovah shall be many." Thus also Zechariah in a remarkable prophecy (xiv. 12), which it is utterly impossible to interpret literally, describes such a pestilence as consuming the bodies, melting the eyes of the many nations that desired to look on the nakedness of poor Zion (Micah iv. 11), and also as rotting the tongues of the blasphemers who dared to blaspheme the God of Israel.[1]

Among the instrumentalities by which the avaricious confederacy is to be overthrown are "the great hailstones, fire and brimstone" (xxxviii. 22) often mentioned in earlier days. By fire and brimstone Sodom and Gomorrah were overwhelmed; and in Joshua's great battle with the five kings their hosts were discomfited at Azekah by hailstones from heaven (Josh. x. 11). A storm of hailstones repeatedly recurs in the symbols of the Book of the Revelation (xi. 19, xvi. 21), though for many reasons we abstain here from citing illustrative passages from that book. But it should be specially

---

[1] See the *Bampton Lectures on Zechariah*, where the numerous absurdities are pointed out which beset any attempt to explain literally the prophecy of Zech. xiv.

noted that in Isaiah's predictions of the ruin of Sennacherib and his army, which was mainly caused, according to the writer of the Book of Kings, by means of an awful pestilence, the prophet speaks of fire, hail, and thunder: "And Jehovah shall cause His glorious voice (comp. Ps. xxix. 3) to be heard, and shall show the lighting down of His arm, with the indignation of His anger, and with the flame of a devouring fire, with scattering and tempest and hailstones" (Isa. xxx. 30, 31).

The confederacy is also spoken of by Ezekiel as broken up by internecine conflict. The Lord shall call for a sword against Gog through all the mountains of Israel, and every man's sword shall be against his brother (xxxviii. 21). In the great battle at Michmash, the Philistines in a heaven-sent confusion turned their swords against one another, and so added to the terrible slaughter of that day (1 Sam. xiv. 20 ff.). Similar events happened in earlier days in the war against Midian (Judg. vii. 22), as well as repeatedly in later days (2 Chron. xx. 23). Hence the prophets introduce this feature into their description of the future overthrow of "the armies of the aliens." It forms a striking future in Zechariah's description of the great conflict (Zech. xiv. 13).

Gog is also represented as overthrown by an earthquake in the land of Israel. By the earthquake mountains are overturned, craggy rocks fall, and every wall is levelled with the ground (xxxviii. 19, 20). Earthquakes are introduced into all the prophetic pictures which represent the overthrow of the Lord's enemies and the salvation of the Lord's people. The earthquake is vividly depicted on the canvas of Zechariah; and the terror of the beasts of the field, of the fowls of the heaven and even of the fishes of the sea, occasioned by the dreaded phenomenon is mentioned in the Book of Hosea (Hos. iv. 3).

In our Lord's great prophecy of the latter days (Matt. xxiv., Mark xiii., Luke xxi.), which comprehends the great period which reaches onward from the time of His ascension into heaven to His return again to earth, these several features are blended together into one grand picture. That prophecy is not a prediction only of the end of the world, it is a faithful sketch of human history during the whole of the Messianic period. It is as it were a sketch and study drawn by the hand of the great Master of all the prophetic painters. It describes in a few masterly touches the wars and commotions, the fearful sights, the great signs, the pestilences, famines, earthquakes, internecine slaughter, nation rising against nation, kingdom against kingdom, the false prophets, false teachers, abounding iniquity, the declining love exhibited on the part of the Church towards its Lord, the increasing hate of religion manifested on the part of the world, the afflictions and sufferings of the righteous, and their triumph even in death, —all which have characterized, and will continue to characterize, this portion of the world's history, notwithstanding the advent of "the Prince of peace," and in spite of the preaching of the everlasting gospel.

Ezekiel gives a graphic description of the great feast which was to be provided by means of the slaughter of Gog's army for the ravenous birds of prey and the wild beasts of the field (xxxix. 4, 5). The prophet was commanded to invite all the birds and beasts of prey to assemble upon the mountains of Israel to partake of the great sacrifice of human flesh and blood. The animals thus assembled are described as gorged with the flesh and fat of mighty captains and princes of the earth. They drink their blood until they become drunken, and are satisfied to the full at that fearful table of the Lord (xxxix. 20) with the sacrifice prepared by God for their enjoyment (xxxix. 17–20).

The description given by Ezekiel is, however, a repetition, with greater fulness of detail, of the equally vivid picture drawn by the prophet Isaiah (xxxiv.) of the sacrifice in Bozrah, and the great slaughter in the land of Idumea or Edom. In Isaiah's picture the mountains are represented as melted down by the blood of the slain, and the anger of the Lord is spoken of as poured out upon all nations of the earth, and His fury upon all their armies. The same imagery is made use of in the description of the final conflict with the beast and the kings of the earth and their armies in the nineteenth chapter of the Book of Revelation.

No Old Testament description of a field of battle (even as presented in the allegorical descriptions of the prophets) would be complete without some mention of the spoil of the foe. Ezekiel in his prophecy speaks first of the spoiling of Israel, and then of the spoiling of the enemies by the Israelites. Similarly Isaiah records the spoils of Israel first as gathered by the Assyrians, and then further describes how the Assyrians were to be spoiled in their turn (xxxiii. 1). Zechariah also predicts the plundering of Jerusalem, and afterwards speaks of the spoil of the foe, consisting in gold, silver, and garments, being gathered up by the men of Judah (Zech. xiv. 1, 2, 14). It is, however, a feature peculiar to Ezekiel that in his prophecy the weapons of the enemies (which are fully described in ch. xxxviii. 4, 5, xxxix. 9, and all of which, with the exception of swords, have long since been discarded by modern armies) are represented as carefully gathered up from the fields of battle, and stored up in order to be used for the useful purpose of firewood. The Israelites, restored to a land the trees of which were cut down by the foe, are represented in the prophecy as provided in this manner with the fuel required for domestic purposes for seven long years.

In one of his graphic predictions of the overthrow of Sennacherib's army, in sight of its long looked-for goal, namely, the holy city Jerusalem, Isaiah depicts Tophet in the valley of Jehoshaphat in front of the city as the place where the great pile of fire and wood would be ignited by the breath of Jehovah in order to consume the bodies of the slain. That natural pit, deep and large as it was, was ordained of old for the purpose, fitly prepared for the haughty king who dared to blaspheme the God of Israel who was his Maker. The Assyrian soldiers, cut down in their ranks like sheaves of corn, were gathered in that spot into the threshing-floor (Micah iv. 12), and laid in their last earthly beds along the sides of that deep valley. Sennacherib's death at Nineveh was the direct result of his discomfiture before Jerusalem (Isa. xxx. 33, xxxviii. 37, 38). In another prophet picture, Joel speaks of the same valley of Jehoshaphat as the place where the final victory should be gained over the enemies of Jehovah, although that prophet does not describe the burial of the foe (Joel iii. 11–17).

In Ezekiel's prophecy, Gog is described as vainly conceiving in his heart that he would get the land of Israel for a possession. No possession in the land of Israel should, however, according to Ezekiel, be accorded to him or his soldiers, but the possession of a place of sepulture (Ezek. xxxix. 11). It is useless to inquire what particular valley the prophet thought of as the special place of burial, whether it was the district lying along the shores of the Dead Sea, the valley of Salt, where Chedorlaomer and his confederate kings were overthrown by Abraham (Gen. xiv. 8–10), and where in later days David, and afterwards Amaziah, won victories over the people of Edom. Ezekiel probably had in view in his ideal description some place within the territory of the Holy Land. Some critics have conjectured the place to have been the valley of Megiddo, where the pious Josiah fell wounded by the Egyptian archers; and others some vale along the side of the Lake of Galilee. It appears, however, more likely that the valley of Hamon-Gog, where the multitude of Gog is described as buried, was probably localized ideally as situated along the Mediterranean or the great sea, the sea of nations.

The translation in the Authorized Version of chap. xxxix. 11,—"And it (the valley with its stink) shall stop the *noses* of the passengers,"—is the rendering given by some Jewish critics. If that were the meaning, the passage would be somewhat parallel to the description in Joel (ii. 20): "I will remove far off from you the northern army, and I will drive him into a land barren and desolate, with his face toward the east sea and his hinder part toward the utmost sea: and his stink shall come up and his ill savour shall come, because he hath done great things." But it is more probable that the meaning of the whole passage (xxxix. 11) is: "And it shall come to pass in that day that I will give to Gog a place for burial in Israel, the valley of passers through, east of the sea, and it shall stop (or hem up) those who pass through, and they shall bury there Gog and all his multitude, and they shall call it the

Valley of the Multitude of Gog."[1] The multitude of Gog is to be identified with "the multitudes" pourtrayed by Joel "in the valley of decision;" and the result of the decisive judgment there given by the overthrow of the foe is that Jerusalem shall be holy, and strangers shall not pass through her any more (Joel iii. 17; or, in the Hebrew, iv. 17).

For Ezekiel describes the fate of Gog as identical with the fate of all the other enemies of the Lord. He shall pass through the land of Israel, but he shall only be a passenger going through the land, for a grave there shall be his only portion. Hemmed up in the Valley of Multitude, he shall no more return, his armies shall be like mere hordes of passers through. His hosts shall come up like a storm and pass through it, covering the land for a while like a cloud (xxxviii. 9). Men appointed to pass through the land shall bury them, and men shall perpetually pass to and fro over the graves of those avaricious passers through the land. Thus shall Jehovah be magnified. There is, it will be observed, all through the passage a play upon words. Gog and his multitudes, however numerous and mighty they may appear, are but passengers—they shall be buried as passengers—passengers shall bury them, and passengers shall walk over their graves.

The burial itself is described as a gigantic undertaking. Notwithstanding the ravenous beasts and

---

[1] The rendering of the Revised Version is substantially the same. We have rendered a little more literally in order to avoid ambiguity.

birds gathered together to consume the corpses, the burial of the transgressors is represented as occupying seven weary months, during which one might almost use the language of Isaiah: "They shall go forth and look upon the carcases of the men that have transgressed against me; for their worm shall not die, neither shall their fire be quenched, and they shall be an abhorring unto all flesh" (Isa. lxvi. 24). The burial is described as a tedious and hateful work, though necessary according to the Law: "Whosoever toucheth in the open field one that is slain with a sword, or a dead body, or a bone of a man, or a grave, shall be unclean seven days" (Num. xix. 16). Seven months shall all the people of the land be burying the army of Gog, that they may cleanse the land (Ezek. xxxix. 12, 13). Even after that period, for a long and undefined space of time, men shall be set apart and separated for the constant work of burying the bodies which still remain unburied, and for the purpose of collecting together the bones scattered over the fields. Over these remains "signs" were to be set up and erected, in order that the bones thus found might ultimately be conveyed in due course of time to the valley of Hamon-Gog, where a new city to be built should serve by its very name Hamonah (or, "Multitude") to keep in everlasting remembrance the memory of the vengeance taken by the Most High upon the foe, and the salvation granted to the people of Israel.

"Ah! the tumultuous-multitude of many peoples,

like the tumult of the seas they are tumultuous; and the roar of nations like the roar of mighty waters they roar! The nations—like the roar of mighty waters they roar, but He rebuketh them, and they flee far away, and are chased like the chaff of the mountains before the wind, and like whirling-dust before the hurricane. At eventide, behold terror! before morning, it is gone! This is the portion of those who spoil us, and the lot of those who plunder us!" (Isa. xvii. 12–14).

In his description of the destruction of the last enemy of Israel, Ezekiel availed himself largely of the phraseology used in the Book of Exodus in reference to Pharaoh, Israel's first great enemy. If the heart of Pharaoh is represented in the Book of Exodus as hardened by Jehovah, even so does Ezekiel speak of Gog as prepared by the same overruling power to rush madly onward to his own destruction. The writer of Exodus depicts Pharaoh as raised up by Jehovah to lofty estate in order that by his fall the divine power might be more clearly manifested (Ex. ix. 16); and Ezekiel describes God as for a similar reason permitting Gog to exalt himself for a little season. The Egyptians are described in the Book of Exodus as learning at last by the destruction of their king and army that Jehovah was God (Ex. vii. 5, xiv. 4, 18), when God had gotten Him honour upon Pharaoh and all his host in the waters of the Red Sea. Ezekiel similarly says that Jehovah would in the same way be sanctified, known, and honoured in the eyes of many nations by the glorious overthrow of the confederacy of Gog and Magog. "The nations shall know that I am Jehovah" (Ezek. xxxviii. 16, 23); and it is specially noted that this should be the case not only with the peoples in the Holy Land, but also with those in the islands (Ezek. xxxix. 6). God's holy name shall be acknowledged in the midst of Israel, "and the nations shall know that I am Jehovah the Holy One in Israel" (Ezek. xxxix. 7, 22, 23, 28).

The various points already noticed all tend to prove that Ezekiel does not describe in the prophecy any special foe of Israel, who has already appeared, or who is to appear at some future period, whose armies are to be literally armed, overthrown, devoured, and buried in the particular manner described. The prophecy is a sort of allegory, in which a picture is presented of the ultimate ruin and utter overthrow of all those enemies who, when Israel is restored to their land, seek for the sake of greed and gain to destroy the people of Jehovah. If the prophecy were regarded as literal, its fulfilment would be in many points impossible, nor can it, regarded as a literal prophecy, be brought into harmony with other predictions which treat of the same period.

On the other hand, regarded as a description of real events, pourtrayed in allegorical language, the picture is grand and impressive. Ezekiel represents, in the thirty-seventh chapter, under the figure of the resurrection of dry bones in the valley, the restoration of

Israel from the Babylonish captivity, and points out that the twelve tribes would thenceforth form one nation, to be ultimately ruled by "David, my servant," or the great Messiah. The conversion of Israel forms the subject of the thirty-sixth chapter; and at the close of the thirty-seventh the prophet returns to the same theme, and gives a short but vivid account of Israel's conversion: "My tabernacle shall also be with them; yea, I will be their God, and they shall be my people. And the nations shall know that I, Jehovah, do sanctify Israel when my tabernacle shall be in the midst of them for evermore" (xxxvii. 27, 28).

The invasion of Gog is then related as an episode, which is to occur after the restoration and before the final national conversion of Israel, which latter point is again predicted in glowing language at the close of chap. xxxix. Some English interpreters have devised a theory of "breaks" or "gaps" in prophecy; but the hypothesis merely shows how utterly such writers, led astray by their imagination, have failed to comprehend the principles which underlie all prophecy. The history of the human race presented in the sacred writings is simple, but its very simplicity is profound. The universal apostasy of the Gentiles from the true God led to the call of Abraham, and to the selection of Israel, as a holy people. The duty appointed to Israel was to preserve the light amid darkness, and by Israel's instrumentality the nations were at last to be brought back to the true God. But though Israel was the chosen people, guided and taught by Jehovah, their unfaithfulness led to their repeated punishment. Israel was chastised and finally overwhelmed by the world-power, first as ruled over by Assyria, afterwards as swayed by Babylon. But forasmuch as the nations which conquered Israel imagined in their folly that their gods had triumphed over Jehovah, the prophets foretold that Israel should be delivered by divine power out of captivity, and restored to the land of their possession. The restoration of Israel and the subsequent coming of Messiah is the theme of the later prophets. The sufferings of Messiah and the glory that should follow (1 Pet. i. 11), as seen by the prophets of Israel, were viewed as part and parcel of one grand picture. The sufferings of Messiah were to be the "birth throes" of the world, its "regeneration," as our Lord expresses it (Matt. xix. 28). The Messianic age in its length and breadth is identified with the "latter days." That age or dispensation is "the day of the Lord," in the morning of which Messiah comes to suffer, and in the evening of which He returns to reign. In the New Testament picture the great Dragon was seen waiting for the birth of the wondrous Child, who was to rule all nations with a rod of iron. The Dragon's expectations were thwarted, for the Child when born was caught up to God, and His throne (Rev. xii.). Thus closed the first half of the Seven Times of the Gentiles, which began with the victory of the world-power over Israel, and to the eyes of the world closed with the victory of that power over Christ. For the triumph of Christ at His resurrection and ascension was a triumph only witnessed by a few. The Dragon, though foiled in his attempt to overcome Christ, is not, however, yet wholly vanquished. He still makes war with the remnant of the woman's seed which keep the commandments of God, and hold the testimony of Jesus Christ. The second portion of "the Times of the Gentiles," or the mystical "time, times and a half," is the period during which this war lasts; and the conflict began when Christ ascended from Mount Olivet, and will not be ended until He shall be manifested as King of kings and Lord of lords.

Ezekiel beheld only part of this scene of conflict and victory. But the portion he was permitted to see was a picture complete in itself. He saw Israel restored from captivity, he saw them settled in a land of unwalled villages. He next saw the foe advancing from all quarters, hoping to gain an easy victory. He was permitted to behold "the conclusion of the matter," the overthrow of the foe, the burial of the mighty, the salvation of Israel, the conversion of the world, and the Messiah seated on His throne! The picture was one which the prophet could fully comprehend. It was drawn upon the lines of the old dispensation. He was permitted further to behold the hidden springs of human action, the reality which often lies deep below the surface. The hostility of the world against Israel often sprang, not so much from hostility towards God, as from the love of gain. As Christ more than once emphatically points out, God and Mammon ever compete together for human souls. Riches, money, wealth, is often the real idol which men worship. Religion is used as a stalking horse, behind which as a shelter money is greedily sought to be acquired. "Money, money, money!" this is the cry which awakens the nations! The wail of Demetrius the silversmith (Acts xix. 24 ff.) over his foreseen and sadly dreaded losses, is the shout that always collects together a sordid mob who would hinder the progress of truth. From all parts they gather, they come; they scent money from far as keenly as the vulture scents the carrion it loves to devour. It was the prosperity and wealth of restored Israel, often exaggerated by report, which attracted the cupidity and aroused the animosity of their foes, whether Persian, or Grecian, or Roman. But had the Israelites not been unmindful of the Rock that begat them, of the God that formed them (Deut. xxxii. 18), how should one have chased a thousand and two put ten thousand to flight? (Deut. xxxii. 30.) Israel's forgetfulness of God at one time, their rejection of Messiah at another, caused that people to be left helpless under the assaults of their enemies both ancient and modern. Stripped of their real defence, their strength gone, Israel, whether in the Land of Promise in unwalled villages, or scattered among the nations, has been plundered and spoiled by foes from every quarter, from the north and the south, and the east and the west.

But a brighter day will, we trust, soon dawn. The days of oppression are well-nigh past. The day of Israel's conversion is to come. Ezekiel's prophecy opens with the restoration of Israel from the Babylonish captivity, and reaches on to the time of the end. It does not delineate all the sad events of Jewish history; it sums them up in one picture. There may be another restoration of Israel to the Land of Promise, and such a restoration is probable, but Ezekiel does not speak in this prophecy of that restoration. His prophecy is not unfulfilled. It has had many a fulfilment in the oppression used against the poor Jew, and in the vengeance that by Divine Providence has fallen upon his oppressors. There are no grounds whatever to expect a more full accomplishment in the future. There is no reason to expect the rise of another such confederacy as that of Gog and Magog. At all events "the mission of Russia" is certainly not pourtrayed in the prophecy.

There is indeed a portion of Ezekiel's prophecy which awaits a future fulfilment, namely, that which speaks of the blessed day of grace and glory. Israel is to be converted; the Jews will shake off the sleep of forgetfulness, and once more remember their Lord. The promises, the fulfilment of which was stayed, because when Christ "came unto His own, they that were His own received Him not" (John i. 11), are yet to have their full accomplishment. The "mystery" which the apostle reveals is that "a hardening in part hath befallen Israel until the fulness of the Gentiles be come in, and so all Israel shall be saved, even as it is written—

"'There shall come out of Zion the Deliverer;

He shall turn away ungodliness from Jacob'" (Rom. xi. 25, 26). And "if the casting away of them was the reconciling of the world, what shall the receiving of them be but life from the dead?" (Rom. xi. 15). "The kingdom of the world shall become the kingdom of our Lord and His Christ, and He shall reign for ever and ever" (Rev. xi. 15).

IV.

THE SPIRITS IN PRISON.

A STUDY ON 1 PETER III. 18-20 AND IV. 6.

THE publication of Dean Plumptre's work on *The Spirits in Prison*[1] has awakened in this country fresh interest in the exegesis of the remarkable passage in 1 Pet. iii. 17–22. Dean Plumptre upholds the dictum of the late lamented Professor Dorner, that "it may be accepted as a result of modern exegetical research" that St. Peter in his Epistle alludes to the descent of Christ after His death on the cross into Hades, or the unseen-world of spirits, and to the work which the Redeemer carried on in the region of the dead previous to His resurrection on the third day.

In face of the formidable consensus of opinion on this point, which exists among the scholars and theologians of the present time, it may appear rash, on critical and exegetical grounds, to impugn the cor-

---

[1] *The Spirits in Prison and other Studies on the Life after Death.* By E. H. Plumptre, D.D., Dean of Wells. London: Wm. Isbister Limited, 56 Ludgate Hill. 1885.

rectness of such an interpretation. But the general acceptance of the theory which thus regards the passage to refer to the descent into Hades has, in our opinion, been mainly due to the mistakes which have been made by interpreters on the other side. The latter have too often sought to defend untenable positions, and have failed to perceive the strong points on the maintenance of which their efforts should have been concentrated. On the other hand, those who refer the passage to a preaching of Christ in the other world, have not really faced the difficulties of the passage, and, even on their own showing, have generally gone beyond the statements of the sacred text. The last word has not been spoken on the controversy; and we hope to be able to show that it is more than doubtful whether St. Peter either in the passage before us, or in the other passage in chap. iv. 6, makes any allusion whatever to Christ's descent into Hell.[1]

[1] It may be well to notice our article on this subject, entitled "Scripture Revelations on the Intermediate State," published in the *Journal of Sacred Literature* for April 1866. That article in a slightly revised form was reprinted in the appendix to our work on *The Fatherhood of God* (T. & T. Clark, 1867). A more careful consideration of the subject led to the rejection of several of the minor positions there maintained, and the subject was more carefully handled in an article on "The Spirits in Prison and the Son of God," which appeared in the *British and Foreign Evangelical Review* for January 1876. The same position there defended is maintained in the present study, though with more fulness and, possibly, more clearness of detail. We have not, however, thought it advisable to embarrass the argument by any discussion of the passage in Gen. vi. 4, 5, though still denying, on exegetical grounds, the correctness of the view which considers that there is an allusion there to an intermarriage of angels and women in the days before the Flood. See pp. 9, 10.

It must not be thought that we have been led to the conclusions indicated by theological prepossessions, or by an inveterate unwillingness to admit the conclusions arrived at on some points by the scholars referred to. Some of their conclusions are in themselves probable, when viewed from a speculative point of view. Thus it may be admitted that it is likely that the descent of Christ into the unseen-world was an event necessarily fraught with momentous consequences to the dwellers in that spirit-land. If the Gospel of St. Luke (xxiii. 24), drawn up under special Pauline influences, contains the beautiful prayer uttered on the cross by Christ for His murderers, "Father, forgive them for they know not what they do;"[1] it is only natural to conceive that the entrance of Christ into "the congregation of the dead" must have been accompanied by some manifestation of love and mercy towards many who in "the times of ignorance" (Acts xvii. 30) had sinned against the divine law. But we assert, that the Holy Scriptures contain no revelation whatever with regard to that and other mysterious subjects; that they do not afford any information with respect to Christ's doings in that region termed in the Old Testament language "Sheol" (or the "Under-world"),

---

[1] This prayer on the cross is no doubt omitted by some ancient Western authorities, and the fact is noted in the margin of the Revised Version, but the omitted words may in this case be "confidently accepted" as genuine, and are marked as such by Westcott and Hort. See their Greek Test. vol. i., Text; vol. ii., Introduction and Appendix, p. 295.

or spoken of in New Testament Greek as "Hades," or "the Unseen."¹ It may be necessary and useful sometimes to speculate on the subject of the state of the dead, like Socrates, who so touchingly conversed on the subject with his friends in the short interval between his condemnation and execution. But we have been left almost as much in the dark as was Socrates. It is quite lawful "with reverence and godly fear" (Heb. xii. 28) to "desire to look into" the mystery, as the angels are described as seeking to penetrate (1 Pet. i. 12) into the mysteries of redemption. But if it can be shown that the Holy Scriptures afford no definite information on the subject, the conclusions at which we may arrive from reasonings outside Scripture can be at best only speculations, based, it may be, on very imperfect knowledge. The so-called orthodox divines of past ages, in their dogmatic teaching on the great question of "eternal punishment," went far beyond the statements of Scripture, and endeavoured to bolster up their dogmas constructed upon a very slight founda-

---

¹ The Hebrew word *Sheol* (שְׁאוֹל), which used to be so commonly explained as connected with the verb *to ask*, and as consequently signifying "the insatiable Orcus," has been recognised by the best modern Hebraists as connected with the root *to sink down, to be sunk*, (שאל, שעל, שׁל), and, therefore, signifies properly *depression, depth*, that is, in other words its proper rendering would be "that which is beneath," "the Under-world." See the latest editions of Gesenius' *Heb. Handwörterbuch*, by Muhlau and Volck. On the other hand, the Greek Hades, ᾅδης, is best translated by "the Unseen," and it is a pity that the words were not so rendered in simple English by the Revisers.

tion of Scripture with buttresses derived from false metaphysics. On the other hand, the modern advocates of "the larger hope" have equally erred in demanding assent to theories built upon as weak foundations. In the interests of true theology we protest against all attempts to found upon speculations, however specious or probable, any doctrines whatever affecting faith or practice, such as the doctrine of a purgatory after death or that of prayer for the dead. The doctrine of purgatory is now boldly asserted as true by many of the modern school of Anglican theologians, although the purgatory they teach may be of a nobler and more generous character than that depicted by Roman Catholic theologians. The doctrine of prayers for the dead is in the present day clearly and distinctly advocated by the former divines as part and parcel of primitive Christianity.[1]

Dean Plumptre's interesting chapter on the subject of "the descent into hell" is divided into two sections, the first treating of the historical tradition, the second of the Scripture foundation on which that article of the Apostles' Creed is based. In the latter the Dean specially notices the views put forward by those theologians who maintain that St. Peter refers

---

[1] See the able work of Rev. H. M. Luckock, D.D., *After Death, the State of the Faithful Dead and their Relationship to the Living*. London. Dean Plumptre in the ninth "study" of his book expresses sympathies in the same direction. Several other Anglican divines have written even more strongly in defence of prayers for the dead, as for instance Dr. Frederick G. Lee in his work on *The Christian Doctrine of Prayer for the Departed*, 2nd ed. 1875.

to Christ's "descent into hell" in his 1st Epist. iii. 18–20. The history of the exegesis of the passage presented by the Dean is far from complete; and, indeed, it professes to be only an outline. But even considered as a mere outline, it is faulty and misleading. The authority of Bishop Horsley is rated too highly,[1] and scant justice is dealt out to the eminent theologians of past days who have rejected the interpretation advocated by the Dean. The expositions of the passage given by these scholars are summarily dismissed with the somewhat supercilious remark that "were it not for the tendency of superficial interpretations, which seem to avoid difficulties, to reappear with a strange vitality after they have been again and again refuted, it might seem superfluous, after Horsley's masterly treatment, to indicate its intimate connection with the doctrine of the 'descent into hell'" (p. 111). It is probable that Dean Plumptre, when he wrote this severe criticism of his opponents, was unacquainted with the remarkable treatise of Professor Schweizer of Zürich on the subject,[2] which is very far from being "superficial" in

---

[1] The advance of scholarship has exploded not a few of Bishop Horsley's most original interpretations, and, notwithstanding that Horsley's writings are highly suggestive, his expositions, especially of Old Testament passages, require always to be carefully examined in the light of modern criticism.

[2] *Hinabgefahren zur Hölle als Mythus ohne biblische Begründung, durch Auslegung der Stelle, 1 Pet. iii. 17-22, nachgewiesen von A. Schweizer, Dr. und Prof. theol. Zürich, Verlag von Friedrich Schulthess, 1868.* Three important articles by Rev. Professor Salmond, D.D., Aberdeen, on this subject, entitled "The Dogma of the Triduum," appeared in the *British and Foreign Evangelical*

its character. Although we do not coincide with all that has been written by that eminent Swiss theologian, his essay is one of the most important contributions to the literature of the passage, and we shall in the present "study" call attention to the critical arguments which he has advanced against the interpretation of the passage advocated by Horsley, Alford and Plumptre among the English divines. It must be noted that our review of the interpretation of the passage is to be regarded merely as a small contribution towards the English literature on the subject. It does not pretend to be an exhaustive treatise on such an important point, or to give anything like a complete sketch of the writings of German scholars on the question.

It is no longer denied that the translation of the passage given in the English Authorized Version is incorrect in several important particulars. The issue of the Revised Version has placed the state of the case in its true light before the intelligent English reader. The contrast intended between the "being put to death in the flesh" and the "being quickened in the spirit" is too clear to be disputed. It is consequently impossible any longer to interpret the

---

Review for October 1872, January and April 1873. Bishop Horsley's sermon on the subject, "On Christ's Descent into Hell, and the Intermediate State," was appended to his *Translation of Hosea, with Notes explanatory and critical*, London 1804. It is also to be found in the edition of his *Sermons*, London 1826, as well as in the collected edition of his works. His "masterly treatment" of the subject, when that which is common to all interpreters is excluded, occupies less than four pages.

former clause as stating the nature in which Christ suffered, and the latter as pointing out the instrumental means whereby Christ was made alive. The clauses are in the Greek identical in form and evidently antithetical in meaning. Hence the translation "quickened by the Spirit," that is, made alive again by the operation of the Holy Ghost, and the explanation of the relative clause in the next verse as referring to a preaching of the Holy Spirit through Noah to the world of the ungodly, must once for all be set aside as erroneous.[1]

For, if the "spirit" mentioned in ver. 18 (contrasted as it is with the "flesh" spoken of in the former clause) signifies the personal spirit of Christ, then the relative in the beginning of ver. 19, "in which" (ἐν ᾧ), must also be referred to Christ's spiritual nature. The other translations, "wherefore," "through which," "at which time," are here inadmissible, although (considered apart from the context) all more or less defensible.

The well-balanced statements of ver. 18, "put to death in the flesh" and "quickened in the spirit," must be interpreted as mutually contrasted. The former expression can only mean that Christ endured

---

[1] The ζωοποιηθεὶς δὲ πνεύματι closely corresponds to the θανατωθεὶς μὲν σαρκί, and even the reading of the Textus Recept. τῷ πνεύματι, which is found in very few of the cursive, but in none of the uncial MSS., would not much alter the matter. It may, however, be fairly doubted whether the translation of our Authorized Version, though incorrect, merits Alford's sweeping denunciation as in defiance of all grammar. But we are not disposed to go into any special pleading on that point.

death in consequence of having become "partaker of flesh and blood" (Heb. ii. 14). By becoming man Christ became subject to the law of death, with the distinct object in view (as stated in the Epistle to the Hebrews) of overcoming death by dying, and not only so, but with the further object of making mankind "partakers of the divine nature" (2 Pet. i. 4). The expression "quickened in the spirit" cannot therefore refer to the spiritual or pneumatical body (1 Cor. xv. 44) with which our Lord rose from the dead;[1] because (as Schweizer observes) the resurrection from the grave which includes the idea of the reunion of the spirit with the soul and body cannot be correctly spoken of as a "being quickened in the spirit."[2]

[1] It ought, however, to be observed that Huther (in Meyer's *Comm.*) does not exactly identify the pneuma of Christ with His spiritual body. He rather understands the pneuma in this place to signify the new spiritual life into which Christ entered when He was raised from the dead. That life began in such a manner that the pneuma united itself again with the σῶμα, so that the σῶμα itself became a pneumatical body. According to Huther's explanation, the preaching of Christ ἐν πνεύματι took place after His resurrection, and not previous to that event.

[2] The object sought to be attained by this explanation of the passage is the preservation of ζωοποιέω in its proper signification, *made alive* after death, the word being constantly used in reference to the revivification of the dead (John v. 21 ; Rom. iv. 17 ; 1 Cor. xv. 22 ff.). The pneuma of Christ in its proper signification can never be thought of as suffering death. One of the difficulties of the passage is that in order to preserve intact the full antithesis between the σαρκί (*in the flesh*) in the first member of the sentence, and the πνεύματι (*in the spirit*) in the second, it seems necessary to understand the verb ζωοποιέω in a sense, not elsewhere to be found in the New Testament writings, of being *kept alive*. There is, however, in the Epistle of Barnabas, chap. vi., a remarkable parallel. In attempting

The phrase "quickened in the spirit," therefore, refers to the spirit-life into which Christ entered when He surrendered up His spirit to the Father. Death put an end for a season to His bodily life; that event was, however, the beginning of a higher and spiritual life, in which His spirit asserted its power and put forth its energies. Death has its effect on the body of Christ. He submitted to death to fulfil the will of the Father. He had power to lay down His life, and had power to take it again (John x. 18). But the latter life (the resurrection life) is not that referred to in the text. St. Peter speaks of the life of which man cannot deprive his fellow in any case whatever, namely, the life of the pneuma or spirit, by virtue of which the man exists even in the disembodied state. In other words, the apostle alludes to the life of the Redeemer in the intermediate state

to explain spiritually the promise of the possession of a land flowing with milk and honey, Barnabas asks: "What then mean the milk and honey?" and replies: "This, that as the infant is kept alive first by honey and then by milk (ὅτι πρῶτον τὸ παιδίον μέλιτι, εἶτα γάλακτι ζωοποιεῖται), so also we being quickened (τῇ πίστει τῆς ἐπαγγελίας καὶ τῷ λόγῳ ζωοποιούμενοι ζήσομεν) by the faith of the promise and by the word, shall live ruling over the earth." Here is the same connection between the datives μέλιτι and γάλακτι, met with in the passage in S. Peter, while the verb is used in the double sense of *quickened* or *made alive*, and of *kept alive* or *preserved in life*. The difficulty, however, as to the meaning of the verb is not really serious, because the apostle speaks of the death mentioned in the first clause as affecting the whole man, Christ Jesus, as a person, although that death in reality only affected His body (His flesh); and similarly the quickening was a fact which concerned Christ's whole personality, although in reality He was made alive and entered into a new phase of existence "in the spirit." Hence it is not of much consequence whether the ζωοποιηθείς is rendered "*made alive*" or "*kept alive*."

prior to His resurrection. As that life was the awakening of a new existence for the man Christ Jesus, S. Peter speaks of it as a being "quickened in the spirit."

Before, however, entering on the inquiry as to what is meant by Christ's "preaching in the spirit," it is of importance carefully to note the general drift of the part of the Epistle in which the statement occurs, and to examine the peculiar phraseology employed in the 19th verse.

The object which the apostle had in view in the context, was to encourage the Jewish Christians to whom he wrote to stand firm amid the trials by which they were surrounded, and to be consistently jealous for that which was good. They were not, like their unbelieving forefathers in the days of Ahaz, to allow themselves to be terrified (Isa. viii. 11–13) when they heard of conspiracies formed against them on account of their religion. Men might seek to root Christ's people out of the land of the living. But believers in Christ, like the faithful saints "who nobly fought of old," should fear the Lord of hosts alone, and not be unduly moved by the plots of mortal men who are only able to kill the body. In the hour of trial they should fear and reverence that God who is able to destroy both body and soul in hell (Matt. x. 28). The followers of Jesus should never forget to sanctify in their hearts Christ as Lord. For if it be the will of God it is better for Christians to suffer for well-doing than for evil-doing.

"A disciple is not above his master, nor a servant above his lord" (Matt. x. 24). If the great Master suffered for His people, He has, even in His submission unto death, left them an example that they should follow in His steps.[1] He did no sin, neither was guile found in His mouth. When reviled He did not revile His revilers, but committed His cause to Him that judgeth righteously. He suffered for us that He might bring us to God. He was put to death in the flesh, the body, in which He suffered on the cross; but He was kept alive or quickened—raised in either case to a higher life—"in the spirit," that is, in the higher part of His nature. Thus was He "justified in the spirit" (1 Tim. iii. 16). Therefore they that suffer with Him here will be similarly "justified," and will be finally "glorified together" (Rom. viii. 17). For when Christian martyrs, "faithful unto death," put off their mortal bodies, in the way that the Lord Jesus Christ oft foretold, "Ye shall be hated of all men for my name's sake" (Luke xxi. 17), they like their Master enter into a higher life "in the spirit." Their enemies cannot kill their souls; and since the believers who are faithful unto death shall assuredly receive the crown of life (Rev. ii. 10), those of them that suffer according to the will of God may with confidence commit their souls in well-doing unto a faithful Creator (1 Pet. iv. 19).

---

[1] The line of thought presented in the passage is in many respects a repetition of that in chap. ii. 19 ff., and hence it is quite lawful to illustrate it by the phraseology of the earlier part of the Epistle.

If this be a fair *resumé* of the exhortations of the apostle which precede and follow the passage specially under discussion, it is clear that his object was to prepare the believers to whom he wrote for the fiery trial which he foresaw would try their faith, and test the vitality of their Christian profession (1 Pet. iv. 12 ff.). The example of Christ who suffered for well-doing was, therefore, repeatedly urged upon their consideration, and Christ's patient endurance when He was led as a lamb to the slaughter was specially dwelt upon (ii. 21 ff.). For in that day of trial the Redeemer committed His cause and its justice into the hands of God, without permitting any denunciations against His enemies to fall from His sacred lips. The example of Christ on the cross is, therefore, first of all set before the believers as a model of suffering patience, and the apostle then mentions, as it were, a second instance of a similar kind, namely, that Christ went in the spirit and preached to the spirits in prison.

The question, therefore, at once suggests itself: Is the new fact adduced in the 19th verse—connected as it is with the former illustration by the use of the conjunction "also" (καί)—another example of Christ's long-suffering patience? If so, some illustration in harmony with the context would be expected. Otherwise the allusion in the 19th verse (whatever be its special meaning) would be an interruption in the solemn and earnest admonition to the saints to persevere in well-doing.

Before entering upon a more minute examination of the disputed passage, it is necessary also to call particular attention to the point that whatever be meant by Christ's preaching to the spirits in prison, the fact to which the apostle refers was evidently considered a matter with which his readers were acquainted. The apostle does not exhibit the slightest consciousness in the Epistle that he was setting forth any new and hitherto unknown truth, which had been by the power of the Holy Ghost specially revealed to him. He does not preface his statement by any announcement like that of St. Paul: "Behold I show you a mystery" (1 Cor. xv. 51). He takes it for granted that the preaching of Christ to the spirits in prison was well known and believed in by all his readers.

It is certain that no preaching of Christ to departed spirits, whether before or after His resurrection, is alluded to in any other passage of the New Testament. Even if it be conceded that all the passages generally adduced in proof of the descent into Hades are correctly interpreted, as directly or indirectly referring to that event,[1] nothing is contained in any of those texts, beyond the general statement that Christ went down into the depths of the Under-world, and that He was with the

---

[1] Dean Plumptre refers to Acts ii. 27 (including, of course, Ps. xvi. 8); Luke xxiii. 43; Matt. xxvii. 52, 53; Eph. iv. 8, 9; Phil. ii. 9, 10; Rev. v. 1-18, together with the passages in 1 Pet. iii. 18-20, and 1 Pet. iv. 6. The latter two we maintain contain no reference at all to the Descent. Dean Plumptre also considers

penitent thief in Paradise. Not one of them contains any allusion whatever to the work which Christ performed "in the spirit," during the interval which elapsed between His death and resurrection.

It will be of importance here to digress a little in order to notice the "historical tradition" concerning Christ's descent into hell, current in the Church of the early ages. Although Dean Plumptre considers that the opinions of the Fathers throw much light on the verse of St. Peter, we maintain that a survey of their opinions distinctly proves that the Church of the early ages was left as completely in the dark on the subject as we are.

Hermas is the only one of "the Apostolic Fathers" who alludes to the matter. He speaks mysteriously of a preaching (κηρύγμα) to those who were asleep carried on by "the apostles and teachers." But that writer nowhere mentions any preaching of Christ Himself to the dead. In the vision of the Church militant and triumphant, represented under the similitude of the building of a great tower, Hermas asks the Shepherd (*Sim.* ix. 16): "Why did also the forty stones"—which in the previous chapter are explained to be "the apostles and teachers of the preaching of the Son of God"—ascend out of the deep having already received the seal (of baptism)?

---

references to the event less distinct, but still highly probable, occur in Ps. cxix. 82, Ps. cxlii. 7, and in Zech. ix. 11, 12, none of which in our opinion, and least of all the last mentioned passage (to which he frequently refers), contain any allusion whatever to the point. See the *Bampton Lectures on Zechariah*, pp. 249-251 and p. 572.

In other words, why were these stones seen in the vision to ascend with the holy spirits or virgins (named Faith, Continence, Purity, Truth, Love, etc.), represented as building the tower? The answer of the Shepherd was as follows: "Because, said he, these, the apostles and the teachers, who preached the name of the Son of God, after having fallen asleep in the power and faith of the Son of God preached (ἐκήρυξαν) even to those who had fallen asleep, and they gave to them the seal of the preaching.[1] They descended, therefore, with them into the water, and again ascended. But these (the apostles and teachers) descended when living, and again ascended living, but the others who had previously fallen asleep descended dead, but ascended living. Through these, therefore, (the apostles and teachers) they were quickened (ἐζωοποιήθησαν) and made to know the name of the Son of God. For this cause also did they ascend with them, and were fitted along with them into the building of the tower, and untouched by the chisel, were built in along with them. For they

---

[1] For as the Shepherd had already explained in the passage immediately preceding: "They were obliged to ascend through water in order that they might be made alive; for they could not otherwise enter into the kingdom, unless they laid aside the deadness of their life. Therefore, even those who had fallen asleep received the seal of the Son of God. For before, said he, the man carries the name of the Son of God, he is dead, but when he receives the seal, he lays aside his deadness, and obtains life. The seal, therefore, is the water: they therefore go down into the water dead and they ascend living. And to them, therefore, was this seal preached, and they made use of it in order that they might enter into the kingdom of God."

slept in righteousness and in great purity, but only they had not this seal." In other words, the persons referred to were not among those who had received Christian baptism in their lifetime.

The designation "apostles," in this and other passages of Hermas, is not restricted to the Twelve Apostles, as the mention of the typical number "forty" proves. Professor Harnack of Giessen has conclusively shown, from a comparison of the *Didache* with the earliest Christian writings, that the apostles of the early period were simply itinerating missionaries.[1] However this may be, it is tolerably clear that the persons of whom Hermas speaks as having heard the "preaching" of the gospel and having received "the seal" of baptism in the other world, were none other than the saints of the Old Dispensation. For he remarks of those persons that "they slept in righteousness and in great purity, but only they had not this seal." All, therefore, they needed was Christian baptism. For Hermas believed in the regenerating power of Christian baptism, and in the absolute necessity of such regeneration, in order to qualify any persons for entrance into "the kingdom of Christ." There is no necessity here to discuss the truth or falsehood of this theory. Hermas was,

---

[1] On the wider use of the term "apostle," see Bishop Lightfoot on *The Epistle to the Galatians*, p. 93 ff., in which reference *inter alia* is made to the passage above quoted from Hermas. See also Harnack, *Lehre der Zwölf Apostel, nebst Untersuchungen zur ältesten Geschichte der Kirchenverfassung und des Kirchenrechts* (Leipzig: Hinrichs, 1884), Prolegomena, p. 111 ff.

however, led by it to affirm that believers under the Old Dispensation were, through the instrumentality of Christian teachers, made partakers after death of the blessings not previously granted under the Old Covenant. The perfection spoken of in Heb. xii. 23, 24 as ultimately bestowed upon "the spirits of just men"—of whom it was said that "apart from us they should not be made perfect" (Heb. xi. 40)—seems to lie at the foundation of the interesting bit of "Christian speculation" set forth in this part of Hermas' vision. But, be it noted, Hermas does not say a word about Christ Himself having preached in the Unseen-world, or of the gospel having been preached to sinners who had died in their sins.

Clement of Alexandria (*ob. circa* 216) has, indeed, ventured to interpret the expressions of Hermas in a wider sense. In his *Stromata* (or *Miscellanies*), ii. 9, vi. 6, Clement specially refers to Hermas, and expounds his words as having reference to the pious Gentiles who lived in the ages prior to Christ, as well as to the saints of the Old Testament. But the interpretation assigned by Clement does not correctly express the meaning of the original writer. Clement maintains that the gospel was preached in the Unseen-world to the Gentiles, at least to those who lived prior to the days of the Christian dispensation. And it must be carefully noted that even Clement speaks of the gospel as having been preached only to such of the Gentiles as had "lived in righteousness according to the law and philosophy," who were "possessed of greater worth in righteousness," and "whose life had been pre-eminent," who were "confessedly of the number of the people of God Almighty," and who were "ready for conversion" (*Strom.* vi. 6). Not even such a bold thinker as Clement dreamed of the gospel being preached to all men, whether they had lived righteously or unrighteously on earth.[1]

The Biblical passages cited by Clement in support of these views are, together with that quoted from Hermas, Isa. xlix. 8, 9; Job xxviii. 22; and 1 Pet. iii. The first passage has nothing whatever to say to the question. The second is strangely quoted, possibly from memory, and does not agree with any known text.[2] He remarks as follows on

---

[1] The words of Clement are: Τουτέστι τοὺς ἐν δικαιοσύνῃ τῇ κατὰ νόμον καὶ κατὰ φιλοσοφίαν βεβιωκότας, . . . ἐπί τι τοῖς πλημμεληθεῖσι μετανενοηκότας, κἂν ἐν ἄλλῳ τόπῳ τύχωσιν, ἐξομολογουμένως ἐν τοῖς τοῦ Θεοῦ ὄντας τοῦ παντοκράτορος κ.τ.λ., and again: Τοὺς ἐξ ἐθνῶν ἐπιτηδείους εἰς ἐπιστροφὴν εὐηγγελίσαντο.

[2] Clement quotes it (*Strom.* vi. 6): "Accordingly the Scripture saith: 'Hades says to Destruction: we have not seen his form, but we have heard his voice'" (φησί γ' οὖν ἡ γραφή, λέγει ὁ ᾅδης τῇ ἀπωλείᾳ· Εἶδος μὲν αὐτοῦ οὐκ εἴδομεν, φωνὴν δὲ αὐτοῦ ἠκούσαμεν). He comments on it as follows: "It is not plainly the place, which, the words above say, heard the voice, but those who have been put in Hades, and have abandoned themselves to destruction, as persons who have thrown themselves voluntarily from a ship into the sea. They then are those that hear the divine power and voice. For who in his senses can suppose the souls of the righteous and those of sinners in the same condemnation, charging Providence with injustice? But how?" Then follow the words quoted above in reference to 1 Pet. iii. The English reader can examine the passage in the excellent translation of Clement of Alexandria in the *Ante-Nicene Library*, published by T. & T. Clark, Edinburgh.

the third passage: "Do not they (the Scriptures) show that the Lord preached the gospel to those that perished in the flood, or rather had been chained, and to those kept 'in ward and guard'?[1] And it has been shown also, in the second book of the *Stromata* [by the quotation cited from Hermas], that the apostles, following the Lord, preached the gospel to those in Hades." Further on he says: "It is evident that those, too, who were outside of the law, having lived rightly, in consequence of the peculiar nature of the voice [of God], though they are in Hades and in ward, on hearing the voice of the Lord, whether that of His own person, or that acting through His apostles, with all speed turned and believed."[2]

Such are the entire of the remarks made by Clement on 1 Pet. iii. Although that Father quotes the text as referring to a preaching to the antediluvians, he comments on it as if it had spoken of Christ preaching generally to the Gentiles. The drift of his argument is to show that the Gentiles, who had not the law, but who walked faithfully according to the light they had, namely, that of philosophy, were also blessed in due time in the Underworld by a revelation of the gospel.

---

[1] Τί δέ; οὐχὶ δηλοῦσιν εὐηγγελίσθαι τὸν Κύριον τοῖς τε ἀπολωλόσιν ἐν τῷ κατακλυσμῷ, μᾶλλον δὲ πεπεδημένοις, κα τοῖς ἐν "φυλακῇ" τε καὶ "φρουρᾷ" συνεχομένοις.

[2] Δηλόν που καὶ τοὺς ἐκτὸς νόμου γενομένους διὰ τὴν τῆς φωνῆς ἰδιότητα ὀρθῶς βεβιωκότας, εἰ καὶ ἐν ᾅδῃ ἔτυχον ὄντα; καὶ ἐν φρουρᾷ ἐπακούσαντας τῆς τοῦ Κυρίου φωνῆς εἴτε τῆς αὐθεντικῆς, εἴτε καὶ τῆς διὰ τῶν ἀποστόλων ἐνεργούσης, ᾗ τάχος ἐπιστραφῆναί τε καὶ πιστεῦσαι.

It ought to be carefully observed that, in setting forth these views Clement teaches them as, in his opinion, fairly deducible from Scripture. They are propounded by him as personal deductions, resting partly on Scripture and partly on "Christian speculation." Clement of Alexandria, it is evident, knew nothing whatever of any "historical tradition" current in the Church, and derived from sources outside of Scripture, on the question of Christ's having preached in the disembodied state to "the spirits in prison." Had such a tradition then been current that Father would have appealed to it. Clement had in reality only the text of St. Peter, and no other authority, on which to base his theories on the subject, whether true or false.

It is admitted that there was a general belief in the ancient Church that Christ's death on Calvary had a beneficial effect on the Old Testament believers. The existence of such a belief appears not only from the quotations already cited from the Shepherd of Hermas, but also in passages of other Christian writers prior to Clement of Alexandria. That belief, however, casts no real light on the passages in the First Epistle of Peter.

Thus Justin Martyr (*ob.* 165), in his *Dialogue against Trypho* (cap. 72), among the passages which he incorrectly accuses the Jews of having fraudulently removed from the text of the Holy Scriptures, enumerates one, which he asserts originally formed part of the Book of Jeremiah, namely: "The Lord

God, the Holy One of Israel, remembered His dead who slept in the sepulchre, and descended to them to preach the glad tidings to them of salvation.[1]

The same apocryphal prophecy is twice referred to by Irenæus in his work *Against Heresies* (cir. 182–188). It is quoted by him in one place (lib. iii. 20. 4) as a proof that Christ was not a mere man, and is there ascribed to Isaiah. But in another place (lib. iv. 22. 1) he quotes it as a prophecy of Jeremiah. In the latter chapter Irenæus maintains that Christ came to save all men "who from the beginning, according to their capacity, in their generation have both feared and loved God, and practised justice and piety towards their neighbours, and earnestly desired to see Christ and to hear His voice."

In another passage (lib. iv. 27. 2) Irenæus also refers to the descent of our Lord to the regions beneath the earth, and to His preaching there the remission of sins. But in that passage he only speaks of "the righteous men, the prophets, and the patriarchs" as those to whom Christ preached in Hades.

Nor does the summary of faith of the Apostle Thaddæus go further, to which Eusebius refers in his *Ecclesiastical History* (*Hist. Eccl.* i. 13), as found

---

[1] Ἐμνήσθη δὲ κύριος ὁ θεὸς ἅγιος Ἰσραὴλ τῶν νεκρῶν αὐτοῦ, τῶν κεκοιμημένων εἰς γῆν χώματος, καὶ κατέβη πρὸς αὐτοὺς εὐαγγελίσασθαι αὐτοῖς τὸ σωτήριον αὐτοῦ. The same passage is ascribed by Irenæus (*Hær.* iii. 20. 4) to Isaiah, and elsewhere to Jeremiah (*Hær.* iv. 22. 1). See von Otto in his note on the passage in Justin.

"in the public archives of Edessa, in connection with the apocryphal correspondence between Abgarus, the toparch of that city, and our Lord."[1] Thaddæus, according to this story, preached to the people about Jesus, how He was sent from the Father, and "about the power of His works, and the mysteries which He had spoken in the world, and in what power He had done thus, and about His new preaching, and about His humility, and His humiliation, and how He had humbled Himself, and died, and minimized His Godhead,[2] and was crucified, and descended into Hades, and burst asunder the barrier that from the beginning of the world had not been burst, and brought up the dead with Him. For having descended by Himself alone, He raised up many with Him, and brought them to His Father, and then He ascended into heaven."

In all this "summary of faith" there is not a sentence which alludes to Christ having preached in the Under-world to any sinners cut off in their

---

[1] On this apocryphal correspondence see *Die Edessenische Abgarsage kritisch untersucht*, von Richard Adelbert Lipsius. Braunschweig, Schwetschke u. Sohn (M. Bruhn), 1880. Also: *The Doctrine of Addai the Apostle*, now first edited in a complete form in the original Syriac, with an English Translation and Notes, by Rev. George Phillips, D.D., President of Queens' College, Cambridge. London: Trübner & Co., 1876.

[2] The Greek is καὶ ἐσμίκρωσεν αὐτοῦ τὴν θεότητα, which Dean Plumptre thus renders. Compare the Pauline expression ἑαυτὸν ἐκένωσε, Phil. ii. 7. The Syriac, however, as translated by Dr. Phillips, is: "He humbled His exalted divinity by the body which He took," and this, perhaps, expresses the real sense in which the Greek of Eusebius ought to be understood.

iniquity, such as the antediluvians in the age of Noah. The "summary" simply lays emphasis upon the fact noticed in Matt. xxvii. 52, 53, that at our Lord's resurrection and prior to His ascension, Christ "raised up many with Him and brought them to His Father."

There is no dispute whatever as to the doctrine of "the Descent into Hades" having formed part and parcel of the general creed of the Churches of the East in the middle of the third century. But no Christian writer of that period, save Clement of Alexandria, seems to have dreamed of salvation having been offered by Christ to any persons cut off in a state of alienation from God. The silence of the Fathers on this subject cannot have been accidental.

In order, however, further to illustrate the point, Dean Plumptre has recourse to the apocryphal Gospel of Nicodemus. He quotes with approbation Tischendorf's opinion that this curious compilation of legends is "derived or copied from a very ancient apocryphal Gospel of the second century."[1] The Dean, therefore, argues that "the antiquity of the

[1] "Sermonem si spectas, mea quidem sententia nihil est quod originem actis Pilati aut Jacobi evangelio posteriorem probet. Idearum vero ratio ea est ut græcum certe textum examinanti, non varie interpolatum latinum, nulla homini ab ætate apostolica proximo aliena inveniantur. . . . Ex ipso vero libello nostro, qui tum nondum cum actis Pilati conjunctus esse videtur, præ aliis multis hausit, nulla quidem alieni mentione facta, Eusebius Alexandrinus. . . . Quæ omnia conjuncta ejusmodi sunt ut libellum nostrum ex antiquissimo scripto apocrypho secundi sæculi haustum vel transcriptum existimem."—*Evangelia Apocrypha*, edid. Constantinus Tischendorf (Lips. 1853), Prolegomena, pp. lxvii xviii.

belief which the legend presupposes is carried up to the immediately sub-Apostolic period."

The main cause, however, which induced Tischendorf to assign such an early date to the *Gospel of Nicodemus*, was that he thought the *Acts of Pilate*, referred to by Justin Martyr and other Christian writers, were to be identified with the first part of the said Gospel. That identification is, however, more than questionable; and notwithstanding, therefore, the weight which generally belongs to the authority of Tischendorf, it is now generally considered that the said apocryphal Gospel cannot have been composed earlier than the third, or more probably in the fifth century after Christ.[1]

To whatever period, however, it may be assigned, the Gospel of Nicodemus throws no further light upon the opinion of the early Christians on the point in which we are specially concerned. The second portion of that Gospel purports to give an account of the descent of Christ into the lower world. It describes in glowing language (borrowed mainly from Isa. xxv. 7, 8, xxvi. 19; Hos. xiii. 14, and Ps. xxiv. 7–10, cvii. 16) the manner in which Christ rescued "the patriarchs and prophets and forefathers" (Part

---

[1] The reader will find a very succinct account of the whole matter in the Introduction (pp. lxxxv.–cii.) to Mr. B. Harris Cowper's very useful work, *The Apocryphal Gospels and other Documents relating to the History of Christ*. Translated from the originals in Greek, Latin, Syriac, etc., with Notes and Prolegomena. Williams & Norgate, 1867. See also *The Apocryphal Gospels, Acts and Revelations* (Introd. p. xi.), in the "Ante-Nicene Library," vol. xvi. T. & T. Clark. Edinburgh, 1870.

ii. chap. 8) of the Old Testament (Adam among the number) from the power of Hades and Satan. It further relates how Michael the archangel escorted those saints into Paradise, where they met with Enoch and Elijah, who had not seen death, and where also they encountered the penitent thief, to whom the Saviour on the cross had promised the boon of admission to that place of rest.

The Gospel of Nicodemus contains no reference to Christ having preached to the rebels of the antediluvian world. It does not allude to "the spirits in prison" of whom St. Peter speaks. The omission is peculiarly significant. For it proves that at the period in which the second part of that Gospel was drawn up,—and the second part is unquestionably a composition even of a later date than the earlier portion,—the Church did not entertain the idea that Christ preached in the Unseen-world to sinners overwhelmed in the act of rebellion against God. Had such an idea been afloat in the days of the writer, had such an interpretation been then generally put upon the language of the apostle, the idea would have materially expanded the conceptions of the author of the apocryphal Gospel on the subject of the work of the Redeemer in the intermediate state, and would, no doubt, have been decked with the bright colours of the "over-luxuriant imagination" of that writer.

It is unnecessary to pursue the matter further, or to examine the opinions put forward by the later Fathers. It is abundantly clear that there is no evidence whatever to show that the Church ever generally believed that Christ preached in Hades to the heathen or to the antediluvians. The Church, no doubt, held the doctrine of Christ's descent into Hades, and freely expressed its belief that His entrance into the spirit-world was an event fraught with blessing for the saints of the old dispensation, and that it was the means of their removal from a place of comparative discomfort and gloom into the blissful fields of Paradise. No stream can rise higher than its fountain, and the opinions of the later Fathers on the subject are all distinctly derived from their interpretation of 1 Pet. iii. 19. There is not the slightest evidence that there was any "tradition" on the subject current in early days, that is, any tradition which was not entirely dependent on the expressions used by S. Peter in that single verse.

On the other hand, it is clear that S. Peter in that text propounds no new revelation which had been made to him by the Holy Spirit, but simply refers to facts well known to all those whom he addressed. Inasmuch, therefore, as there is no evidence that any Christian writer, prior to Clement of Alexandria, believed in Christ having preached in the intermediate state to sinners who had been previously impenitent, and since the sentiments expressed by Clement and the later Fathers are avowedly based on speculations deduced from that text, and from that text only, it is highly probable that a closer examination of that text will show those writers to have misconceived the meaning of the apostle.

The statements of Augustine on the point afford additional evidence tending in the same direction. For although Augustine considers it highly probable (*non immerito creditur*) that the soul of Christ descended into Hades to effect a work of redemption,[1] that Father does not regard even that to be a subject of express revelation. The salvation of Adam, the father of mankind, is confessed by Augustine to be a matter simply of high probability.[2] On the other hand, it is well known that Augustine opposed the interpretation of 1 Pet. iii. 19 (now advocated by Dean Plumptre and others), and that he explained the "prison" there spoken of to be spiritual darkness (referring to Isa. xlii. 7), and considered "the preaching" to have been that of Noah to the antediluvian world.[3] In setting forth his opinions to this effect, Augustine does not evince the slightest suspicion that he was running counter to any Church "tradition"

---

[1] "Et Christi quidem animam venisse usque ad ea loca, in quibus peccatores cruciantur, ut eos solveret a tormentis, quos esse solvendos occulta nobis sua justitia, non immerito creditur."—August. *De Gen. ad litt.* xii. 63.

[2] "Et de illo quidem primo homine patre generis humani, quod eum inde solverit, Ecclesia fere tota consentit; quod eam non inaniter credidisse credendum est, undecumque hoc traditum sit, etiamsi canonicarum Scripturarum hinc expresse non proferatur auctoritas."—August. *Epist.* clxiv. *Ad Evodium*, 6.

[3] "Quia dixit, conclusis in carcere spiritibus prædicatum, quasi animæ non possint intelligi spiritus, qui tunc erant in carne, atque ignorantiæ tenebris velut carcere claudebantur; de quali carcere se desiderat liberari ille qui dicit, *educ de carcere animam meam ut confiteatur nomini tuo* (Ps. cxli. 8); quæ alibi umbra mortis appellatur:

whatever, otherwise he would not have gone so far as actually later to place the opinion he opposed among the list of "heresies."[1]

Having thus ascertained that no "historical tradition" was current in the early Church on the subject of Christ's preaching to the spirits in prison, we return to examine in detail the phraseology used in 1 Pet. iii. 19, on the interpretation of which verse alone all theories on the point necessarily depend.

The expression "spirits in prison" occurs in no other passage in Scripture. The Greek word rendered "prison" ($\phi\upsilon\lambda\alpha\kappa\acute{\eta}$) is the expression ordinarily used in that sense by the writers of the New Testament. Their constant use of the word in that signification is fatal to the interpretation which assigns the meaning to it of "watch" or "safe-keeping," proposed by Schott and Wiesinger among the German, and by Bishop Horsley and Bishop Harold Browne among the English divines.[2] The word, though frequently used in the sense of "prison," occurs only in one other passage, or possibly in two, of a prison in the Spirit-world. The "abyss" into which Satan is represented as hurled for a season (Rev. xx. 1–3), is termed "his prison" (ver. 7). It

de qua non utique apud inferos, sed hic liberati sunt de quibus scriptum est, *qui sedebant in umbra mortis, lumen ortum est eis* (Isa. ix. 2). Illis autem in diebus Noe frustra prædicatum est, quia non crediderunt cum expectaret eos Dei patientia per tempus tot annorum quibus arca eadem fabricata est," etc.—*Epist. ad Evod.* 16.

[1] *De Hæres.* lxxix.

[2] See Bishop Harold Browne's work on the *Thirty-Nine Articles*, p. 94 ff.

is, moreover, possible that a similar sense may lie beneath the literal signification of our Lord's expression: "Thou shalt be cast into prison" (Matt. v. 25). If, however, it be so, the reference of our Lord is not to any "purgatory" (to which no previous allusion is there made), but to "the Gehenna of fire" immediately before referred to (ver. 22). S. Peter (2 Epist. ii. 4) speaks of "pits of darkness," or, as another reading has it, "chains of darkness,"[1] which latter would correspond with the expression in Jude 6, "everlasting bonds." These are the only passages in the New Testament writings in which mention is distinctly made of a prison in connection with the Spirit-realm.[2]

But there is a remarkable passage in the Old Testament which must not be left out of sight, namely, Isaiah xxiv. 21, 22. The prophet there states that "Jehovah shall punish the host of the high ones on high, and the kings of the earth upon the earth." The double contrast renders it impossible (as Delitzsch has well observed) to explain "the host of the high ones on high" to be a designa-

---

[1] Σειραῖς ζόφου or σιραῖς ζόφου. Σιρός is regarded by the Revisers as another form of σιρός, and hence is translated "*pits.*" But the reading σειροῖς may easily have arisen from a copyist's blunder. The Alex. and Sin. have σειροῖς ζόφοις, and the latter word in this connection must be an adjective signifying *hot*. See Huther in Meyer's *Krit. exeg. Comm.* p. 350.

[2] There are, of course, a number of passages in which mention is made of binding and casting forth transgressors, such as Matt. xxi. 13. But as these passages cannot be properly adduced to explain the phrase "the spirits in prison," they are of no account in our present argument.

tion of any earthly powers. The phrase must, therefore, indicate either the host of the stars (Isa. xl. 26), or the host of angels (1 Kings xxii. 19; Ps. cxlviii. 2).[1] But as it is more natural to think of persons on earth and persons in the heavens as there contrasted, the passage is correctly interpreted to refer to the evil angels who seduced the nations of the earth into rebellion against the Most High. Hence the final overthrow by Jehovah of the kings of the earth brings with it in its train the downfall also of "the spiritual hosts of wickedness in the heavenly places" (Eph. vi. 12).[2]

The overthrow of those combined hosts of earth and heaven on the field of battle (described in the 21st verse) is followed by a description of the imprisonment of the rebels against the Divine power. "They shall be gathered together as prisoners are gathered in the pit,[3] and shall be shut up in the prison, and after many days shall

---

[1] Cheyne (*The Prophecies of Isaiah*, in his note on the passage) calls attention to the remarkable interpretation of the passage which is found in Enoch xviii. 13–16, where the angel is described as pointing out to Enoch "the place where heaven and earth are at an end; it serves for a prison for the stars of heaven and for the host of heaven. And the stars which roll upon the fire are those which transgressed the command of God before their rising, since they did not come in their appointed time. And He became wroth with them, and bound them unto the time when their guilt should be complete, in the year of the secret."

[2] Compare also Isa. xxxiv. 5, and our remarks thereon on p. 52.

[3] A pit (בּוֹר) was often used for the purposes of a prison. So in the case of Joseph (Gen. xxxvii. 24 ff.), Jeremiah (Jer. xxxviii. 6 ff.), etc. The word used in Isa. xxiv. 22 for *prison* is מַסְגֵּר,

they be visited." The overthrow is exactly parallel to that spoken of in Rev. xix. 19–21, where, immediately after the great battle on earth, an angel is represented (Rev. xx. 1–3, 7–10) as laying hold on Satan, the prince of darkness who deceived the nations, and shutting him up in prison. The "visitation" spoken of in Isaiah is, therefore, a visitation of wrath and judgment (like those in Isa. xxix. 6; Ezek. xxxviii. 8; Isa. xxvi. 14, 21), and is probably identical with that set forth at the close of Rev. xx. 10, 14, 15. The "visitation" of the transgressors, angelic and human, is followed, both in the Old and New Testament passages, by a manifestation of the Divine glory and a revelation of grace to God's faithful and redeemed people.

The passage, therefore, in Isaiah may fairly be cited as explanatory of the phrase in S. Peter, "the spirits in prison." It is quite possible (though the point cannot be pressed) that the phraseology used in the Old Testament prophet may have suggested the very phrase "spirits in prison" to the apostle's mind. For the "prison" in both cases is that in which the unrighteous dead are thought of as awaiting their final doom and punishment.

With the light obtained from the Old Testament parallel, we are now in a better position to examine

which occurs also in this signification in Ps. cxlii. 8; Isa. xlii. 7. The LXX. in Isa. xxiv. 22 render the Heb. word meaning *pit* by δεσμωτήριον, and the word designating a *prison* by ὀχύρωμα, so the φυλακή of the apostle cannot be directly drawn from that passage.

the statement of S. Peter. The apostle does not say that Christ after His resurrection went and preached to the spirits in prison, but that Christ "in the spirit," *i.e.* Christ as pneuma or spirit, went and preached to the individuals whose disobedience is recounted in ver. 20. According to our view of the passage, the apostle, after mentioning the fact that Christ, though put to death in the flesh, was quickened or kept alive in the spirit, was led on to adduce, as another instance of His long-suffering patience with ungodly sinners, Christ's action "in the spirit," not indeed Christ's work in His disembodied state in the interval which elapsed between His death and resurrection, but Christ's work at a previous period afterwards fully described (ver. 20), when "in the spirit," prior to His incarnation, Christ as the Pre-incarnate Word (the λόγος ἄσαρκος), preached to the antediluvian race, "the world of the ungodly" (2 Pet. ii. 5).

It would, indeed, be soaring into a region of speculation, where we have no guide to direct us, to maintain that the pneuma which Christ had in His disembodied state was identical in all respects with the pneuma which He, as "the Angel of Jehovah's presence," possessed prior to the incarnation. We are not forgetful of the fact that in His disembodied state the Redeemer had not only pneuma (spirit), but also the "reasonable soul," spoken of in the Athanasian Creed. Though we emphasize the statement of man's tripartite nature, "body, soul, and spirit," as set forth in 1 Thess. v. 23, we are very far from asserting that we can dogmatize much on the question of the distinction between soul and spirit, or on the powers which severally belong to each of those parts of man's higher nature.[1] By "spirit" in the passage the apostle evidently signified the higher nature of man, that higher nature which was unscathed and unharmed, even when the Redeemer's body succumbed to the stroke of death. The apostle was not, however, writing on psychology or pneumatology, and inasmuch as he had mentioned the higher nature or pneuma, it was quite natural that he should refer to the long-suffering exhibited by Christ "in the spirit," whether the "spirit" then possessed by the Divine Logos was identical or not with that which afterwards became united to the flesh and soul of the Son of Man. For the distinction, if any, existing between the one spiritual nature and the other, is a matter utterly beyond human cognisance, or human power of conception.

It seems, however, highly probable, from the hints afforded in the Scriptures, that prior to our Lord's incarnation, that is, prior to His taking upon Himself "all things appertaining to the perfection of man's nature," Christ was manifested to the angels in an angelic nature, and became in some special manner

---

[1] That, however, we can understand something even of this distinction, will be evident to all who have read Delitzsch's *Biblical Psychology*, or Heard's *Tripartite Nature of Man*.

an angel or "spirit." Dogmatism on subjects belonging to a sphere man can have little comprehension of, is of course impossible. But the statement in John i. 18,[1] and indirectly that in 1 Tim. vi. 16, seem to imply that the knowledge of the Infinite God cannot be directly made known to any finite being. Hence even in the upper spheres, the mediation of the Second Person of the Trinity may have been necessary in order that God might be revealed to His creatures.

There is, no doubt, in certain quarters a popular notion that Christ did not take on Him the nature of angels, and that Christ's incarnation as man was something absolutely unique. The opinion is based on the mistranslation of Heb. ii. 16, which occurs in the Authorized Version. The sacred writer in that place (as can be seen from the Revised Version) makes no such affirmation. He simply states that angels were not caught hold of, and redeemed from the consequences of their sin, like the seed of Abraham, for whose redemption primarily Christ came. The Pre-incarnate Word was certainly manifested in angelic form in the days of old. It was He who styled Himself "the captain of Jehovah's host," and was spoken of as Jehovah (Josh. iv. 13, v. 2). That was the Angel of Jehovah, also termed by the incommunicable name Jehovah (Zech. iii. 1, 2), and designated elsewhere "the Angel of the

---

[1] Θεὸν οὐδεὶς ἑώρακεν πώποτε, "No one (not simply *no man*) hath seen God at any time."

Covenant" (Mal. iii. 1), etc. Scripture lends no support to the idea that such manifestations were merely phenomenal and not real, and such a theory is akin to the semi-Sadducean idea, broached by several Jewish authorities, that angels themselves were only phantom appearances and not real entities.[1]

Thus it may fairly be affirmed that the Second Person of the Trinity was, like the angels (Heb. i. 14), a "spirit" prior to His incarnation, and appeared, as angels often did, in bodily form to men. He was recognised on certain occasions by the patriarchs, and worshipped by them as God (*e.g.* Gen. xxxii. 24–30; Hos. xii. 3–5). Christ as the Angel of Redemption (Gen. xlviii. 16), Christ "in the spirit," wrought in the world before the Flood, and preached grace and mercy, although then in vain, as far as the majority of mankind were concerned.[2]

---

[1] Dr. J. H. Biesenthal, in his very valuable and suggestive work, *Das Trostschreiben des Apostels Paulus an die Hebräer* (Leipzig, Fernau 1878), on Heb. i. 7, referring to the Midrash Rabbah on Exod., remarks: "God performs His will through His angels, whom He sometimes makes into winds and sometimes also into fire, as it is written, 'He makes His angels winds.' In these appearances of nature they embody themselves in order to perform the will of God. But that alone is their calling, which when they have discharged, they return again to their nothingness. For only the fulfilment of this calling is their existence. When it ceases, the existence ceases also. . . . The angels, the Talmud teaches, are daily, when God pleases, created anew; they have only existence so long as they serve, as they are busied with the fulfilment of their task. After their work is ended they fall back into their former nothingness. They are never again called into being."

[2] It ought perhaps also to be noted that the spirit of Christ, considered as part of His tripartite nature, was not itself "of man nor by man." The human ego, or personal consciousness of man, has probably

The disobedience of "the spirits in prison" consisted in their refusal to listen to the warning afforded to them, which warning was continued for the space of upwards of a hundred years. This was the instance of the long-suffering patience of Christ which the apostle desired to deeply impress on the attention of his readers. For if Christ as the Pre-incarnate Word endured "with much long-suffering" such "gainsaying of sinners against themselves" (or "against Himself"), His people ought not to wax weary or faint in their souls (Heb. x. 3), even though, like their Master, they should be called to stretch out their hands all the day long unto a disobedient and gainsaying people (Rom. x. 21).

The passage, however, does not speak of the Spirit of Christ preaching through Noah, as Augustine and others after him imagined, although Noah is in another passage styled "a preacher of righteousness" (2 Pet. ii. 5). Nor are the words of the apostle explained by reference to Gen. vi. 3, as if an allusion was made in the text to the saying of Jehovah there recorded: "My spirit shall not strive with man for ever." For the term "spirit" in Genesis is not to be

---

its centre in the *soul*, and Christ's incarnation probably consisted in the Pre-incarnate Word taking to itself a human body and soul of the substance of the Virgin Mary, to which the pre-existing pneuma, which had manifested itself to angels, was united. We do not, however, desire to rest our interpretation of 1 Pet. iii. 19 on any uncertain basis of psychology. But see Delitzsch's *Biblical Psychology*, English translation, T. & T. Clark, Edinburgh 1867, and Heard's *Tripartite Nature of Man: Spirit, Soul and Body*, 5th ed., T. & T. Clark, 1882.

identified with the "spirit of Christ" mentioned by
S. Peter. Moreover, the apostle reckons Noah and
his family among the persons to whom the preaching
was made, for they were the "few" who believed
the preaching of "Christ in the spirit," and were
saved in the ark from perishing by the waters of
the Deluge.

S. Peter does not specify the manner in which
the preaching of Christ in the spirit took place. In
the Book of Judges mention is, perhaps, made of a
discourse delivered by the Angel of Jehovah to a
large number of Israelites assembled together. We
refer to the preaching which took place at Bochim
(Judg. ii. 1–5). If that be the correct interpretation of that remarkable passage, it would be quite
in accordance with analogy to conceive that some
similar transaction took place in the days of Noah.
The objection to such a view is, however, that no
such preaching is recorded in the Book of Genesis,
while the apostle refers to an event well known to
his hearers. But the Book of Genesis states that
God spake to Noah. And since whenever a detailed
account of God speaking with man is recorded
in Genesis, it is generally stated that the Most High
appeared in angelic or human form, it is in accordance
with analogy to suppose that the Angel of Jehovah
appeared to Noah, and gave him directions concerning
the building of the ark. The building of the ark,
commanded by the Divine voice, may well be regarded
as a continuation of the Divine preaching. By that

ark "regeneration" was preached to the world.[1] It spoke of judgment and of mercy, though few accepted the salvation offered thereby. The threatened judgment was long deferred, and hence ungodly sinners went on in transgression until the day of wrath overtook them unawares.

S. Peter speaks in another passage of the "spirit of Christ," which worked in and through the prophets of bygone days (1 Pet. i. 11). This is in full accordance with the saying of Amos: "Surely the Lord Jehovah will do nothing, but He revealeth His secret unto His servants the prophets" (Amos iii. 7). A similar statement occurs in the commencement of the New Testament book of wrath and judgment, "the Revelation of Jesus Christ," which was given to show "the things which must shortly come to pass," and was "signified by His angel unto His servant John" (Rev. i. 1). The gospel of warning and mercy preached by the Pre-incarnate Word to "the spirits in prison," was not less His even if it were made known to them prior to their punishment by the prophets of that era, whether Enoch, Noah, or others whose names are unrecorded.

The expression "went" ($\pi o \rho \epsilon v \theta \epsilon i \varsigma$), used of motion from one place to another, presents no difficulty in the way of our interpretation. The employment of

---

[1] "Noah being found faithful by his ministry, preached ($\pi \alpha \lambda \iota \gamma$-$\gamma \epsilon \nu \epsilon \sigma i \alpha \nu \ \kappa \dot{o} \sigma \mu \omega \ \dot{\epsilon} \kappa \dot{\eta} \rho v \xi \epsilon \nu$) regeneration to the world."—Clem. Roman. 1 Epist. 9. Again in Clem. Rom. i. 8, "Noah preached repentance ($\dot{\epsilon} \kappa \dot{\eta} \rho v \xi \epsilon \nu \ \mu \epsilon \tau \dot{\alpha} \nu o \iota \alpha \nu$), and those who listened to him were saved."

the same word and form in ver. 22, in the phrase "having gone into heaven" (πορευθεὶς εἰς οὐρανόν)—though the identity of the expression cannot without harshness be retained in English,[1] shows that the apostle mentally contrasts the two events, the going "up" into heaven, and the going "down" to earth. For the descent referred to signifies necessarily no more than that mentioned in Gen. xi. 5, 7, where Jehovah is represented as "going down" to confound the builders of the tower of Babylon. The expression "went" would be employed with equal propriety, whether used of Christ's going down from heaven in order to preach to the antediluvians on earth, or of Christ going down after death to the place of departed spirits.

The meaning of the term "prison" has been already discussed (see p. 166 ff.). But the question is, what idea is conveyed by the phrase "the spirits in prison"? Does it signify "the spirits *who are* in prison," *i.e.* who in consequence of their sin were "cast into prison," and therefore were regarded by the apostle as still there? The preaching in that case must necessarily be thought of as having taken place previous to their imprisonment. Or does the phrase signify "the spirits *who were* in prison," the apostle leaving his readers mentally to draw the inference, that possibly all, or at least considerable numbers of the transgressors, were by means of the preaching of

---

[1] The literal translation would be: "in which, also, having gone to the spirits in prison, He preached."

the gospel[1] released out of their prison? But even if "the spirits in prison" be understood to signify "the spirits *who were* in prison," the release of these spirits out of prison is by no means distinctly stated.

The awful character of the transgressions committed prior to the Flood, and the universality of the apostasy which then took place, is spoken of in the strongest manner in the Book of Genesis. The story is several times referred to in the New Testament,[2] and the deliverance of Noah and his family is generally referred to along with the punishment of the ungodly. The outlines of the entire narrative are distinctly set forth in the context of the passage in S. Peter (ver. 20). But, if the apostle was speaking of Christ's preaching in the Under-world, it is remarkable that he should say nothing definite about the outcome of that preaching, especially as he refers to "the spirits" of those who perished in the Flood as "in prison." It will scarcely be maintained that the long-continued impenitence and hardness of heart

---

[1] The word κηρύσσω in the New Testament generally conveys the idea of the preaching of good tidings. It signifies, as von Zezschwitz notes, properly the preaching of the kingdom of God, and hence is used, as in the case of the preaching of our Lord and of John the Baptist, of a preaching in which warnings of judgment and offers of grace were commingled. It is never, however, used of a simple announcement of wrath, though used, on the other hand, to denote a preaching in which mercy only was the theme. See *Petri Apostoli de Christi ad inferos descensu sententia ex loco nobilissimo* 1 *Ep.* iii. 19 *eruta exacta ad Epistolæ argumentum.* Scripsit C. A. G. von Zezschwitz. Lipsiæ: Doerffling et Francke, 1857.

[2] As in Matt. xxiv. 37–39; Luke xvii. 26, 27; Heb. xi. 7; 2 Pet. ii. 5, iii. 6; Jude 13–15, and in the passage before us.

of those spirits on earth peculiarly fitted them for the reception of the gospel preached to them "in prison," and consequently that it was unnecessary for the apostle to do more than mention the fact.

There may be, and no doubt are, good reasons why men are kept by God in ignorance with regard to the secrets of the Unseen-world. But we can conceive no reason why so much should be said about the marvellous results of converting grace achieved by the descent of the Spirit on the day of Pentecost, while such a stupendous fact as the conversion of the whole antediluvian world, by the preaching of Christ in the intermediate state, should be left to be deduced by a mere chance inference from the apostle's words.

It is strange, indeed, that the apostle should refer to Christ's preaching in the Under-world as a point with which presumably his readers were acquainted, while no allusion is made to the subject by any other writer of the New Testament.

The interpretation of the passage first given by the speculative Clement of Alexandria, and now affirmed to be the most simple and natural sense, is, however, in reality beset with difficulties on every side.

It is no small difficulty to read of Christ's proclaiming the gospel to the deep-dyed transgressors who perished in the Deluge. Their former obstinate rejection of the Divine revelation can, as Prof. Schweizer observes, surely not have been the reason why the gospel should have been specially preached to them. No mention is made of an offer of salvation having been similarly made to others. Were the antediluvians the only "spirits in prison" in the Unseen-world? Are we to believe that there are "many prisons" in the Under-world corresponding to the "many mansions" in the Father's house? The assertion that the preaching of Christ to the antediluvians is only mentioned "as a sample of a like precious work on others," is the last resort of an exegesis driven to despair. Not a tittle of evidence can be adduced to justify such an assertion. But assertions of such a kind are often made with the greater boldness, the smaller the basis really is on which to construct an argument.

The persons to whom Christ preached are described as "the spirits in prison which aforetime were disobedient." If the clause "the spirits in prison" be regarded as the principal, and that which in the Revised Version is the relative clause be the subordinate, the phrase may be interpreted to mean: "The prisoners who were in prison who aforetime had been disobedient in the days of Noah."[1] In that case the reference of the passage

---

[1] Τοῖς ἐν φυλακῇ πνεύμασιν ... ἀπειθήσασιν. The article τοῖς in such a case would have been naturally expected before the participle. In that case the disobedience in former days would be contrasted with an *implied* submission in later time. The second dative (the participle) must then be regarded as the less important part of the clause, serving more exactly to define those signified by "the spirits in prison" in the preceding part.

must be to the descent of Christ into Hades. The second clause may, however, with equal propriety be regarded as expressing the principal idea present to the apostle's mind. In that case the clause ought to be rendered, " Christ went and preached to the spirits in prison, disobedient aforetime, when the long-suffering of God waited in the days of Noah."[1] The idea conveyed is then: "Christ went and preached to the spirits now in prison on account of their disobedience aforetime in the days of Noah.'

---

[1] The aorist participle (ἀπειθήσασι) simply indicates that the disobedience contemplated by the apostle was exhibited in past time. It does not convey the idea that those who were then disobedient had ceased to be disobedient. There is no reference to the condition of the individuals at the time at which the apostle wrote. Had he meant to refer to them as then actually disobedient, he would have used the present participle (ἀπειθοῦσι) instead of the aorist. But he passes no judgment whatever on their actual condition, unless it be contained in the expression "the spirits in prison" (τοῖς ἐν φυλακῇ πνεύμασι). It is, however, to their past disobedience rather than their present condition that the apostle mainly directs attention. In order to avoid the introduction of an interpretation into the translation of the words of the apostle, the whole should be rendered "the spirits in prison" (or "the imprisoned spirits"), "disobedient aforetime, when the long-suffering of God waited," etc. Even the introduction in the Revised Version of the relative "which" into the clause, and the breaking up of the participle into two words, "were disobedient," impart a particular turn in English to the passage which is not necessitated by the Greek. If it should be argued that the same remark would apply to rendering the participle by an adjective, we reply, that the objection does not hold good, because the adjective "*disobedient*" in connection with the adverb "*aforetime*" must refer to an event long past, which is the true grammatical force of the aorist participle. The ambiguity lies simply in the phrase "the spirits in prison," and the sense of that expression is to be determined from the context and that only. The participle which follows does not afford any help to the understanding of that clause.

So far from being a "superficial" interpretation, this is in reality the true explanation of the passage. It brings the whole into close connection with the immediate context. It justifies the use of the connective particle "also" (καί) in the 19th verse, which unquestionably suggests that the illustration thereby joined to the preceding is akin to what had been already mentioned.

The passage thus understood contains several distinct statements. In the first the apostle affirms that the spirits of whom he speaks were "in prison." Secondly, he states that their imprisonment was caused by their former obstinate disobedience. He next mentions the long-suffering of God, which it was his main object to illustrate by the reference to the history of the antediluvian world. The disobedience of the "spirits in prison" took place in former days; "aforetime" (πότε), "when (ὅτε) the long-suffering of God waited in the days of Noah." The apostle speaks of those transgressors as "kept under punishment unto the day of judgment" (2 Pet. ii. 9),[1] *i.e.* as "spirits in prison." But he does not enter into any details as to what that punishment consisted in. He hurries onward to speak of their disobedience during life, and to compare the deliverance offered to believers in Christ by true

[1] It is well to note the important variation in translation in the Revised Version, as quoted above, from that of the Authorized Version, which renders that passage, "to reserve the unjust unto the day of judgment to be punished." We cannot here discuss the correctness of the alteration.

entrance by baptism into "the ark of Christ's Church," with the salvation which had been once offered in the ark of Noah to the antediluvian world. Christ, as the Pre-incarnate Logos, was the cause of the latter deliverance, and hence the reference by the apostle to the mercy and long-suffering of the Son of God in former days was no real digression from his argument; while the allusion to the fate of "the spirits in prison" was a wholesome warning to those to whom the Epistle was addressed, lest they should "fall after the same example of disobedience" (Heb. iv. 11).

At the close of our argument it is necessary also to notice the passage in iv. 1–6. For as mention is there made of the gospel having been preached to the dead, it is of importance to consider that statement in the context in which it is contained. The whole paragraph runs thus:—

"Forasmuch then as Christ suffered in the flesh, arm ye yourselves also with the same mind; for he that hath suffered in the flesh hath ceased from sin; that ye no longer should live the rest of your time in the flesh to the lusts of men, but to the will of God. For the time past may suffice to have wrought the desire of the Gentiles, and to have walked in lasciviousness, lusts, wine-bibbings, revellings, carousings, and abominable idolatries: wherein they think it strange that ye run not with them into the same excess of riot, speaking evil of you: who shall give account to Him that is ready to judge the quick and the dead. For unto this end was the gospel preached even to the dead, that they might be judged according to men in the flesh, but live according to God in the spirit."

To enter, indeed, fully into the exegesis of the remarkable passage in ver. 6, would necessitate a lengthened discussion. Its explanation depends, as will be presently seen, materially upon the interpretation assigned to 1 Pet. iii. 19. The very forms of expression made use of by the apostle clearly show that reference is made to what had been previously stated, and prove that there is a distinct comparison between the subjects treated of in chap. iii. and those brought under notice in chap. iv.

The preaching of the gospel referred to in the latter passage was (as appears from the tense used in the original) a transaction conceived as having already happened in past time.[1] The gospel was, at some time prior to the date at which S. Peter wrote, preached to the individuals described as "dead," in order that they might be judged according to men in the flesh ($\sigma\alpha\rho\kappa\acute{\iota}$), but might live according to God in the spirit ($\pi\nu\epsilon\acute{\upsilon}\mu\alpha\tau\iota$). Whether the gospel, however, was preached to those persons in life or after death, is the question now to be investigated.

Several points are distinctly noticed in this remarkable verse.

---

[1] The Greek of the whole passage is important to be before the eye of the reader : εἰς τοῦτο γὰρ καὶ νεκροῖς εὐηγγελίσθη, ἵνα κριθῶσι μὲν κατὰ ἀνθρώπους σαρκί, ζῶσι δὲ κατὰ Θεὸν πνεύματι.

1. The preaching of the gospel, as far as there alluded to, was an act performed at some past time. The words of the apostle are too precise to admit of their being regarded as referring to an habitual act. They, therefore, do not convey the meaning put upon them by some, that the gospel is, as a matter of ordinary occurrence, preached even to the dead. For although the persons preached to are not specially particularized in the verse, it is to a preaching which took place in past time that the apostle speaks.

2. The "gospel," in the New Testament sense of that term (as Huther has well observed), could not have been preached until after the work of redemption was complete, and consequently not until after Christ had died, or had risen from the dead. The apostolic statement cannot, therefore, mean (as Schweizer seems to maintain) that the gospel, loosely explained as the manifestation of divine mercy, has been at all times preached in some form or other to men in this world; and that this has been effected by the operation of "Christ in the spirit," or of the Logos, in the ages prior to the incarnation of the Son of Man. Such a theory, whether true or false, is not contained in the words before us. Schweizer considers the argument of the apostle to be: the dead may well without injustice be judged by Christ, for all men have in this life opportunities for manifesting their disposition towards the Son of Man (comp. Matt. xxv. 40, 45); and He is not only the

judge, but the law whereby men shall finally be judged.¹

3. The whole drift of the apostle's exhortation (see p. 187), and the language of this verse, make it abundantly clear that a comparison is drawn in the passage between that which had happened to certain followers of Christ, and that which had befallen their Divine Master. He was put to death in the flesh (σαρκί), but was quickened in the spirit (πνεύματι). His followers were judged according to men in the flesh (σαρκί), they lived according to God in the spirit (πνεύματι). The comparison (as Schweizer has justly remarked) would lose much of its force, if the preaching, spoken of as preceding the judgment mentioned in the text, had not taken place while the persons referred to were still "in the flesh," or in the very same state or condition in which Christ was "found" (Phil. ii. 8) when He was "put to death," even to "the death of the cross."

4. The objects for which the gospel had been specially preached to the followers of Christ contemplated by the apostle, were (a) that they might be judged according to men in the flesh; (b) that they might live according to God in the spirit.²

---

¹ The gospel is sometimes spoken of as if it had been preached even in apostolic days to every individual. Thus, St. Paul in Col. i. 23 speaks of the gospel as "preached in all creation under heaven" (τοῦ εὐαγγελίου, τοῦ κηρυχθέντος ἐν πάσῃ κτίσει τῇ ὑπὸ τὸν οὐρανόν), comp. Mark xvi. 15. Such language is, however, the language of faith, which looks on that as already accomplished which is actually in course of being accomplished.

² Huther (in Meyer's *Commentar, in loco*) observes that according to the grammatical construction, κριθῶσι and ζῶσι are co-ordinated

The gospel was preached to these early believers with the design on the part of God that they should be witnesses even unto death, and should glorify Him by their death. The idea which underlies the apostolic statement is akin to that expressed by our Lord (Matt. xxiii. 34): "Therefore, behold, I send unto you prophets, and wise men, and scribes, some of them shall ye kill and crucify; and some of them shall ye scourge in your synagogues, and persecute from city to city." The gospel was preached to the believers in question that they might be "partakers of Christ's sufferings" (1 Pet. iv. 13). For it was "no strange thing" that had happened unto them (1 Pet. iv. 12) when they were called to "drink of the cup" that Christ drank of, and were "baptized with the baptism" that He was baptized with (Mark x. 38, 39). "He that hath suffered in the flesh hath ceased from sin," or "sins," that is, has finally broken off with sin; sin has no longer any power over him (ver. 2). The followers of sin hated the followers of

together, and are both equally dependent on ἵνα; but, according to the sense, ἵνα refers only to the ζῶσι, and the first clause is to be regarded as a parenthesis. The latter supposition is not necessary. The strict grammatical construction is always to be followed when it affords a good sense. Huther calls attention to the use of the aorist κριθῶσι, as showing that the judgment referred to is one which had already taken place, and, therefore, ought not to be identified with the judgment of the last day. If κριθῶσι be regarded as really dependent, even in sense, on ἵνα, the judgment referred to must needs be a judgment which took place after the gospel had been actually preached to the persons concerned. But as this is the very point Huther will not admit, he consequently maintains that according to the sense the ἵνα can only refer to the ζῶσι. But see above.

Christ, and spoke evil of them; they reproached them, persecuted them, and said all manner of evil against them falsely for Christ's sake (Matt. v. 12). For they thought it strange that Christ's people would not run with them into the same excess of riot (ver. 4). Consequently Christ's followers were condemned by the judgment of men, though acquitted and rewarded by the judgment of God.

5. The contrast between the ways of God and the ways of men in the passage has not been generally noticed with sufficient accuracy. The judgment referred to in ver. 6 is the same as that spoken of in the end of the chapter (vers. 17, 18), where the apostle says, "The time is come for judgment to begin at the house of God; and if it first begin at us, what shall be the end of them that obey not the gospel of God? And if the righteous scarcely be saved, where shall the ungodly and the sinner appear?" The judgment meant was the fiery trial, which, owing to the hostility of men, had already begun to try the reality of the faith of the followers of Christ. The judgment, therefore, was inflicted by the hands of men according to their malicious desires, although at the same time in accordance with the "determined counsel and foreknowledge of God" (Acts ii. 23). The servants of Christ were only treated like their Master. If Christ was put to death "in the flesh," Christians experienced similar ill-treatment. But "he that endured to the end was saved" (Matt. xxiv. 13).

When Christ on the way to the cross beheld with the eye of a prophet the approaching judgment on Jerusalem and her people, He drew attention to the contrast between the judgment inflicted on Himself "according to men," and the awful judgment to be inflicted on the guilty nation "according to God." "If they do these things in the green tree, what shall be done in the dry?" (Luke xxiii. 31). With a similar prophetic instinct the apostle exclaims: "If the righteous scarcely be saved, where shall the ungodly and the sinner appear?" For S. Peter considered "the end of all things" to be "at hand" (chap. iv. 7). Christ having been raised from the dead and at the right hand of God was, said he, ready (comp. Acts xxi. 13; 2 Cor. xii. 14) to judge the quick and the dead. The adversaries of Christ's people would, therefore, have to give account unto Him (ver. 5) for the manner in which they persecuted His chosen ones; for he that toucheth them toucheth the apple of Jehovah's eye (Zech. ii. 8).

There is no difficulty whatever in understanding the expression "according to men"[1] to mean in the

[1] Compare the meaning of κατὰ ἄνθρωπον in 1 Cor. iii. 3 and Gal. i. 11. The plural κατὰ ἀνθρώπους, found in the passage in 1 Peter, is used possibly to denote more distinctly the plurality of the adversaries. We subjoin here the interpretation of the passage given by Dean Alford in his Greek Testament as that generally held by the commentators who oppose our view, in order that the reader may compare it with the interpretation given above. The parentheses in the following note are Dean Alford's own :—"Our Lord is ready to judge the dead : and with reason : for even they have not been without opportunity of receiving His gospel : as the example adduced in iii. 19 shows. For this end the gospel was preached even to the dead, that

manner peculiar to men, who are wont to judge according to the appearance, and who do not judge righteous judgment (John vii. 24). Nor is there any difficulty in understanding "according to God" to signify, according to the peculiar manner in which God judges. For, as St. Paul says, " it is a righteous thing that God should recompense affliction to them that afflict you, and to you that are afflicted rest with us at the revelation of the Lord Jesus" (2 Thess. i. 6–9). God bestows life on His people, and grants them even in the intermediate state "rest yet for a little time, until their fellow-servants also and their brethren, which should be killed even as they were, should be fulfilled" (Rev. vi. 11).

It would be introducing a new idea into the passage to explain the expression "live according to God" as signifying eternal life, in opposition to the condemnation mentioned in the text. The "living in the spirit" is better explained as equivalent to the "quickening in the spirit" (iii. 18). The idea, therefore, is identical with that found in Rev. xx. 4, in

they might—not indeed escape the universal judgment on human sin, which is physical death—but *that they might be judged* [aor.; be in the state of the completed sentence on sin, which is death after the flesh] *according to* [as] *man as regards the flesh* [this first clause following ἵνα being the subordinate one, of the state which the ἐπαγγελίσθη left remaining], *but* [notwithstanding] *might live* [pres.; of a state to continue] *according to God* [a life with God and divine] *as regards the spirit:* so that the relation of these two clauses with μέν and δέ is precisely as in Rom. viii. 10, where the former clause in the apodosis is not the consequence of the protasis, but an abiding fact, seeming to militate against, but not really hindering that consequence."

which passage "the souls of them who had been beheaded for the testimony of Jesus, and for the word of God," are represented after their sufferings as living and reigning with Christ during the "thousand years."

The only difficulty with which the above exposition has really to contend is the use of the expression "was preached to the dead." The article is not found in the Greek, but is required by the English idiom. It is omitted also in the Greek, in the expression "ready to judge the quick and the dead," immediately preceding, and in the similar expression in Rom. xiv. 9; 2 Tim. iv. 1, etc. It cannot be denied that "the dead," without the article, is sometimes used to indicate the dead in general, as in Luke xvi. 30; Acts x. 42, etc.

The difficulty, however, is not by any means insuperable. For the expression "*the dead*" may also be used in a more restricted sense, as referring to the persons of whom special mention had been made in the context, and to them only. The fact that "the dead" are spoken of immediately after in the phrase "the quick and the dead," is not sufficient to prove that the word must be understood in the wider sense of the dead in general. For the phrase "judge of quick and dead" is a common expression, used in reference to those who shall be alive or dead at the time of the Second Advent. But inasmuch as in this passage of S. Peter reference is made to a past transaction, and not to the time of the future

Advent, the expression "the dead" in ver. 6 is not to be regarded as identical in meaning with the same expression found in a different collocation in the previous verse. Huther has virtually conceded what is here contended for when he remarks: "Had Peter meant the νεκροῖς (*dead*) in a wider sense, he would have certainly given in some way an intimation of his meaning." That critic adds: "One might at the most find an indication in the εὐηγγελίσθη (*was preached*), in that the gospel could have been preached only to the living and not to the dead. But iii. 19 is opposed to this assertion."

The reference Huther here makes to iii. 19 is quite fair. For it is quite true that the interpretation of iv. 6 depends to a great extent upon that assigned to the former passage. If it can be proved that the apostle there refers to a preaching of the gospel to the antediluvian race in the Unseen-world, it is quite possible that a preaching of the gospel to the dead in general might be alluded to in chap. iv. But it would be strange that the apostle should there have spoken of a preaching to the antediluvian world, and not have dropped a hint concerning the mercy offered in the Under-world to the whole human family. We maintain, however, that the former passage is not rightly so interpreted. Neither is it necessary, to explain iv. 6, to assert that the gospel was preached to any person after death. Such an interpretation is moreover opposed to the other statements contained in that verse. And inasmuch as the preaching spoken of was one which had occurred in past time, we are in no case entitled to draw from the terms of the verse any deduction that the dead in general have the gospel preached to them.

The introduction of any such idea is foreign to the whole scope of the apostolic exhortation. The apostle speaks of believers, and believers only as receiving the reward of faithfulness unto death, namely the crown of life, which is the crown of righteousness. This reward includes the gift of life in the intermediate state, of "rest" during "the little while" which elapses between the resurrection morn, and includes life in its fullest sense in the great day of the Lord Jesus (Rev. ii. 10 ; 2 Tim. iv. 8). Such a hope was an encouragement which might well lead those "that suffer according to the will of God" to commit their souls in well-doing unto a faithful Creator (ver. 19). The sufferings of the martyrs might well be regarded as in one sense " according to the will of God," for though they were inflicted by the hands of evil men, their trials were foreseen and predetermined by God.

The apostle had, therefore, given clear and distinct indications in the context who the persons were of whom he spoke. There is consequently no real objection to "the dead" in the passage being understood of the martyred brethren, who had already by the cruel judgment of men passed on to their rest in the Paradise of God. Their brethren who were still in life were bidden to remember the faith of the martyrs who had gone before, and were exhorted to emulate their fidelity. The introduction into such an exhortation of any doctrine concerning the salvability of all men, or of a statement of a gospel to be proclaimed to the dead, even if the idea was in perfect harmony with other passages of Scripture, would have been most extraordinary, and utterly out of place.

It would be interesting and not unprofitable to review the history of the interpretation of the passage. There are several points in the exposition of von Zezschwitz and Wiesinger on the one side, and of von Hofmann and Weiss on the other (not to speak of other scholars), to which we would fain have directed attention. But we must forbear. Though our review does not profess to be exhaustive, we have striven to act fairly with the views presented on the other side, and are not aware of having passed over any argument adduced by English theologians in defence of the exposition which regards the passages in St. Peter to refer to a proclamation of the gospel to any portion of the dead. The passage in 1 Pet. iii. 19 gives no support to the strange doctrine that our Lord preached in the Under-world a *concio damnatoria*, that is, went and proclaimed judgment to the lost spirits in hell. But the passage, critically examined, says just as little of His having preached a *concio evangelica* to trembling spirits kept bound " in prison." There is from a speculative point of view much to be said in favour of the opinions held in the early

Church as to the state of the dead before Christ, and the change in their position brought about by virtue of His death upon the cross. The views often propounded by Roman Catholic theologians concerning the *Limbus Patrum* may have been in many points crude, because the speculations of the early teachers of the Church were too often dressed up in mediæval clothing, which did not become them. But at the bottom there is a solid substratum of sound thought which rests on some basis of Scripture (see p. 155). *Limbus Patrum*, however, is not "purgatory;" and in defence of the latter doctrine not the slightest solid argument can be drawn even from the broadest interpretation of any Scripture passages.

The advocates of "the larger hope" do not really strengthen their position by attempts to ground their "hopes" on the passages in St. Peter's Epistle. There may be mercy extended to persons in another world who have not been here made partakers of the blessings of the gospel. But Scripture affords no solid foothold for any definite theory on the subject. It is not at all necessary to suppose, however, that Scripture has given us full information on such points. The Sacred Writings warn sinners here to "flee from the wrath to come." They tell us that "the wrath of God is revealed from heaven against all ungodliness and unrighteousness of men" (Rom. i. 18), and that "it is a fearful thing to fall into the hands of the living God" (Heb. x. 31). The so-called orthodox theologians, however, following in the wake of Minutius Felix and Tertullian, have been too fond of mapping out the fields of Paradise and the plains of woe, with as much precision as if they had been escorted through both localities by some revealing angel. But the dreams of a Milton and the visions of a Dante ought not to warp our theological opinions. Evangelical preachers, in order to alarm the unconverted and to arouse them to repentance, have not unfrequently dared to picture out the "eternal horrors" of "the second death." In doing so they have gone beyond the simple statements of Scripture, and have often unwittingly transformed the God of the Bible into a cruel and arbitrary tyrant. The preacher may, indeed, warn men of the advent of "the day of wrath, that awful day." But he must be on his guard not to go a single step beyond what is written in Scripture. In transgressing the limits prescribed, he may find himself doing the work of the antagonists of Christianity. Scripture does not by any means afford us as much light on this mysterious subject as many superficial thinkers imagine. The sober-minded theologian, who compares Scripture with Scripture, will find many a gap in Scripture revelation, which he will not venture to fill up dogmatically from his own reasonings. If desirous to speculate on the subject, he will modestly advance his opinions as speculations, but as nothing more. He will do wisely to abstain from setting forth as Scripture teaching any dogma of "universal restitution," or even of "conditional immortality." He will candidly admit with the Psalmist that there are "clouds and darkness" round about the Infinite Jehovah, although "righteousness and judgment are the foundation of His throne" (Ps. xcvii. 2).

V.

THE KEY TO THE APOCALYPSE, PRESENTED IN THE VISION OF REV. XII.

IT would be impossible in the compass of a short "study" to attempt anything like a review of the various interpretations of the Book of the Revelation, or even a satisfactory outline of the history of the exegesis of a single chapter. But, paradoxical as the assertion may appear, there is, notwithstanding the differences of opinion which exist among expositors, a far more general agreement among them than is usually supposed. The real differences, indeed, between those commentators who believe in the inspiration of the book, and who are really worthy of notice, are to be found in the explanation of the subordinate details. There is a general agreement among expositors on the question of the main object and teachings of the book itself.

On no book of the Sacred Scriptures has a larger number of worthless "expositions" been written, and on none has such an amount of perverse ingenuity been expended. The multitudes of pamphlets also which have been issued, all giving more or less discordant explanations of the Book of the Revelation, have, indeed, like Egyptian flies, "shadowed" the book "with their wings" (Isa. xviii. 1), and have lighted down, like the Assyrian bees, on all the "rocks and pastures" of this "holy land" (Isa. vii. 18, 19), not a little obscuring for ordinary Bible readers the sacred teachings of the book. We cannot profess any reverence for those busy nobodies whose ignorance is generally equalled by their dogmatism, and must claim the right even in a popular essay simply to brush them off without any detailed notice. For it would be hopeless to attempt as much as an enumeration, even of the titles of the productions which have teemed forth from "the prophetical writers" of our own country, not to speak of those of other lands.

The object of the present study is to point out that the Book of the Revelation itself contains a key wherewith the darker rooms in that castle may be unlocked, and presents a clue which may enable the ordinary Biblical student to penetrate many of the winding passages in that apparent labyrinth of Scripture.

Interpretations of the Book of the Revelation which claim to be entirely new and original ought not to be regarded with any favour. The very claim to originality ought to be sufficient to condemn them unheard. For the book was no doubt understood in its general outlines by the Churches for whose instruction it was penned, and to whom it was first sent by the Apostle. Though it contains also prophecies of later times, and points out the working of principles, which have been exhibited in the Church and in the world in all ages, yet to understand it aright we must try and transport ourselves back to the days in which the Apostle tarried in Patmos, and from that rocky isle surveyed the conflict in which the Church was engaged, as well as those struggles into which she was shortly to enter.

Zahn in his recent *Apokalyptische Studien*[1] has called attention to the importance of recognising this truth, and has shown how important the principle is when used in the defence of the apostolic authorship of the last book of the New Testament. He observes, as many expositors have done before him, that the author of the Apocalypse expressly put the reader on his guard not to regard his book as "sealed" (Isa. xxix. 11), like the Book of Daniel (xii. 4, 9), the Book of Enoch (i. 2), or the Fourth Book of Ezra (xii. 36–38, comp. xiv. 26, 45–47).[2]

---

[1] See Zahn's articles in Luthardt's *Zeitschrift für kirchliche Wissenschaft u. kirchl. Leben* for 1885, pp. 523 ff., 561 ff.; also in the *Zeitschrift* for the present year 1886, p. 32 ff.

[2] It is much to be regretted that the apocryphal books of the Old Testament are so seldom read in the present day, and that many even of the clergy have never perused them. They afford on many points important "side-light" on Biblical subjects. We can scarcely avoid commending the Rev. W. R. Churton's valuable edition of these books, *The Uncanonical and Apocryphal Scriptures*, with introduction and notes. London: J. Whitaker, 1884; as well as the popular commentary on the Apocrypha issued by the Christian Knowledge Society; and, above all, Bissell's valuable commentary.

The Apocalypse was not therefore a book intended only for later ages, and for the reading of the "learned" (Isa. xxix. 12) and "wise" (Dan. xii. 10), but from the beginning to the end of the book St. John distinctly contemplates his work being used by Christians in general even of the earliest ages.[1]

The visions of the Apocalypse have a voice which has spoken comfort to the Church in all trials and tribulations she has been called upon to endure from the very earliest period. The glowing hopes therein set forth, and the expectations of coming victory, have cheered the soldiers of Christ in many of their arduous combats. Mistakes have, no doubt, been constantly made as to the interpretation of many of the details of the book, owing in great part to the tendency of persons in every age to exaggerate the importance of the events in which their own lot is cast, and to view events which occur in their day too much either from an optimistic or pessimistic standpoint.

It appears to have been designed by Divine wisdom that the Church of the Old Dispensation should be kept always in anticipation of the first Advent of the Messiah; and on all occasions the prophets anticipated the speedy coming of that Deliverer. The Church of the New Dispensation has likewise been kept in constant expectation of the second Advent of the Redeemer; and the Apostles, under the influence of the Holy Ghost, expected even

[1] Rev. i. 3, ii. 7, 11, 17, 29, iii. 6, 13, 22, xxii. 7, 10, 18.

that Advent to take place in their own day. They were thus kept watching and waiting for the advent of the Son of Man, and such an expectant attitude was most befitting the servants of the great Master. Christ has not permitted His people to know the day or the hour of His coming; their duty is simply to "watch"—which implies that they are to work as men who expect His arrival—"and pray."

In the same way the Book of the Revelation, written in the light of the Neronic persecutions, was designed not merely to encourage the Christians of that age, but to be a blessing to the Church in all ages. It was not intended to be a history written in advance, a history so general and so precise, that if its starting-point were once clearly ascertained, the intelligent and God-led believer would be able to track out the history of the Church to the end of the world. It is a mistake to affirm that all fulfilled prophecy is clear and distinct, and unfulfilled prophecy is dark and obscure. Prophecy was scarcely ever "history written in advance," and consequently many prophecies generally assumed to have been fulfilled, are, when examined, found to be difficult and obscure. The careful student of the prophecies of Isaiah and Jeremiah will fully endorse this statement; and we cannot tarry here to give proofs sufficient to convince the gainsayers.

It is a fact, however, patent to the student of Church history, that the Book of the Apocalypse has afforded hope and encouragement to the Church in

all periods. It nerved her for her early struggles
with those adversaries who said they were Jews and
were not, but were of the synagogue of Satan (Rev.
iii. 9). It comforted the Church during the oppressions and persecutions late and early to which it was
subjected at the hands of pagan foes, as is evident
from the writings of Hippolytus and the commentaries of Victorinus at the close of the third century.
It acted as a warning voice to many within the
Church in the days of her decline, when she had
gotten the victory over the Roman power. It supported the hearts of Christians in the terrible struggle
of Christianity against the Mohammedan enemy, and
in that day of darkness it spoke of deliverance.
The Abbot Joachim founded on an exposition of the
book a strong but ineffectual argument in favour of
the reformation of the Church in the twelfth century.
The Waldenses in their warfare with the Church of
Rome appealed to its visions. Birgitta, the saint of
the North, in the fourteenth century made earnest
appeals to the Popes to purify the Church, which were
partly founded on its solemn warnings. Wickliffe a
little later expounded more fully its teachings. Huss
followed in his train. It is needless to remark that
from the dawn of the great Reformation in the
sixteenth century down to very recent times, Protestant expositors of no mean ability have been wont to
trace in its pages the history of the great defection
from the faith of the gospel, against which that
Reformation was a protest. This exposition of the

Apocalypse, whether correct or not, helped to support the martyrs and confessors of the Reformation in their struggles against the Papal power, while the gallant but ineffectual insurrection of the Camisards in France was greatly promoted by the remarkable expositions of Jurieu on the same prophetical book.

But it is quite possible to discover a certain harmony in all these divergent interpretations, when sifted to the bottom. It is however impossible to harmonize those expositions, if the Apocalypse be regarded as a prophetical compendium of the history of the Church to the end of time, in which the events are supposed to be arranged one after another in chronological order.

The events depicted in the Book of the Revelation were necessarily represented in vision as succeeding one another in consecutive order. But it does not at all follow that the order of fulfilment should necessarily be that in which the events were presented to the view of the Apostle. It is quite conceivable that a similar series of events might in the process of time often recur in a similar order, or in the course of the world's history even reappear in an inverted order.

Thus the four seals, the opening of which is described in chap. vi., cannot be satisfactorily explained in any other way than as representing the operation of the judgments upon earth which follow in the wake of the great Conqueror (comp. Rev. vi. 2 with xix. 11 ff.), namely, the sword, scarcity, famine, and pestilence—all of which are preceded by the cry "come" arising from animate creation (comp. Rom. viii. 22). Those judgments are closely akin to the "four sore judgments" mentioned by Ezekiel (xiv. 21), which are, indeed, included in the series mentioned in this part of the Apocalypse (vi. 8). All those judgments, which have again and again fallen upon the earth, have, in accordance with our Lord's prophecy (see p. 123), been preparations for the revelation of the Son of Man in His day.

The same might be affirmed of the vision of the martyred saints presented under the fifth seal. The blood of the martyrs is there, like that of Abel, depicted as crying out against their murderers for vengeance. For the earth upon which their blood was poured out like water is God's altar, and the death of Christ's saints, "slain for the word of God and for the testimony which they held," was in very deed a sacrifice (Phil. ii. 17; 2 Tim. iv. 6). The blood of the saints re-echoes the cry of suffering creation, "Come, Lord Jesus!" That piercing cry has been raised as often as Christian soldiers have fallen under the merciless hands of their foes, and may, for aught we know, yet be heard again "in the street of the great city" (Rev. xi. 8). The earth has often witnessed the repetition of the terrible scene; and the names of many a martyr unknown in Christian annals will be made known in that day when "the earth shall disclose her blood, and shall no more cover her slain" (Isa. xxvi. 21).

Even the sixth seal depicts a state of things which may repeatedly recur. For the imagery made use of in Rev. vi. 12–17 is not by any means confined to descriptions of the final day of wrath. Almost all the details there mentioned are used in the Old Testament in passages which refer to judgments which have already fallen on the nations. The sixth seal, although it probably depicts the great day of the destruction and perdition of ungodly men, may also be referred to seasons of judgment which have taken place in various ages and in various lands. A recent writer has well remarked that "imagery, which, if literally verified, would involve the total dissolution of the fabric of the globe, and the destruction of the material universe, may really mean no more than the downfall of a dynasty, the capture of a city, or the overthrow of a nation."[1]

The correctness, therefore, of the eulogium pronounced upon the learned Joseph Mede by Bishop Hurd is more than questionable.[2] Mede maintained

[1] *The Parousia: A Critical Inquiry into the New Testament Doctrine of our Lord's Second Coming* (London: Daldy, Isbister, & Co. 1878), p. 352.

[2] Speaking of the earlier interpreters of the Reformation era, Hurd remarks: "As each interpreter brought his own hypothesis along with him, the perplexities of the book were not lessened but increased by so many discordant schemes of interpretation. And the issue of much elaborate inquiry was, that the book itself was disgraced by the fruitless efforts of its commentators, and was on the point of being given up as utterly impenetrable, when a sublime genius arose in the beginning of the last century, and surprised the learned world with that desideratum, *A Key to the Revelation*. This extraordinary person was Joseph Mede."—Hurd's *Warburtonian Lectures* (Sermon x.), London, 1772.

that if the real time of any one vision could be discovered, the relative time of the other visions could, from such data, be easily ascertained. For, although the visions were not regarded by him as all arranged chronologically (inasmuch as several refer to the same event), yet he regarded it as quite possible, by arranging first the coincident portions in a series of what were termed "synchronisms," to ascertain the precise order in which the events prophesied would occur; such as preceded a special vision were to be regarded as matters preceding the events therein depicted, while those things that followed were to be explained as subsequent transactions.[1]

It may be fully admitted that the scheme propounded by Mede in his *Clavis Apocalyptica* imparted a peculiar definiteness to the more detailed exposition of the Revelation which that writer published shortly afterwards, especially when compared with former works on the subject. But there is little doubt that Mede was carried too far by his love of system. Several of his "synchronisms" have been disproved by later writers, among whom Vitringa is peculiarly worthy of mention, whose work on the subject, *Anacrisis Apocalypseos* (Amsterdam, 1719), notwithstanding many errors, has not after more than a century and a half lost its value for the real student of the Revelation.

With these prefatory remarks we turn to a consideration of the remarkable vision which forms the

[1] See Mede's Works, *Clavis Apocalyptica*, p. 432.

subject of Rev. xii. The chapter opens with the statement: "And a great sign was seen in heaven."[1] The use of the word "sign" has been rightly regarded as an indication that the vision which follows is of a peculiarly allegorical character. Düsterdieck maintains that the expression implies that the vision is different from such visions as those of chap. vi. and chap. viii. 7-9, which in his view are not entirely of an allegorical character, since they contain descriptions of literal events, such as the shedding of blood, the occurrence of earthquakes and of other plagues. Without, however, fully endorsing Düsterdieck's opinion of those passages, we agree with him in regarding the vision contained in chap. xii. as in the main allegorical.[2]

The Book of the Revelation, as Auberlen has observed, starts with the assumption that the Church of Jesus Christ has the special work assigned to her of converting the nations of the world. That is the duty set before the Church; that is her distinctive mission. The Church, too, is represented throughout the Book of the Revelation as more or less successful in the discharge of the work assigned to her, although she is depicted as retarded at every step by

---

[1] The translation of σημεῖον by "*sign*" given in the Revised Version is more correct than that of "*wonder*" which occurs in the Authorized Version. The reading σημεῖον μέγα, in place of ἄλλο σημεῖον, has been adopted by all recent critics.

[2] *Kritisch-exegetisches Handbuch über die Offenbarung Johannis*, von Friedrich Düsterdieck, in Meyer's *Krit.-exeget. Kommentar*, 2te Aufl., Göttingen, 1865.

her spiritual adversary. At one time she is represented as confronted by one set of dangers, at another by difficulties of a different kind. She is often described as persecuted by the world-power, stirred up by Satanic agency. But though tried and harassed by persecution, the Church in those struggles came off victorious. Her members overcame the Evil One "because of the blood of the Lamb, and because of the words of their testimony," and because "they loved not their life even unto death" (Rev. xii. 11). Baffled in open conflict, the Adversary is represented not as relaxing his efforts, but changing his tactics. Victorious over open force and over the false religions of the world, the Church was tempted and overcome by the allurements of "the pomps and vanity" of earth.—The heathenism which could not overthrow her from without, seduced and corrupted her from within. The chaste woman of Rev. xii. and the bedizened harlot of Rev. xvii. are both pictures of the visible Church, though of course under different aspects: the former represents the Church in its pure state persecuted by the world-power; the latter is a picture of the Church corrupted and led astray from the simplicity toward Christ (2 Cor. xi. 3). In consequence of such a transformation she appears in the next scene as upheld by the world-power, and even as ruling and directing its operations. The mission of the Church is, however, represented as ultimately successful, though retarded for a time by the world-power, which either assumes the part of an open enemy, or acts the *rôle* of a treacherous seducer. In spite of all the machinations of the Prince of Darkness, the work of Christ is carried on in every age, and at the close of the Dispensation the Lamb's wife is finally described as made ready for the marriage-supper of the Lamb (Rev. xix. 7, 8).

There is no doubt that the woman persecuted by the dragon signifies the Church of God. Both in the Old and New Testaments the Church is spoken of under the figure of a woman. In the vision in Rev. xii., the woman was seen "in heaven," not merely because heaven was the place in which the scene was represented, but because the Church, even in its present state, belongs to heaven. "Our citizenship is in heaven" (Phil. iii. 20). The saints of whom the Church is composed are potentially raised up in Christ, by virtue of His resurrection, and are represented even now as seated together with Him "in the heavenly places" (ἐν τοῖς ἐπουρανίοις), that is, in the same places in which Christ Himself is seated at the right hand of the Father (Eph. i. 3, ii. 6, comp. with i. 20). In the same Epistle the manifold wisdom of God is said to be made known by the Church "unto the principalities and powers in heavenly places" (Eph. iii. 10). And at the close of that letter S. Paul warns the believers that "our wrestling is not against flesh and blood, but against the principalities, against the powers, against the world-rulers of this darkness, against the spiritual hosts of wickedness in the heavenly places" (Eph. vi. 12).

There seems to be, then, a peculiar significance in the Church being symbolized by a "woman in heaven." The Church is heavenly in its origin, and its final inheritance is there. It is in this respect like the great sheet seen by S. Peter in his vision, "wherein were all manner of four-footed beasts and creeping things of the earth and fowls of the heavens" (Acts x. 11, 12), which sheet descended from heaven and was drawn up again into heaven. But while the woman was depicted as in heaven, she was also represented bringing forth "the man child" on the earth. The latter is necessarily implied in the statement (Rev. xii. 5) that the child when born "was caught up unto God, and unto His throne." Thus the woman is represented at one time in heaven, and at another time on the earth, although no mention is made of her removal from the one place to the other. Similar changes of scene constantly occur in ordinary dreams, and excite no surprise on the part of the dreamer. Hence it is not strange that rapid changes of scene should occur in allegorical visions, in which they have often peculiar significance. That the woman was on earth, when seen "travailing in birth and in pain to be delivered," is plain from the sequel of the vision, in which she is described as fleeing into the wilderness (ver. 6, comp. vers. 13, 15, 16). The wings of the great eagle, mentioned in ver. 14, were bestowed upon her in order that she might fly swiftly over the surface of the earth from the face of her enemy, and not in order to enable her to descend from heaven.

It is also to be noted that in like manner the great red dragon, the adversary of the woman and her child, is represented in ver. 3 as in heaven, while described in ver. 4 as lying in wait on earth to destroy the child as soon as it should be born. In the intermediate paragraph (vers. 7–12), which, as shall be seen presently, represents under other figures the same great realities, "the great dragon," or "the Devil and Satan," is depicted as carrying on "war in heaven," and as "cast down to the earth" after his defeat in the heavenly places along with those angels who espoused his cause. At the close of the vision (vers. 13–17), he is described burning with rage at his defeat, and seeking on earth to destroy the woman and the rest of her seed, because the child he had specially longed to devour had been so wondrously delivered out of his hands.

When the apocalyptic seer at first beheld the woman she appeared to shine forth arrayed in heavenly light. Her appearance was similar to that of Christ upon the Mount of Transfiguration, when He was clad in the heavenly glory, His face shining as the sun, His garments white as the light (Matt. xvii. 1), or, as another evangelist expresses it: "His garments became glistering, exceeding white; so as no fuller on earth can whiten them" (Mark ix. 3). When the Son of Man revealed Himself in vision to His servant John in Patmos, "His head and His hair were white as white wool, white as snow; and His eyes were as a flame of fire; and His feet like unto burnished brass, as if it had been refined in a furnace; and His voice as the voice of many waters," "and His countenance was as the sun shineth in his strength" (Rev. i. 14–16). So in the Old Testament God is described as covering Himself with light as with a garment (Ps. civ. 2). And the Church of Israel is addressed by Isaiah: "Arise, shine; for thy light is come, and the glory of the Lord is risen upon thee. For, behold, darkness shall cover the earth, and gross darkness the peoples: but the Lord shall arise upon thee, and His glory shall be seen upon thee" (Isa. lx. 1, 2).

The "sun" with which the woman in the vision appeared clothed must not be interpreted to signify Christ Himself; because He is represented in the vision as the child born of the woman. Hence the light with which the woman is arrayed is better explained, like the light spoken of by Isaiah, of the glory of God in general. Malachi speaks of the sun of righteousness as arising on the people of God (Mal. iv. 2), and the Psalmist describes Jehovah as a "sun and shield" who gives "grace and glory" to them that walk uprightly (Ps. lxxxiv. 11). In the allegorical vision of S. John those very gifts are pictured as abundantly bestowed upon the Church in the days of her travail and sorrow. We may also compare the teaching of Ps. xix., in which the glory of the natural sun in the expanse of heaven, which is a gift bestowed upon all men, is contrasted with the light of the Law of Jehovah and its precepts, which was the peculiar gift vouchsafed to the nation which God had chosen to be His inheritance.

The "moon" which was seen under the feet of the woman can hardly, in accordance with Old Testament language, be explained as the symbol of earthly glory or of mutable things, as "the venerable Bede" was wont to interpret it. Nor can it be interpreted to signify that "all reflected light" is too mean to be characteristic of her upon whom the glory of God Himself has been bestowed,[1] which explanation could not have been understood in the days of S. John. Still less can we view it, with Ebrard, as a figurative description of the night, the darkness of which is pourtrayed as chased away and overcome.[2] The passage, too, can scarcely be regarded as based on Cant. vi. 10, as Dean Alford supposed, for the language of the Song of Songs is certainly not used by the New Testament writer. The introduction of the moon into the vision may be regarded as simply part of a poetical description in which all the light-giving bodies are united — sun, moon and stars. This is the view of Düsterdieck, and the dream of Joseph might be cited in some respects as a fitting parallel (Gen. xxxvii. 9). But there appears even

---

[1] Dean Vaughan in his Lectures on the Revelation of S. John.
[2] See Ebrard's Comment. in Olshausen's *Bibl. Comm. über sämmtl. Schr. des N.T.*

more probability in the explanation given by J. P. Lange (in his *Bibelwerk*), to wit, that Diana of the Ephesians, goddess of the moon, and the symbol of nature, was so familiar to the Apostle and to the members of the Seven Churches of Asia, for whose benefit the book was primarily intended, that they could scarcely avoid interpreting the symbol of the woman clothed with the sun and the moon under her feet otherwise than as indicative of the subjugation of heathenism by the Church of Jesus Christ. Such an incident in the vision would have been interpreted by them in the same manner as Constantine is said in the well-known story to have interpreted the appearance of the cross above the sun which he saw in the heavens.

Upon the head of the woman there was "a crown of twelve stars." This symbol also has been variously interpreted. Those expositors who regard the woman to mean the Church of Christ naturally think of "the twelve apostles of the Lamb" (Rev. xxi. 14); those who explain the woman to typify the Church of Israel naturally interpret the diadem of stars to mean the twelve patriarchs; while those who view the whole as a picture of the Church of God in general, in both its Old Testament and New Testament aspects, regard the twelve stars to be significant of the twelve tribes of Israel, emblematic of "the Israel of God," composed of both Jews and Gentiles. In proof of this combination of the old and the new ideas the vision of Rev. vii. may be quoted, and the scene of the harpers on the glassy sea depicted in

Rev. xv. 2, as "singing the song of Moses the servant of God and the song of the Lamb."

The key to the solution of the allegory, and to the correct comprehension of the larger portion of the Book of the Revelation itself, lies in the right understanding of "the man child" to whom the woman gives birth. It is to be noted that several interpretations of the symbols made use of in the allegory are given in the chapter itself. The dragon is explained to be Satan (ver. 9), the contest represented at one time as waged in heaven is explained to be that which has taken place on the earth, the angels of Michael are described as "our brethren," and the weapons of their warfare are in ver. 11 said not to be carnal but mighty before God to the casting down of strongholds (2 Cor. x. 4).

Similarly the sacred writer explains (ver. 5) the "man child" to be Him "who was to rule (ποιμαίνειν), *feed, guide* as a shepherd (ποιμήν) all nations with a rod of iron." There is a reference here to Ps. ii. 9, where the LXX. translate the Hebrew by the words quoted by S. John.[1] That Psalm is Messianic, and

---

[1] The Hebrew of the Psalm is no doubt correctly pointed in the Masoretic text תְּרֹעֵם from רעע, and has unquestionably the meaning of *breaking*, which idea not only agrees better with the *rod* or *sceptre of iron* spoken of, as well as with the word *break-in-pieces* used in the parallel clause. But the consonants could also be pointed תִּרְעֵם from רעה, which is what was read by the LXX. and Syr. The word שבט, *rod*, is used both of the sceptre or rod of power and of the staff of the shepherd (Ps. xxiii. 4; Micah vii. 14); and the Son of Man, when He exercises to the full His authority as Shepherd, is represented not only as opening the kingdom of heaven to all

is frequently expounded as such in the New Testament (Acts iv. 25–27, xiii. 33). It is quoted again in Rev. xix. 15, where "He shall rule them with a rod of iron" forms part of the description of Him who is "Faithful and True," whose name is called "the Word of God," and who is there described riding forth to victory over His foes, having on His garment and on His thigh a name written, "King of kings and Lord of lords." If, then, Rev. xii. 5 is to be explained in accordance with those passages, "the man child" can be no other than God's "holy Servant Jesus" (Acts iv. 27).

Many interpreters, however, maintain that the actual birth of Christ is not the event referred to. They explain the passage of the birth of Christ mystical (Gal. iv. 19), that is, the birth of the Church in general, or of some particular Church composed of true believers in Christ. They seek to remove the incongruity of regarding the woman and her child to mean one and the same thing, by referring to Isa. lxvi. 8 (which passage is also quoted by S. John, as shall presently be noticed, see p. 221). In the latter passage Zion and her children are virtually identical. S. Paul also makes use of the expression "the Jerusalem that is above is free, which is our mother" (Gal. iv. 26). In support of such an inter-

---

believers, but also as punishing with an everlasting destruction those who are workers of iniquity. See Matt. xxv. 31 ff., xxi. 44. These are the two aspects of the rule of Messiah over the nations set forth both in Old and New Testament Scriptures, and neither must be lost sight of. See Delitzsch's remarks on the Psalm in question.

pretation the promise in Rev. ii. 26, 27 is appealed to: "He that overcometh and he that keepeth my works unto the end, to him will I give authority over the nations: and he shall rule (ποιμανεῖ) them with a rod of iron, as the vessels of the potter are broken to shivers; as I also have received of my Father." The promise of Christ is: "He that overcometh, I will give to him to sit down with me in my throne, as I also overcame, and sat down with my Father in His throne." But such promises, which are only to be fulfilled in the day of Christ's appearing, can hardly with propriety be cited as explanatory of an event represented as taking place long prior to that day. For the reign of the "man child" over the nations commences in the allegory when the child is caught up to God and His throne, and invested there with the power of the Divine majesty.

It has been frequently maintained that, inasmuch as Christ is uniformly represented in other parts of Scripture as Lord and Husband of the Church, He cannot be described in the Revelation as the Son of the Church. But the answer to this objection is easy. There is nothing inconsistent in Christ being represented in an allegorical vision as the Church's son, although He be in very deed her Lord and Master. The Messiah was similarly described in prophecy as both David's Lord and David's son. The Pharisees could not explain the enigma, but to the instructed Christian it presents no difficulty (Matt. xxii. 41-45). The two cases are analogous, and even if no parallel text could be adduced, in which Christ is actually represented as the Son of the Church, that would not in itself be any objection to explaining Christ to be designated in Rev. xii. by the son of the woman.

There are, however, other passages in which Christ is represented as the Son of the Church. The proto-evangelion (Gen. iii. 15) may be regarded as an approximation to this manner of speaking. The birth of the Messiah was the event to which the Church before His advent looked forward with intense longing and expectation. The Synagogue was wont to use the expression: "the pains of the Messiah" (חֶבְלֵי הַמָּשִׁיחַ) to indicate not only the sufferings which the Messiah should endure in His own person, but also the sorrows of His people which were to precede and accompany His advent, "the birth-throes" (comp. Micah iv. 9, 10), as it were, of the Church of the Messiah.[1] Thus the Messiah is spoken of by the prophets in the following language: "For unto us a child is born, unto us a son is given" (Isa. ix. 6). The passage of Isaiah is, we admit, not wholly free from obscurity. Delitzsch regards it to refer back to Isa. vii. 14; for he considers the child and son of Isa. ix. to be thought of by the prophet in the latter chapter as the son of "the maiden" of Isa. vii., although the "child" spoken of in chap. ix. is

---

[1] See Dr. Aug. Wünsche, *Die Leiden des Messias in ihrer Ueber-einstimmung mit der Lehre des Alten Tests. und den Aussprüchen der Rabbinen in den Talmuden*, etc. Leipzig 1870.

regarded in that passage as a special gift granted to the people of God. But the episode of Isa. viii. 1–5 seems to break off the connection with chap. vii. Consequently the child prophesied of in Isa. ix. appears to us to be there represented as the son of the nation or Church of Israel,—the holy nation and the Church being regarded under the Old Testament dispensation as identical.[1]

A more satisfactory parallel, however, is that in Micah v. 3. In the verse immediately preceding Micah mentions the place where Christ should be born, and adds: "Therefore will He (God) give them up," *i.e.* permit His people to be brought down and subjected to their foes, in order that in man's greatest extremity the Divine power and grace might be more gloriously exhibited. Messiah was to be born of the royal house of David after the Davidic family had sunk into obscurity, when the home of the family was no longer the royal city of David, but the inconsiderable town of Bethlehem from whence the family originally came. There the great Messiah, like his forefather David, was, in accordance with the counsels of the Eternal, to be born in utter obscurity.

The people of Israel were, however, only to be given up for a season "until the time that she which travaileth hath brought forth." The travailing woman

---

[1] The student who is desirous of understanding these prophecies should consult not only Delitzsch's Commentary, but also Cheyne's notes on these passages, which abound with valuable matter.

of Micah, whose pains "in travail" are described in Micah iv. 9, 10, has been explained by Calvin, Vitringa, Auberlen, and others, to signify the Church of Israel personified as a woman. The explanation is in harmony with the context, in which "the daughter of Zion" is repeatedly mentioned; although the passage has been explained by other interpreters, as Hitzig, Ewald, and Keil, to refer to the mother of the Messiah, "the maiden" of Isa. vii. If the former interpretation, however, be adopted, the expression in the close of the verse (Micah v. 3), "the residue of His (Messiah's) brethren," will be seen at once to have a fitting counterpart in Rev. xii. 5, where the Son of the woman is spoken of, and reference is made at the same time to "the rest of her seed" (ver. 17).

There is little doubt but that Rev. xii. 5 contains a quotation from Isa. lxvi. 7, 8:[1] "Before she travailed, she brought forth; before her pain (חֵבֶל) came, she was delivered of a man-child. Who hath heard such a thing? who hath seen such things? Shall a land be born in one day? shall a nation be brought forth at once? for as soon as Zion travailed,

---

[1] The LXX. translate the last clause of ver. 7 by ἐξέφυγε καὶ ἔτεκεν ἄρσεν, and the text of Rev. xii. 5 embodies the last words, interpolating the noun υἱόν as an explanation, καὶ ἔτεκεν υἱὸν ἄρσεν. This may possibly account for the grammatical incorrectness of the Greek text. The reading ἄρρενα, which smooths over the grammatical mistake, is now generally recognised to be a correction. The neuter may be explained as caused by a mental reference to the τὸ τίκτον which precedes and follows, as has been suggested by Düsterdieck. The grammatical peculiarity of the Greek might be rendered literally in English, "a son, a male *thing*." The ἄρσεν may also be explained

she brought forth her children. Shall I bring to the birth, and not cause to bring forth? saith the Lord: shall I that cause to bring forth shut the womb? saith thy God."

The "man-child" spoken of by Isaiah to be brought forth by Zion with such rapidity and ease, must (with Delitzsch and Cheyne) be identified with the "children" afterwards mentioned. The meaning of the prophet is that the Holy Land will once more be full of people who shall acknowledge Zion as their mother. Nägelsbach imagines that the earlier prophecy of Isaiah (ix. 5) was present to the mind of the prophet when he wrote those words, although it is of course impossible to regard the prophecy in chap. lxvi. as a prediction of Messiah's birth. The blessings there predicted were, however, to be brought unto Israel by means of the Messiah, and Isaiah describes there the fulness of Messianic times. The Zion travailing in birth of Isa. lxvi. is to be identified with the travailing Zion of Micah v. 3, and, as Delitzsch has observed, is also identical with the woman clothed with the sun of the Book of the Revela-

---

as a kind of apposition. But it seems more probable that the word *son* was interpolated to explain the ἄρσεν which immediately follows. On the expression itself, apart from its grammatical irregularity, Düsterdieck compares בֵּן זָכָר, Jer. xx. 15, where the LXX. have simply one word, ἄρσεν. It may be well to note that the idea "man child" is in Isa. lxvi. expressed by one word, זָכָר, literally "*a male.*" Hence it would have been better in the Revised Version to have united the words in Isaiah by a hyphen, "man-child," in order to note the difference between that and the "man child" in Revelation.

tion; notwithstanding that the "man child" in the New Testament passage is the Shepherd of the nations, who bears the iron rod, who was to be brought forth by Zion at the commencement of the Messianic dispensation, while the "man-child" of the Old Testament prophet is the new Israel, "the faithful" nation which is to be born at the close of the Messianic age. For, as Delitzsch observes, "the community which has been saved through all tribulations is as truly the mother of the Lord who overthrows Babylon, as she is the mother of the Israel which shall inherit the blessing."

But if the "man child" of Rev. xii. 5 be no other than "the Christ of history," a fixed point is secured from whence to start in the interpretation of the passage. The visions of the Revelation depict not merely the present and the future, but in some cases the past also. The correct comprehension of the past history of the Church is often absolutely necessary in order to understand either its present or its future. The travailing woman is no other than the Church of God, the Church founded in the days of the Old Testament, and which exists still in New Testament times. The Church is built upon the foundation of patriarchs and prophets and apostles, Jesus Christ Himself being the chief corner-stone. Jews and Gentiles, if properly enlightened, would mutually regard one another no more as strangers and foreigners, but as fellow-citizens and as fellow-members of the household of God (Eph. ii. 18–22). The woman of Rev. xii. is identical with the Zion represented by

Isaiah and Micah as travailing with child (Isa. lxvi. 7, 8; Micah iv. 9, 10), although "the pains" in Isaiah and Micah iv. represent the birth-throes of Israel as a nation; while the pains spoken of in Rev. xii. were the birth-throes of the Messiah. The two ideas are apparently combined in Micah v. 3. For Messiah and "His brethren" are there spoken of as if they were born at the same period, and the connection between Messiah and Israel throughout those passages is similar to that already noticed in our study on Jonah, pp. 62–65, 70.

The pictorial vision of Rev. xii. 4, 5 is founded upon the opening and the closing scenes of the history of our Lord. The Dragon even prior to the birth of the Redeemer attempted the destruction of that great Son of the Church. But in spite of all the efforts of the Evil One to destroy the Saviour Himself, to mar His work, and to make the incarnation valueless for the purposes it was designed to effect, Christ was "saved" from his malice (Zech. ix. 9; see pp. 65, 66), and "sat down on the right hand of the Majesty on high" (Heb. i. 3). Düsterdieck is correct in maintaining that no precise historical fact corresponds to the prophetico-ideal representation of the dragon waiting to devour the child as soon as it was born, but the facts recorded in the evangelical history of the attempt on the part of King Herod (who was a Roman vassal) to destroy the infant Christ in His cradle (Matt. ii.), and the subsequent murder of the infants of Bethlehem, gave rise to the particular conception in the vision by which the Apostle sought to represent the deadly hostility of Satan against the Christ of God.

For it was not only during the infancy of Christ, but all through His short but eventful life, the Redeemer was assaulted by the Foe. The temptation in the wilderness was a device to destroy the value of the incarnation of the Son of God. Foiled in his efforts at that time, Satan departed, but only " for a season " (Luke iv. 13). He renewed his onslaughts when he sought to overcome Christ by means of the weakness of His disciples, the carnal expectations of the Jewish people, the hypocritical temptations of the scribes and Pharisees, and of other adversaries. The Apostles in their solemn prayer and thanksgiving to God, recorded in Acts iv. 27, called to mind how " of a truth in this city (Jerusalem) against Thy holy Servant Jesus, whom Thou didst anoint, both Herod and Pontius Pilate, with the Gentiles and the peoples of Israel, were gathered together." To the malignity of Satan in the bitter hour of His last earthly conflict Christ referred when He said to His disciples: " Now is the judgment of this world : now shall the prince of this world be cast out" (John xii. 31), or exclaimed at a later period : " The prince of the world cometh ; and he hath nothing in me " (John xiv. 30). Similarly He remarked to those that came to seize Him in the Garden of Gethsemane, " This is your hour, and the power of darkness " (Luke xxii. 53). Both at the commencement and the close of

Christ's earthly career, "the great red dragon," the "murderer from the beginning" (John viii. 44), seated on the throne of earthly power, sought to devour "the child as soon as it was born."

Similarly, as Düsterdieck has also noticed, no fact in the history of Christ corresponds exactly with the words of the Revelation: "the child was caught up to God and His throne." But the event of the ascension of the Lord on Mount Olivet afforded in like manner the form with which to clothe the idea of how inexpressibly glorious was the manner in which the Child of the Church was preserved from the attacks of Satan, and how fully Satan was put to shame. Despite the tremendous efforts of the great enemy by open attack and by crafty guile to destroy the Redeemer, despite the fact that he persecuted Him to the death, even the death of the cross, Christ by His own death brought to nought him that had the power of death, that is, the devil (Heb. ii. 14); the seed of the woman bruised the serpent's head (Gen. iii. 15); "the child of the woman" was, in very deed, as described in the allegory, "caught up to God and His throne."

If, however clothed in allegorical language, it was the history of the work on earth of our blessed Lord (which began with His incarnation and closed with His ascension), which is set forth in the vision of Rev. xii., a number of interpretations more or less ingenious must be at once set aside. The "man child" cannot be explained, with Sir Isaac Newton,

to be the empire of Rome, secured to the Christian
Church by the victory won by Constantine over
Licinius (A.D. 323), by which victory Sir I. Newton
imagined "the child was caught up to God and His
throne."[1] Nor is the modification of the same theory
adopted by Rev. E. B. Elliott in the third volume of his
Horæ Apocalypticæ much better, by which Constantine
himself is regarded to be "the man child caught
up to the throne," or raised to political supremacy
in the Roman empire.[2] Constantine, the great
Christian emperor, was not even baptized until the
agonies of death came upon him, and although styled
by some fulsome Orientals "equal to the apostles"
($ἰσαπόστολος$), he cannot, as Niebuhr well remarked,
be termed "a saint" without "a profanation of the

---

[1] *Observations on Daniel and the Apocalypse*, Lond. 1733.

[2] Elliott has called attention to the fact that Constantine himself in his letter to Eusebius speaks of his victory as an overthrow of the dragon. Elliott also refers to the coin struck by that emperor, in which the cross (the labarum with the monogram of Christ) is represented as standing above the dragon. Elliott exhibits a peculiar fondness for catching hold of such apparent literal fulfilments of prophecy, which mars some of the best portions of his really able work. The overthrow of Paganism was, no doubt, an eventful period in the Church's history; and with the Book of the Revelation in their hands it is not surprising that its phraseology was made use of by Christian writers in describing the wonderful change which then took place in the position of Christianity. But the admission of such a fact by no means obliges us to see in such incidents any fulfilment of the special prophecy. Great as was the importance of the ascent of the throne of the Cæsars by a Christian prince, the importance of the event was (as was very natural) overestimated by the writers of the period. In giving, however, that explanation of the prophecy, Elliott only treads in the footsteps of many commentators who were prior to his day, and his explanation is substantially that given by Vitringa.

word." Notwithstanding the fact that at the Council of Nice, which was convened by his authority, he solemnly subscribed to the dogma of the proper divinity of Jesus Christ, Constantine does not appear to have had any real understanding of the matter in dispute; and it is scarcely possible to regard such an event as his elevation to the emperorship as worthy to be described in the terms used by the sacred writer.

The explanation of George Stanley Faber (a writer whose works, once read with avidity, are now, perhaps, too little regarded) is highly ingenious, but little more.[1] He regards the vision of chap. xii. to be synchronical with that of the two witnesses in chap. xi., and considers the casting down of the stars by the dragon's tail (xii. 4) to symbolize the apostasy of some of the professed adherents of the Church of Christ. The birth of the man child, according to his view, is the setting apart of the Vallensico-Albigensic Church from the general body of the Faithful, and "the abreption of the man child to God's throne" the protection of that Church from extinction during the 1260 prophetic days or years. The war in heaven is the warfare in the visible Church, the casting down of Satan from heaven the success of the Reformation in Europe; while the flood, which at the close of the vision is represented as cast forth out of the mouth of the dragon after the woman, symbolizes the rise and progress of secular infidelity during the close of the great prophetic times.

[1] In his *Sacred Calendar of Prophecy*, vol. iii., London, 1844.

Of more importance is the view taken by J. Chr. K. von Hofmann. That scholar explains the woman to mean the Jewish Church which gave birth to our Lord.[1] The Church of Israel, according to his theory, is depicted in the vision in two distinct stages, first as it existed immediately before Christ and at the time of His Ascension; and secondly, as it will be in the days immediately preceding the second Advent of the Redeemer. The Church of Israel during the first period was in the Holy Land, and she will be there, according to von Hofmann, when the second crisis arrives. He considers the Church of Israel to be distinct from that of the Gentiles, and to be heir to promises peculiarly her own. The 1260 days during which the woman or Church of Israel is preserved in the wilderness and sheltered from the wrath of the Dragon, are identified by him with the 1260 days during which Jerusalem shall be trodden down of the Gentiles (Rev. xi.). The incongruity of regarding the Holy Land at one time as a place of shelter in the wilderness from the persecutions of the Dragon, and at another as the scene of the hottest persecution, von Hofmann seeks to lessen, by calling attention to the analogy between the sojourn of Israel in the wilderness of Sinai, which, regarded under one aspect, was a place of trial, and under another was the place

---

[1] See von Hofmann's *Weissagung und Erfüllung* (2 vols.), Nördlingen 1841, 1844; and in his more recent work the *Schriftbeweis*, both in the earlier and later editions, in which he notices the objections of Auberlen and others.

in which Israel was concealed and preserved for a season.

The theory of von Hofmann mainly rests upon his explanation of Michael as the Angel-Prince of the Israelitish nation, instead of being an allegorical representation of Christ (see p. 240). Notwithstanding the arguments adduced by von Hofmann in his *Schriftbeweis* in reply to Auberlen, the objections of the latter scholar seem to be destructive of the whole interpretation.

Briefly stated, Auberlen's objections are the following: The Jewish Christian Church has not really been in existence as a separate community during the greater part of the Church-historical period. The writer of the Apocalypse cannot mean by the woman clothed with the sun anything else than a congregation or community of people believing in Christ. No satisfactory proof can be adduced in favour of the idea that the allegory is confined to the representation of the Judæo-Christian Church. The sudden transition in the passage from the time of Christ's birth to the end of the world (when Antichrist, according to von Hofmann, is to be manifested) is arbitrary. The theory of such transitions, which have been too often devised by expositors, has proved a pregnant source of error. The transition in question, as Auberlen remarks, is one "for which there is no ground or connecting link in the words of the text." It is unnatural to regard the vision as pourtraying the woman fleeing from Judæa, where she gives birth to the Saviour, back into Judæa again, without the slightest intimation being afforded of the long intermediate period, which has lasted now more than eighteen centuries.[1]

The anonymous author of *The Parousia* (see note, p. 206), a book of more than ordinary ability, explains the woman to signify the Church of Jerusalem in apostolic days; the "man child" to be the faithful disciples of Christ in Judæa (or those in the city of Jerusalem itself); the flight into the wilderness, the flight of the Christians to Peræa beyond the Jordan during the period of the great Jewish war; and the "man child" caught up to God and His throne to mean probably "the martyred sons of the Church referred to in ver. 11," if the event signified by the latter symbol be not identical with that referred to under the former.

Archdeacon Farrar, in his interesting work entitled the *Early Days of Christianity* (1882), takes sub-

---

[1] The exposition of Ebrard is in many respects similar to that of von Hofmann. He regards the woman as "Israel according to the flesh," and Christ as the Son of Israel. Ver. 5 depicts the birth and ascension of Christ. The woman's flight is the dispersion of the Jewish people, and the events at the close of the vision are supposed to be those which are to take place at the time of the end. But the dispersion of Israel was a judgment from God. It cannot, from a Christian standpoint, like that of the author of the Apocalypse, be regarded as an event caused by the malignity of Satan. The flight of the woman, instead of being rapid (as pointed out in ver. 14), would, according to this exposition, have lasted 1800 years. Nor can the woman in the place of shelter prepared for her by God well be regarded as representing a nation remaining in a state of unbelief, but must denote some community protected, preserved, and nourished by God (vers. 6-14).

stantially the same view. He explains the 1260 days to be the period of the great Jewish war from about A.D. 67 to A.D. 70, when the temple perished amid blood and flame. But Dr. Farrar afterwards explains the forty-two months of Rev. xiii. 5 (which surely must be identified with the 1260 days of Rev. xii. 6, and the "time and times and a half a time" of Rev. xii. 14) as the three years and a half which intervened between the beginning of the Neronic persecution in Nov. A.D. 64 and the death of Nero himself in June 68.

In reply to these interpretations, it must be noted that the object aimed at by the war of the Romans with the Jews was not the extinction of the Christian Church—that terrible war was not a war of religion, certainly not a war against Christianity. The destruction of Jerusalem and its temple was an advantage rather than a disadvantage to the cause of Christianity. That event could not with any propriety be described in a Christian allegory under the symbol of the Dragon seeking to devour the child of the woman, or the Church. Moreover, an expositor ought definitely to make his choice between the two conflicting interpretations of the "man child" in the vision. That symbol must be explained to mean either Christ Himself or Christ's people. An interpreter is not at liberty to explain it at one time to denote the former, and at another time to signify the latter. If the symbol be interpreted to mean the Christian Church, or any company of believers in

Christ, it is incongruous to explain the being caught up to God and His throne to mean the ascent to heaven in the fires of martyrdom. But if, as already shown, Christ Himself be the "man child," the 1260 days, 42 months, or three times and a half, must be supposed to commence shortly after His ascension into heaven. The destruction of Jerusalem, as the author of *The Parousia* has pointed out, was a judicial punishment, and being such we maintain it cannot be viewed as the central point of the vision of the Apocalypse.

There is no doubt but that the discovery in modern times, that the name of Nero may be so written in Hebrew as to make the numerical value of the letters reach the fatal number 666, combined with the fact that a very general belief prevailed in early days that Nero was still alive, or would return to life,—a belief which many suppose referred to in Rev. xiii. 3 and xvii. 11,—have induced many able expositors (Ewald among the number) to consider Nero and his bloody persecutions as the special theme of the Revelation. But it ought to be observed that the correctness of the mode of writing "Nero Emperor" in Hebrew (נרון קסר) so as to bring out the desired result is a matter of grave doubt. For Cæsar or Καίσαρ ought to be written in Hebrew fully with four letters (קיסר), and not defectively with three. The former method of writing, which is more correct, is destructive of one of the chief supports of the hypothesis.[1] Nor can we

---

[1] See the important article on the number of the beast in Zahn's "Apokalyptische Studien" in Luthardt's *Zeitschrift* for 1885, pp. 561–

admit the second assumption on which the theory rests. Consequently although Archdeacon Farrar has put the exposition in the most favourable light before English readers, a close examination of it reveals difficulties which cannot, we maintain, be overcome.

We have no space here in which to give a sketch of other explanations, such as those propounded by Kliefoth and others, by whom the entire vision is relegated to the future. Kliefoth, it may be noticed, interprets even the birth of the "man child" as a prophecy of Christ's Second Advent. Symbols interpreted in that manner might be explained with equal propriety of almost any event in history.

The power of evil in opposition to the woman, is represented in the vision by a "great red dragon." This representation of Satanic power is founded upon Gen. iii., which passage seems also to be referred to in the symbol of the son of the woman. The Dragon is called the old serpent in ver. 9 (comp. also vers. 13—15). His great size symbolizes the greatness of his power, and the colour assigned to him denotes his murderous designs (John viii. 44).[1] The Dragon, however, does not represent the great Adversary himself, but Satan as directing the power of

---

576. Dr. Salmon (Regius Professor of Divinity in the University of Dublin) has some interesting remarks on the whole subject in his *Historical Introduction to the Study of the New Testament*, p. 300, London, 1885.

[1] Düsterdieck has satisfactorily replied to the objection made by Ebrard to this latter explanation.

the Roman empire in his capacity of "the Prince of the world" (John xiv. 30). His seven heads have, therefore, a reference to "the seven mountains" on which Rome was sitting in the days of the Apostle, in the plenitude of her power (Rev. xvii. 9).

The number "ten" in the horns has, of course, a reference to the ten kingdoms into which the fourth world-empire, that of Rome, was to be divided in its second and weaker phase (see Dan. vii. 24 as explained by Dan. ii. 41, 42). For the explanation given in Dan. ii. 41, 42, of the second phase of the fourth monarchy distinctly shows that second period to be far inferior in power and strength to the former.

"It has been too often assumed that the kingdom of Antichrist, supposed to be predicted by Daniel, is described by that prophet as stronger and mightier than all the kingdoms which preceded it. Whatever its strength may have been represented to be, considered in relation to the Church of God, the second stage of the fourth kingdom in the vision of the metallic image is described as the very weakest stage of the last world-monarchy. Nor does the vision of Dan. vii. set forth any other view; for the description of the fourth beast (in verses 7 and 19) as "dreadful and exceeding strong" is the description of the last monarchy in its earlier stage, and is not a picture of that monarchy in its latter phase. On the contrary, even in that chapter (ver. 24), the latter times of that power are represented as weak, so far as material strength is concerned, however violent its rage against the saints of the Most High." [1]

The number "ten" in the horns of the dragon is used as a round number to denote division and plurality. It does not, as commentators have too often explained it, necessarily refer to that precise number of "kings" or "kingdoms." The sole reason why the number ten was employed was that such was necessarily the number of the toes of the great image seen by Nebuchadnezzar in his dream. For in the vision of Nebuchadnezzar, as explained by Daniel (chap. ii.), in which the number ten first occurs, the number is not expounded as significant except so far as indicating that the fourth monarchy in its later phase was to be broken up into a considerable number of kingdoms, which, though possessing a certain unity, should not cohere or cleave together, notwithstanding all efforts to bring about union by the device of matrimonial alliances.

Many prominent features in the great colossus are passed over in Daniel's interpretation as possessing no significance whatever. Nothing is said of the symbolical meaning of the eyes and ears of the image; the number *two* belonging to the arms, thighs, and legs is not regarded as significant. Nor is the number ten found in connection with the fingers and toes explained by Daniel as symbolical. The *plurality* of the toes, indeed, is of significance, for it is alluded to in Daniel's explanation (though no

---

[1] *Bampton Lectures on Zechariah*, p. 132.

stress is laid upon the number), and that feature reappears in the symbols made use of in other prophecies. The number ten was specially selected, because it was that necessarily presented to the eye in the representation of the four empires as a metallic colossus. But inasmuch as no importance was there assigned to the special number, the number chosen is most simply explained to indicate a divided unity, or a plurality of kingdoms, which though severally independent were parts of one great whole.

Hence it is a mistake to look for ten kings or kingdoms in the fourth world-monarchy, while there is even less warrant in Scripture for any interpretation of the number "two" in the two legs of the great image as being in any way symbolical. For if an image of a man had to be divided into four portions, no better division could be made than that given in Dan. ii. It is a sound principle in the explanation of parables and symbols, to refuse to regard any feature as necessarily symbolical which is not distinctly pointed out as having such a meaning.

The seven-headed, ten-horned dragon represents the world-power, symbolized by the Roman empire, and ruled over by Satan, who claims and exercises authority over the kingdoms of the world (Luke iv. 5, 6). The world-power is represented in the vision as hostile to the Church of God in its pure state, even down to the close of the mystical period of the three times and a half.

The description of the dragon casting down a

third part of the stars of heaven (Rev. xii. 4) appears to have no special meaning, but to be a poetical detail, intended to depict his magnitude and fury. The strength of dragons or serpents was supposed to lie in great measure in their tails. The description is partly framed on that in Dan. viii. 10, where "the little horn" is spoken of as casting down some of the stars to the ground. In the latter passage the stars of heaven represent the people of Israel, against whom Antiochus Epiphanes acted with violence and cruelty (see Keil and Kranichfeld on that passage). There is no allusion whatever to the fall of angels, as Arethas and other early Christian writers imagined, although that opinion has been in modern days regarded with favour by Alford and others.

The description of the "war in heaven" in vers. 7 to 9 seems to be an explanation of the truth set forth under different symbols in the opening of the chapter. The passage, indeed, has been often popularly regarded (as by Milton) to be a description of the original fall of angels. But the contest described in the Apocalypse is distinctly connected (vers. 10, 11, 12, 13) with the endeavour on the part of the dragon to destroy the child of the woman. Some commentators (such as von Hofmann, Ebrard, and Auberlen) have argued that the expression "neither was their place found any more ($\check{\epsilon}\tau\iota$) in heaven" (ver. 8), tends to show that Satan and his angels maintained their place in heaven until the ascension of our Lord. Job i., ii., 1 Kings xxii., and Zech. iii. are referred to in proof of this theory.[1] But those passages must not be interpreted as stating historical facts. As illustrative of spiritual realities, they cast light upon the vision of the Revelation. When the seventy disciples returned to Christ with joy and announced the success of the mission on which He had sent them forth, our Lord expressed His assurance of final victory in the remarkable saying: "I beheld Satan fallen as lightning from heaven" (Luke x. 18). That exclamation was probably a reminiscence of Isaiah's song of triumph over the anticipated downfall of the King of Babylon: "How art thou fallen from heaven, O day star, son of the morning!" (Isa. xiv. 12).[2] For Isaiah does not there refer to the fall of Satan (as the Fathers and even some moderns have expressed it), and still less to the fall of Antichrist, to which some commentators are too fond of discovering allusions in parts of the sacred writings, often where the idea could never have entered into the mind of the original author.

A more suitable parallel may be found in Isa. xxiv. 21, 22, a passage already discussed on pp. 167–169. The prophet there also predicts the downfall of Babylon, and speaks of the overthrow on earth of that mighty monarch and his vassal kings,

---

[1] See remarks on these passages in our study on Job, pp. 6–13.

[2] For the words ἐθεώρουν τὸν Σατανᾶν ὡς ἀστραπὴν ἐκ τοῦ οὐρανοῦ πεσόντα are closely akin to the LXX. rendering of the passage in Isaiah, πῶς ἐξέπεσεν ἐκ τοῦ οὐρανοῦ ὁ ἑωσφόρος ὁ πρωὶ ἀνατέλλων; compare with the latter the words of Christ in Rev. xxii. 16, ἐγώ εἰμι ... ὁ ἀστὴρ ὁ λαμπρός, ὁ πρωινός.

and at the same time of the overthrow of the wicked angels who assisted them in fighting against God. The rebels both of earth and heaven, after their defeat on the field of battle, are represented as shut up in prison by Jehovah the King of Israel (Isa. xliv. 6), and reserved by Him for future judgment. When nations that oppose God's truth are overthrown, their spiritual leaders are likewise cast down (Rev. xii. 9, 13,). In his commentary on Isaiah, Delitzsch has aptly cited the Rabbinic saying: "God overthrows no people until He has first overthrown their prince," namely, the angel who has exercised an ungodly influence over particular nations.

But the real passage upon which the description of Rev. xii. 7–9 is founded is that in Dan. xii. Michael is represented by Daniel as standing up for the cause of Israel, "the great prince which standeth for the children of thy people." A day of battle is depicted, like that of Zech. xiv. 3, 4, which, though a day of trouble and darkness, is also a day of deliverance, as pointed out by both of the Old Testament prophets, and also by the New Testament seer (vers. 12, 13, 14 ff.). Michael is, as Hengstenberg and others maintain, a personification of Christ. That view has been strongly opposed by von Hofmann, who, in his *Schriftbeweis*, considers that such an interpretation would render it impossible to explain the vision of Rev. xii. Michael, according to the latter theologian, is the angel-prince of the people of Israel, the guardian-angel of the nation. The interpretation is not in itself opposed to Old Testament ideas. But the New Testament casts a new light upon dark passages of the Old. And, while it was quite natural for "the great prince of Israel" (Dan. x. 21, xii. 1), the Angel that redeemed Jacob from all evil (Gen. xlvii. 16), who guided Israel through the wilderness to Canaan, to be described in Daniel as only "one of the chief princes" (Dan. x. 13),—a comparison of the prophecies, even of the Old Testament passages with one another, show the identity of "Michael your prince" with Messiah the leader of Israel. In Daniel Messiah and Michael are never mentioned together. The vision of Dan. vii. speaks of the Son of Man, the Messiah, appearing in the time of the end for the deliverance of His people. The vision of Dan. viii. pourtrays the Messiah as "the Prince of princes," His adversary having been "broken without hand," assailed (to use the language of Dan. ii. 45) by the "stone cut out of the mountain without hands." In the last prophecy of Daniel, "that which is inscribed in the writing of truth" (Dan. x. 21), Michael assumes the place and discharges the work of Messiah. He is, therefore, to be regarded as an angelic personification of the Messiah. His people are Messiah's people; and Israel, even in the New Testament, remains still the people of Christ,—"His own" people, although as a nation Israel has not yet received Him (John i. 11).

The Angel that stood up for Israel, against Satan, when in the days of the Restoration as in the days of David, that Adversary "stood up against Israel" (1 Chron. xxi. 1), is identified by Zechariah (iii. 2) with Jehovah Himself. This is the interceding Angel seen in Zechariah's first vision (i. 12), this the Captain of the army of Israel who, in days of peril, manifested Himself to Joshua, and having been worshipped and acknowledged by Joshua as his superior (Josh. v. 13–15), gave the directions for the siege of Jericho in the capacity of Jehovah (Josh. vi. 2 ff.).

d There is, therefore, nothing against the analogy of Scripture in the identification of Michael and Christ. The very name of Michael (*Who is like God?*) gives utterance to the glorious challenge of St. Paul in Rom. viii. 33: "Who shall lay anything to the charge of God's elect?" For the apostle adds: "God is He that justifieth, who is he that shall condemn?" which words are a paraphrase of the Old Testament passage in Isa. l. 8, 9. The language of Isaiah throws again fresh light on the scene described in Zechariah's vision (chap. iii.), in which the Angel of Jehovah, who is also called Jehovah, pronounced judgment in favour of Israel in opposition to the demands of the Adversary, and "justified" Joshua, the high priest (Israel's representative), by removing his filthy garments from him, while with his solemn "Jehovah rebuke thee" he put to flight the Adversary of Israel.

The name of Michael, as Hengstenberg remarks in his *Christology*, is a connecting link between the Old

Testament and the New. We do not, however, think with Hengstenberg, that the reason why the name Michael is made use of in Rev. xii. is that the victory described in the vision belongs not to Christ in His human, but in His Divine character.

For it is essential to the very nature of an allegory that the characters therein described should not be directly named, but should be pointed out under significant appellations. There is a special reason in Rev. xii. 7 ff. for a change in the personification employed. For Christ appears in the former part of the vision as the Child of the woman rescued from the great enemy (Ps. xxii. 19–21), and exalted to God's throne. As the child is described as only just born, such an infant could not be fitly represented as the Conqueror of the Dragon. Hence if Christ had to be depicted in the allegory as a victor, it was necessary to represent Him in that capacity by a new personification; and the Divine character of the person represented as Michael is so clear as to make the episode of verses 7–12 introduced into the vision an explanation of the vision itself.

The prophecy of Dan. xi. is an introduction to that of Dan. xii., which forms its concluding portion. When carefully examined, that prophecy appears not to extend beyond the time of Antiochus Epiphanes. Many portions, indeed, of the earlier part of that apparently literal prophecy do not, as Kranichfeld has shown, refer to actual historical events. The destruction of Antiochus Epiphanes at the close is related, not in literal language, but in language more in accordance with the general usage of prophecy. It is a mistake to view the latter portion as referring to the Antichrist of the New Testament.

Daniel in chap. xii. describes the great deliverance fondly expected by the Church of Israel. He speaks of it in connection with the overthrow of the Grecian power, so far as it had come into collision with Israel, which overthrow as represented in Daniel was an ultimate result of the victories of the Maccabean heroes. If Daniel speaks of the Messiah in connection with the downfall of the third world-power, so does Isaiah when he predicts the overthrow of Syria (Isa. vii., viii., ix.), and of Assyria (chaps. x., xi.), and so does Micah when speaking of the overthrow of Babylon (chaps. iv., v.). Many other parallels could be cited. For it was the constant practice of the prophets of Israel to connect the advent of Messiah with any special deliverance they were commissioned to predict.

The victory of Messiah and the establishment of His kingdom was shadowed forth in Nebuchadnezzar's dream (Dan. ii.). It was depicted in the vision of the wild beasts which came up one after the other from the stormy sea (Dan. vii.). In the latter prophecy the Messiah is represented as coming in the clouds of heaven. It is not, however, the second advent but the first which is there described, of which the second advent is but the completion (comp. Dan. ii. 44 with Dan. vii. 27). The standing up of Michael the warrior-prince in Dan. xii. similarly represents the first advent of the Messiah, who then came for "the redemption of Jerusalem" (Luke ii. 38), although that advent "in great humility," owing to Israel's "hardening in part" (Rom. xi. 25), was not only attended by "the raising up" of many sons and daughters through faith in His name, but also resulted in "the falling of many professors through unbelief" (Luke ii. 34).

Christ's first advent, therefore, on account of the sin of Israel, was followed by a time of trouble (Dan. xii. 1), namely, by the great tribulation predicted by our Lord, when Jerusalem for her iniquity was trodden down by the Gentiles (Luke xxi. 24). The two great facts which are prominently mentioned in the sketch presented by our Lord of "the times of the Gentiles," are the fall and punishment of Israel, and the proclamation of the gospel of the kingdom to every nation under heaven (Matt. xxiv.; Mark xiii.; Luke xxi.).

The first advent of Messiah is suitably represented in the Old Testament prophecy by the standing up for warfare of Michael, the captain of the Lord's host (Josh. v. 14, 15), and the captain of our salvation (Heb. ii. 10). For inasmuch as the last prophecy of Daniel is chiefly concerned with the conflict of earthly kings and warriors, Messiah is fitly represented in it as a prince and a warrior.

The prophecy of Dan. xii. no doubt reaches forward to the time of the end. Hence it alludes to the resurrection of the just and unjust, though that event is spoken of by Daniel only as a resurrection of "many" and not as the resurrection of all men. The resurrection of mankind from the dust of the earth is to be brought about by the power of Him who is the Resurrection and the Life; and inasmuch as the swallowing up of death in victory was one of the great objects to be effected by Messiah, Daniel speaks of it in close connection with His advent. Those who live in New Testament days can speak of two advents of Christ; the prophets of the Old Testament knew of but one. They were unable to understand fully their own prophecies, in which at one time the glory and at another time the sufferings of Messiah were depicted (1 Pet. i. 10, 11). It was not granted to them to know about the long period that would intervene between the days of suffering and the time of glory. All was presented to them in one view, in which the sufferings of Messiah were dimly seen by reason of the brightness of the glory also exhibited. Both events were predicted as belonging to one era, inasmuch as they form in reality one grand whole. The sufferings of Christ were to be but temporal, His glory was to be eternal. The prophets before Christ beheld in their visions the first and second advents of Christ as one and the same event; in the ages to come the saints in glory will probably also look back on the two advents as but one.

The war of Michael and the dragon in Rev. xii.

is, therefore, to be identified with the struggle of Michael in Dan. xii. Both passages represent the same contest " in heavenly places" alluded to by our Lord (Luke x. 18; John xii. 31). The expression "cast out" used in John xii. 31 is similar to the phrase "cast down," used of Satan's fall (Rev. xii. 9); and the warning of ver. 12 has its counterpart in the warnings of S. Paul (Eph. vi. 12–16) and of S. Peter (1 Pet. v. 8, 9), which last was no doubt suggested by the warning given by Christ to that Apostle (Luke xxii. 31, 32). The victory of Michael "in heaven" was but a foreshadowing of the triumph of his soldiers on earth (ver. 11). For "this is the victory that hath overcome the world, even our faith" (1 John v. 4). By faith the Church in early days obtained her victories, by it she conquers still. The Adversary with whom believers struggle has been overcome, and vanquished by "the Stronger than he" (Luke xi. 22); and "the God of peace shall bruise Satan shortly under His people's feet" (Rom. xvi. 20).

It is unnecessary further to delineate the explanation of the vision. The flood cast forth by the serpent after the woman represents the attempts made from time to time by the powers of darkness to destroy Christianity; and the help afforded to the woman points to the providential arrangements by which the rage of the adversaries has been as repeatedly checked.

If the events of Christ's life on earth form the

subject of the vision of the Revelation, the "time, times and a half" must commence with the period when the dragon, worsted in the war in heaven, sought to destroy the saints on earth. That period extends from the ascension of our Lord to the time of the end. The vision of chap. xii. is an epitome of the history of the faithful belonging to the real Church of Christ down almost to the close of the gospel dispensation. The "time, times and a half" are not to be explained as three and a half literal years, nor even, according to the "year-day" theory, to mean a cycle of precisely 1260 years. The period spoken of is undefined and indefinable. The expedients resorted to by writers in favour of the literal interpretation, of introducing "breaks in prophecy," or of supposing immense gaps of time to be passed over without mention by the prophecy, or of expounding the flight of the woman as an event lasting for an indefinitely long period, are each and all arbitrary. The period is not a literal but a mystical cycle. It represents a definite time in the Divine reckoning, but man cannot discover its exact duration. Ebrard is not wrong when he maintains that the forty-two months or 1260 days correspond to the Church-historical period, namely, the period which extends from the ascension of our Lord and the destruction of Jerusalem on to the coming of Antichrist, or, as we prefer to express it, up to the period of the destruction of the power of Satan. For the notion that a great Antichrist is to arise at the close of the dispensation is, we maintain, a simple delusion, grounded on a misconception of certain portions of the Sacred Scriptures.

That question cannot, however, be here discussed; we purpose to discuss it elsewhere. We can only here give an outline of our conclusions without entering further into detail.[1]

There are two distinct periods, each spoken of as a "time, times and a half." The first of these is that period during which the fourth monarchy bears rule over the earth. This is the period spoken of in Dan. vii. 25, and must be identified with that in Rev. xii. 14. The second is the period noticed in Dan. xii. 7; the two have been erroneously regarded as identical. For the cycle of Dan. xii. 7 is the time which has already intervened between the days of Daniel and the advent of our Lord, and the "breaking in pieces of the power of the holy people" because of their rejection of Jesus as their Messiah. The coming of Messiah and the destruction of Jerusalem are the great events with which the one cycle begins, and with which the other closes. For the Messiah was to appear in the days of the fourth world-monarchy. The two periods combined make up "the seven times," or "the times of the Gentiles, during which the theocracy has ceased to exist on earth."

---

[1] We hope to discuss the questions more fully in our commentary on Daniel, which is to form part of the *Pulpit Commentary* now in course of publication by Messrs. C. Kegan Paul & Co. of London.

The first half of these times may be reckoned from the period when Israel fell under the power of Babylon, or from the close of the seventy years of the Babylonish captivity. The second period (which is not necessarily equal in length to the first) may be reckoned from the day in which Christ was taken up from the midst of His foes, or from that time in which the gospel was finally rejected by the Jewish nation, and when Christ came in the clouds of wrath to execute vengeance upon Jerusalem. Thus the seven times comprehend the period which began when the world-power, represented then by the king of Babylon, was permitted to overwhelm the professed people of God, who were chastened for their sin, but not given over to utter destruction, according to our Lord's words: "This generation shall not pass away, till all things be accomplished" (Luke xxi. 32).

"The times of the Gentiles," during which Israel is trodden down under their feet, reach onward to the end of the world. In the first half of that period "Israel after the flesh" is described sometimes as rescued from, and at other times as falling under, the power of their adversaries. That half closed with the great transgression of Israel predicted by Zechariah, and with Israel's punishment, also set forth by that prophet.[1] All through that chequered period, in which light and darkness were strangely commingled, there existed "a remnant of Israel according to the election of grace" (Rom. xi. 5). These were delivered

---

[1] See *Bampton Lectures on Zechariah*, chaps. x.-xiii.

in every age, and by their instrumentality the nations were prepared for Christ's first advent, and when He came were converted in great numbers from heathenism.

Thus Israel and Israel's Messiah form the two great subjects about which all prophecy speaks. The second half of the seven times peculiarly belongs to the Gentile Church; for Israel does not exist in the second period as a God-ruled nation, protected and upheld by Divine power. On the contrary, that nation is still trodden down and broken in pieces. Israel is not, however, even during that period, to be thought of as excluded from the blessings purchased by Israel's Messiah. But the Church of Christ composed of all nations is represented during that cycle as identical with the true Church of Israel, "Israel after the spirit," and is described as by faith overcoming the world.

But as "Israel after the flesh" ultimately fell away as a nation from God, so the Gentile Church, the Church of the New Testament in its visible form, is represented in the prophecies of the Revelation as entering into an alliance with the world, and becoming apostate like that of Israel. The second period, therefore, of the seven times closes like the first (comp. Isa. i. 21), with the overthrow of an apostate Church, with the downfall of "the great harlot that sitteth upon many waters" (Rev. xvii. 1 ff.), and with the destruction of the spiritual Babylon.

But as at the close of the first part of the seven times salvation was manifested to Israel, and then, through Israel's instrumentality, to the nations; so at the end of the second portion of that great period, "the mystery of God according to the good tidings which He declared to His servants the prophets" shall be finished (Rev. x. 7), "all Israel shall be saved," and the salvation of Israel shall be the salvation of the world (Rom. xi. 12). The history of Nebuchadnezzar was a remarkable shadowing-forth of the history of the world-power; and the "seven times" of the insanity of that king who finally crushed under foot the theocracy, fitly symbolize the seven times of the Gentiles, when the nations in their madness "give their power and authority unto the beast" (Rev. xvii. 13). But at the end of the dispensation, spiritual reason will be restored to the whole human family, and when the long-lost prodigals shall have been brought home, then shall be "heard as it were the voice of a great multitude, and as the voice of many waters, and as the voice of mighty thunders, saying, Hallelujah: for the Lord our God, the Almighty, reigneth" (Rev. xix. 6).

INDEX OF TEXTS ILLUSTRATED OR EXPLAINED.

OLD TESTAMENT.

Genesis.
	PAGE
iii. 14,	8
iii. 15,	226, 234
iv. 26,	11
vi. 2, 4, 8, 9, 10,	178

Exodus.
x. 20,	3
xx. 5, 6,	82

Leviticus.
xvi. 8,	4

Numbers.
xxii. 9,	55
xxiv. 24,	76

Deuteronomy.
iv. 19, 20,	22
xxxiii. 8, 9, 12,	xxii.
xxxiii. 18, 19,	102

Joshua.
v. 13, 14,	172, 242
vi. 2,	172, 242

Judges.
ii. 1–5,	175

2 Samuel.
xii. 1–7,	xxv.
xiv.,	xxv.

1 Kings.
	PAGE
xviii.,	72
xx. 39–41,	xxv.
xxii. 19–22,	xxv., 6, 12, 36

2 Kings.
xiv. 25,	42, 71
xvii. 24–41,	79

Ezra.
iv. 2,	80
iv. 7–16,	79
vi. 21,	80
ix., x.,	xx.

Esther.
viii. 17,	80, 94

Job.
i., ii.,	13 ff.
ix. 15,	22
xiii. 15,	50
xix. 21, 23–26,	27
xxxviii. 7,	8
xxxviii. 28,	9

Psalms.
ii. 9,	216
xix., xxii.,	213
xcv. 5, 6,	50
cx.,	88
cxxvi. 1–3,	64

Canticles.
	PAGE
ii. 3,	87
ii. 4,	97

Isaiah.
vii. 14,	219, 221
vii. 18, 19,	199
viii. 11–13,	148
ix. 6,	219
x. 5, 6,	47
xi. 9,	8
xiv. 12,	239
xviii. 1,	199
xxiv. 21, 22,	167 ff., 239 ff.
xxvii. 1,	52
xxvii. 19,	70
xxix. 10,	48
xxx. 30, 31,	122
xxxiv. 5,	52
xxxv. 1, 2,	9
xxxvi. 18, 19,	47
xlii. 1,	62
xlii. 19,	62
lii., liii.,	63, 64
lv. 12,	9
lxv. 25,	8
lxvi. 7, 8,	64, 217, 221 ff.

Jeremiah.
xiii.,	xxv.
xiv. 13–15,	7
xviii. 7, 8,	82, 100

253

Index of Texts

JEREMIAH—contd.

	PAGE
xxii. 16,	7
xxii. 24,	87
xxv. 15-31,	76
xxxvi. 2, 7,	82
xlviii. 46, 47,	55
xlix. 6,	55
xlix. 39,	55
l. 17,	53
li. 34, 44,	xxiii., 53, 54

LAMENTATIONS.

iv. 20,	86, 87

EZEKIEL.

xiv. 9,	7
xxiii.,	70
xxvii. 26,	47
xxxiii. 8, 13-16,	82
xxxvii. 1-14,	70, 131
xxxviii. 2,	105
xxxviii. 8,	113
xxxix. 11,	126
xxxviii., xxxix.,	113

DANIEL.

	PAGE
ii. 41, 42,	235
vii. 24,	235
vii. 25,	249
viii. 10,	238
x. 13, 21,	241
xi.,	243
xii. 1,	240 ff., 243 ff., 248
xii. 7,	249

HOSEA.

vi. 1, 2,	54, 65, 70
xii. 13,	56

AMOS.

iii. 6,	2
iii. 7,	176

JONAH.

i. 3,	41
i. 17,	53
i. 18,	172
ii.,	54-60

MICAH.

	PAGE
iv. 9, 10,	224
v. 3,	220, 222, 224
vii. 16, 17,	8

HABAKKUK.

i. 12,	30

HAGGAI.

ii. 23,	86, 87

ZECHARIAH.

i. 8-11,	12
i. 12,	242
iii. 1-3,	4, 6, 13, 172, 242
vi. 5,	8
vi. 9-15,	88
ix. 6, 7,	80
ix. 9, 10,	66, 81, 224
x. 10-12,	59
xiv. 16, 17,	81
xiv.,	8

NEW TESTAMENT.

MATTHEW.

iii. 5, 6,	xxiii.
iii. 7,	92
v. 25,	167
xii. 39 ff.,	xxii., xxiii., 37, 69
xxiv.,	123
xxvii. 4,	49
xxvii. 52, 53,	161
xxviii. 30,	10

MARK.

xii. 35,	10
xiii.,	123

LUKE.

ii. 34,	245
iv. 5, 6,	237
vi. 9,	94
x. 18,	239

LUKE—continued.

x. 30,	65, 91
xi. 29, 30, 32,	xxii., 69
xv.	70, xxi.
xv. 1, 2,	92
xx. 16, 35,	10
xxi.,	123, 245
xxi. 32,	250
xxiii. 24,	140
xxiii. 31,	189

JOHN.

iv. 12,	79
viii. 44,	7
x. 16,	98
x. 18,	147
xi. 49-52,	8
xii. 31,	247
xiv. 30,	235

ACTS.

x. 11, 12,	211
xix. 24 ff.,	135
xxii. 21, 22,	96

ROMANS.

iii. 1, 2,	96, 97
ix. 4, 5,	97
viii. 33,	242

1 CORINTHIANS.

v. 3-5,	8
xv. 4,	70
xv. 35-42,	71

GALATIANS.

ii. 11-14,	94
iv. 19,	217

Index of Texts.

GALATIANS—*contd.*

	PAGE
iv. 21-26,	35
iv. 26,	217
iv. 28-31,	35

EPHESIANS.

iv. 10,	65
vi. 12,	168, 211, 247

PHILIPPIANS.

ii. 4,	100
iii. 20,	210

1 THESSALONIANS.

ii. 16,	92

2 THESSALONIANS.

ii. 10-12,	7

1 TIMOTHY.

	PAGE
iii. 16,	149
ii. 4,	100

HEBREWS.

ii. 14,	65, 226
ii. 16,	172
xi. 40,	155
xii. 23, 24,	155

JAMES.

i. 2-4,	33

1 PETER.

i. 11,	176
iv. 6,	183 ff.
iii. 18,	145 ff.

2 PETER.

	PAGE
ii. 4,	167
ii. 9,	182

REVELATION.

xi. 8,	92
xi. 13,	77
xii.,	133, 209
xii. 7-11,	13
xii. 14,	249
xvii.,	209
xvii. 9,	235
xvii. 11,	76
xx. 1-3,	166, 169
xx. 4,	190
xx. 7-10,	166, 169
xxii. 16,	239

GENERAL INDEX.

AEGAR, apocryphal correspondence, 160.
Abraham and his family, 34.
Abraham's sacrifice of Isaac, xi., xii., 34.
Addai, doctrine of, 160.
Adversary. See under *Satan*.
Advocate, the great, 16.
Afflictions, various views of, 18 ff., 32.
Akiba, Rabbi, 50.
Alford, Dean, *Greek Test.* 144, 145, 189, 214.
Allegories in Scripture, xxv.
Allegory and Divine inspiration, 35.
—— change in personification in, 243.
Amittai, 43, 46.
Angels not called sons of God, 8 ff.
—— and fleshly intercourse, 10 ff.
—— not merely phenomenal, 173.
—— Christ as an, 172 ff.
Antediluvian sinners, 178, 182.
Antichrist, kingdom of, weak, 235.
—— a future, a delusion, 248.
Antiochus Epiphanes, 238, 243.
Apocalypse, worthless pamphlets on, 199; new interpretations, 199; not a sealed book, 200; has always comforted Church, 201 ff.; not depicted chronologically, 204; key to, 199–252.
Apocryphal [books of Old Testament, 200.

Apocryphal Gospels, 162. See under *Nicodemus*.
Apostasy of the Church of Israel and of the Church of Christ, 251.
Assurbanipal, 107, 108, 109.
Assyrian inscriptions, xv., 40, 43.
Athanasian Creed, 170.
Auberlen on *Daniel and the Apocalypse*, 208, 221, 230, 238.
Augustine, 68; on descent into Hades, 165, 174.
Azazel, the evil spirit, 4.

BAPTISMAL regeneration taught by Hermas, 154.
Barnabas, Epistle of, 146, 147.
Bede on the Revelation, 214.
Bergmann, *Jonah*, ix., xxvi., 48.
Biesenthal, J. H., *Das Trostschreiben an die Hebräer*, 173.
Bildad, 21 ff.
Birgitta, 203.
Bissell, *Commentary on the Apocrypha*, 200.
Bloch, J. S., *Studien*, xvii., 53.
Blumenbach, 38.
Bochart, 105.
Booth of Jonah, 84, 85, 96.
Böttcher, *Neue Aehrenlese*, 22.
Browne, Bishop Harold, *Thirty-Nine Articles*, 166.

CALVIN, 221.
Chamberlain, Rev. W., *National Restoration and Conversion of Israel*, 101, 111, 119.
Chebar, 111.

Cheyne, T. K., on *Jonah*, xv., xvii., xviii., xix., xx. *The Prophecies of Isaiah*, xii., 168, 220, 222.
Christ, descent of, into Hades productive of blessing, 140, 160, 162; texts referring to descent, 151; no tradition of His preaching to antediluvians or heathen, 114 ff.; preached as Pre-incarnate Logos, 170 ff., 181-183; neither a concio damnatoria nor evangelica, 194; spirit or pneuma of, 170 ff., 186; quickened in the spirit, 145 ff.; sufferings, 150; as Angel, 172 ff.; temptation of, 225; His coming spoken of in connection with various deliverances, 244; first advent a time of trouble, 241; two advents spoken of as one, 246; His prophecy of the latter days, 123, 245; Christ mystical, 217. See under *Messiah*.
Church, represented as a woman, 209. See under *Woman*. Mission of, 209; early contests of Jews and Gentiles in the Christian, 92 ff.
Churton, W. R., *Apocryphal Scriptures*, 200.
Circumcision, disputes about, 94.
Clement of Alexandria (*Stromata*), 155-158, 164, 179.
Clement of Rome, Epistle of, 176.
Coming struggle, the, 104.
Conditional character of denunciations, 82.
Conditional immortality, 196.
Confusion, Heaven-sent, 122.
Constantine, 215, 227.
Cowper, B. H., *Apocryphal Gospels*, 162.
Cox, Dr. S., on *Job*, viii.
Crimean War, 117.
Cyril of Alexandria, 40.

DANTE, 196.
Davidic throne, the, 89.
Davidson, Rev. Dr. A. B., on *Job*, viii., 4, 5, 25, 27, 29, 31.

Davidson, Dr. S., *Introduction to Old Testament*, xxiv.
Daysman or mediator, 23.
Dead, prayers for the, 142, 192.
—— the gospel preached to, 191 ff. See *Hermas*.
Delitzsch, Prof. Dr. Franz, *Commentary on Psalms*, 217; on *Job*, viii.; on *Isaiah*, 167, 219, 220, 222, 223, 240; *Biblical Psychology*, 171, 174.
Delitzsch, Prof. Dr. Friedr., *Paradies*, 107, 110, 111.
Divine denunciations, conditional character of, 82.
Dorner, Prof. J. A., 138.
Dove, symbol of the, 45 ff., 64.
Dragon, the, 212, 216, 224; attempts of, to destroy Christ, 224, 234, 237.
Düsterdieck, Dr. F., on *Die Offenbarung*, 208, 214, 222, 224, 226, 234.

EARTHQUAKES, 122.
Ebrard on the *Apocalypse*, 214, 231, 234, 238, 248.
Elihu, 29.
Elijah, 42, 72.
Eliphaz, 19 ff.
Elisha, 42, 44.
Elliot, E. B., *Horæ Apocalypticæ*, 227.
Enoch, apocryphal book of, 168, 200.
Eusebius, *Hist. Eccl.*, 159.
Evangelical preachers on "second death," 196.
Ewald, viii., xv., 106, 221.
Exiles, songs of the, 61.

FABER, G. S., *Sacred Calendar of Prophecy*, 228.
Fabricius, *Fauna Grönlandica*, 37.
Farrar, Archdeacon, *Early Days of Christianity*, 231, 232.
Feast for birds and beasts, 124.
Fishes, great, 37 ff.
Fleming, Rev. John, on *Fallen Angels*, 10, 11.
Frederichsen, *Krit. Uebersicht*, 39.

GAMIR, 108.
Gentiles, times of the, 250.
—— willing to learn religion from Israel, 78; unwillingness of early Christians to preach gospel to, 92.
German critical school, xviii.
Gesenius, *Thesaurus*, 22, 105; *Lex. Man.*, 22, 141.
Gimir, 108, 109, 111.
Glassius, *Philog. Sacra*, 119.
Gog and Magog, 104; Gugu and Gagi, 107 ff.; prophecies about, to be fulfilled in latter days, 113; were not designed to be understood literally, 113; scene ideally laid in Palestine, 114; not confined to that land, 114; the theme of all the prophets, 114 ff.; Gog in hands of Providence, 116; confederacy of, not an attempt to extirpate worship of Jehovah, 117; caused by desire of filthy lucre, 118 ff.; mode of destruction of, 120 ff.; the feast for birds and beasts, 124; spoil of foe, 125; weapons used by his army, 125; place of sepulture, 126; burial of, 128 ff.; exaltation of, compared to that of Pharaoh, 130; denotes no special foe, 131; does not refer to Russia, 105, 106.
Gourd of Jonah, 85, 89.
Greed for gain, 118 ff., 134.

HADES, the unseen world, 65, 141; Clement on the gospel preached in, 155 ff.; prison in, 166 ff.
Hailstones, 121; Sennacherib's army partly overthrown by, 122.
Hamburger, *Real-Encyclopädie*, 50.
Hamon Gog, 127 ff.
Hamonah, 129.
Hardt, von der, 53.
Harnack on the *Didachē*, 154.
Heard, *Tripartite Nature of Man*, 171, 174.
Hengstenberg, *Christology*, 240, 242, 243.

Hercules and Hesione, 41.
Hermas, *The Shepherd* of, 152, 153, 154, 155, 156, 157.
Herodian tabernacle, the, 96.
Hippolytus, 203.
Hitzig, 221.
Hofmann, Prof. J. K. C. von, *Weissagung und Erfüllung*, and *Schriftbeweis*, 194, 229, 231, 238, 240; on Michael, 230 ff.
Horsley, Bishop, 143, 144, 166.
Human sacrifices, xii.
Hurd, Bishop, *Warburtonian Lectures*, 206.
Huss, 203.
Huther, in Meyer's *Comm.*, 146, 185, 186, 187, 192.
Huxtable, Comm. on *Jonah*, in *Speaker's Commentary*, xi., xv., xxii., 54.

IDOLATRY, sin of, 61.
Inspiration, 35.
Intermarriages of Israelites and Gentiles, xx., 79.
—— of angels and men, 9 ff.
Interrogative sentences, 114, 119.
Irenæus, 159.
Israel, mission of, 46; represented fitly by a prophet, 50, 55; songs in exile, 61, 64; the only nation elected, 100. See under *Jonah*. Restoration of, 136; great subject of prophecy, 251. "after the flesh" and "after the spirit," 251. Anglo-Saxon race not Israel, 102. Name of Israel not confined to ten tribes, 77. See under *Messiah*.
Ivan and Javan, 111.

JALKUT JONAH, 59.
Javan, 111.
Jehu, 43.
Jeroboam II., 42, 43.
Jerome, 67.
Jesus the son of Anan, 68.
Jews, hostility of, to Christianity, 95.
Joachim, Abbot, 203.

Job, trials of, 12 ff. ; and his friends, 18 ff.
Jonah. See Contents, p. xxix. ; sign of, xxiv., 69 ; booth of, 84, 85, 96 ; gourd of, 85 ; perished in a night, 89 ; book of, 34 ff. ; not confirmed by Assyrian inscriptions, ix., 40 ; mission of, 71, 72 ; sullenness of, 93.
Josephus, 68, 71.
Judgment in the gospel, declaration of, 91.
Jurieu, *on the Revelation*, 204.
Justin Martyr, 158, 162.

KALISCH, *Biblical Studies on Jonah*, 38, 40, 41, 44, 48, 54, 58, 59, 60, 68, 73.
Kaulen on *Jonah*, 53, 54, 67, 72.
Keil, 221, 238.
Kennedy's edition of Ewald's *Syntax*, 106.
Khorsabad, 39.
Kleinert on *Jonah*, 53, 54.
Kliefoth, 234.
Kranichfeld on *Daniel*, 238, 243.
Kuenen, *Religion of Israel*, xx.

LANGE's *Bibelwerk*, 53, 215.
Larger hope, the, 142, 195.
Latter days or years, 113. Our Lord's prophecy of the latter days, 123.
Layard's *Nineveh and Babylon*, 68.
Lee, F. G., on *Prayer for Departed*, 142.
Lee, Dr. S., on *Job*, 12.
Leviathan, 52.
Lightfoot, Bishop, on *the Galatians*, 154.
Limbus Patrum, 194.
Lions, slave-traders compared to, 118 ff.
Lipsius, *Abgarsage*, 160.
Luckock's *After Death*, 142.
Ludicrous and grotesque element in Book of Jonah, x., xi., xiv.
Lycophron, 41.

MAMMON, worship of, 135.

Man-child, the, of the Revelation, 211, 216–223.
Man-child, the, of Isaiah, 221, 222.
Mede, Joseph, 206, 207.
Merx, viii.
Meshach not Moscow, 104, 109, 110.
Messiah a shepherd, 216 ; as son of the Church, 218 ff. ; pains of, 219 ; great subject of prophecy, 251 ; identified with Michael, 242, 245 ; sufferings and glory presented in one picture, 133. Messiah and Israel, 63, 64, 65 ; incidents of their history alike, 70. See under *Christ*.
Michael the archangel, 230 ; the prince of Israel, 240 ff. ; identified with Messiah, 242, 245.
Michaiah, vision of, xviii., 6, 12, 36.
Midrash, 46.
Milton, 196, 238.
Minutius Felix, 196.
Moon under woman's feet, the, 214.
Mühlau and Volck's edition of Gesenius' *Lex.*, 141.
Müller, *Natursystem*, 37.
Mushki, 109, 112.

NÄGELSBACH on *Isaiah*, 222.
Nations disposed to think well of themselves, 99. No nations necessarily foredoomed, 100. Israel the only nation specially elected, 100. Shaking of the nations, 78.
Nebuchadnezzar's penitence, 78, 83.
Nero and his name, 233.
Newton, Sir I., 226, 227.
Nicodemus, the Gospel of, 161, 162, 163.
Nineveh, greatness of, 39 ; warning to, 68, 69, 76, 91, 92.
Ninevites, the repentance of, xxii., 67, 72, 73, 81, 84.
Noah and his preaching, 145 ; Augustine on, 165, 174 ff.
Noldius, *Concord. Particularum*, 119.

OTTO, von, *Justin Martyr*, 159.

PALMCHRIST of Jonah. See under *Gourd*.
Parousia, The, 206, 231, 233.
Passengers of Ezekiel, the, 128.
Penitence. See *Repentance*.
Perowne, Archdeacon, on *Jonah*, 54.
Perseus and Andromeda, 41.
Pestilence and blood, 120.
Pharaoh and Gog compared, exaltation of, 130.
Phillips, Rev. Dr., *Doctrine of Addai*, 160.
Pit and prison, 168.
Plumptre, Dean, *Spirits in Prison*, 138 ff.
Preaching, meaning of New Testament term κηρύσσειν, 178.
Pre-incarnate Logos, the, 170.
Prison in Hades (φυλακή), meaning of, 166 ff.
Prodigal son, parable of, xxi., 32, 73, 96, 97.
Promises stayed, fulfilment of, 136.
Prophecy not history written in advance, 202; theory of "breaks" in, 132, 248; pretended expositions of, 117, 120.
Prophetico-allegorical history, 69, 90.
Prophets accused of unpatriotism, 51; voices of the prophets against the nations, 74 ff.; representatives of Israel, 55; false prophets, 7, 48.
Purgatory, 142.
Pusey on *The Minor Prophets*, x., xi., xii., 37, 38, 40, 41, 54, 60, 61, 68, 85.

QUICKENED in the spirit, 144 ff., 190 ff.; meaning of ζωοποιέω, 146. See under *Christ*.

RASH, land of, 106, 107.
Red Sea, passage of, 59; weedy sea, 58.
Redford's *Studies in Jonah*, ix. ff.

Regeneration of the world, 133; baptismal regeneration taught by Hermas, 154.
Repentance, no, exhibited by Jonah, 61; of Ninevites—see *Ninevites*; of Nebuchadnezzar, 78, 83; of Gentiles, 80 ff.
Resurrection, the, 27, 71; in the Book of Daniel, 246; in Ezekiel only allegorical, 70.
Reuss, *Gesch. d. A. T.*, xxiii.
Revelation, the Book of. See under *Apocalypse*.
Rondelet, 38.
Rosh not Russia, 105 ff.
Russian Empire, Napoleon on, 103.

SALMON, Rev. Prof., *Hist. Introd. to New Testament*, 234.
Salmond, Rev. Prof., 143.
Samaritans, the, 79, 80.
Satan in *Job*, 3 ff.; not a mere minister of God's suffering providence, 14; the Adversary, 12 ff.; challenge of, 14; trials inflicted on Job by, 15 ff. See under *Dragon*.
Schott, 166.
Schrader, Prof., *Keilinschriften*, 40, 43, 107, 110, 111.
Schweizer, Prof. A., on *The Descent into Hell*, 143, 146, 179, 185, 186.
Scythian invasions, 106, 107, 108, 109, 112.
Sea monster, 52.
Seals, the six first, 204 ff.
Sennacherib's overthrow, 122, 125.
Seven Times, the, 133, 248 ff.
Shark, stories of the, 37 ff.
Sheol, the Under-world, 65, 141.
Shepherd of Hermas, the, 152 ff.
Sheshbazzar. See *Zerubbabel*.
Signet ring, the, 87.
Silence of Scripture, xiv., 71, 72.
Slave traders described as young lions, 118 ff.
Smend, *Comm. on Ezekiel*, 106.
Smith, G., *Hist. of Assurbanipal*, 107.
Socrates, 141.
Sons of God not angels, 8 ff.

Spirit, quickened in the, 141 ff. See under *Christ*.
Spirits in prison, 138 ff., 177 ff.
Suffering for well-doing, 148.
Sword of Jehovah, 52, 62.

Tabali, land of, 109, 111.
Targum, 44, 58.
Tarshish not the maritime power of England, 120; merchants of, 118 ff.
Ten horns and ten toes, the, 235 ff.
Tertullian, 196.
Thaddæus, summary of faith, 160.
Thomsen, Prof. V., *Russia and Scandinavia*, 106.
Three, the number, 54, 65, 70, 91.
Time, times and a half, the, 134, 248 ff.
Tischendorf, *Evang. Apoc.*, 161, 162.
Togarmah, 110.
Tophet, place of burial, 125.
Twelve hundred and sixty days, 240.
Two, the number, 54; legs of the Colossus, 236.

Universal restitution, 196.

Vaughan, Dean, *Lectures on the Revelation*, 214.
Victorinus, 203.
Vitringa, 207, 221.

Waldenses, 203.
War in heaven, 238 ff., 247 ff.
Weapons of war, 125.
Weiss, 194.
Whale of Jonah, the, 36.
Wickliffe, 203.
Wiesinger, 166, 194.
Wolff, Rev. Dr. J., *Researches and Missionary Labours*, 111.
Woman, the chaste and unchaste, in the Apocalypse, 209; clothed with sun, 212; with moon under her feet, 214; diadem of stars, 215; in heaven, 210; in travail, 211.
Wright, C. H. H., *Bampton Lectures on Zechariah*, 13, 59, 65, 77, 79, 80, 81, 87, 88, 121, 152, 236, 250; *Donnellan Lectures on Koheleth*, 90; Miscellaneous articles, xii., 111, 139.
Wright, G. H. B., on *Job*, viii.
Wünsche, Dr. A., *Die Leiden des Messias*, 219.

Zahn, Prof. Th., *Apocalyptische Studien*, 200, 233.
Zerubbabel, hopes excited by his governorship, 86; identical with Sheshbazzar, 86; not crowned by Zechariah, 88; early death and removal, 89.
Zezschwitz, Prof. von, 178, 194.
Zophar, 23 ff.

T. and T. Clark's Publications.

Just published, in Two Vols., 8vo, price 21s.,

NATURE AND THE BIBLE:

LECTURES ON THE MOSAIC HISTORY OF CREATION IN ITS RELATION TO NATURAL SCIENCE.

By Dr. FR. H. REUSCH.

REVISED AND CORRECTED BY THE AUTHOR.

Translated from the Fourth Edition

By KATHLEEN LYTTELTON.

'Other champions much more competent and learned than myself might have been placed in the field; I will only name one of the most recent, Dr. Reusch, author of "Nature and the Bible."'—The Right Hon. W. E. GLADSTONE.

Will shortly be published, in demy 8vo,

THE JEWISH
AND
THE CHRISTIAN MESSIAH.

A STUDY IN THE EARLIEST HISTORY OF CHRISTIANITY.

By VINCENT HENRY STANTON, M.A.,

FELLOW, TUTOR, AND DIVINITY LECTURER OF TRINITY COLLEGE, CAMBRIDGE; LATE HULSEAN LECTURER.

Recently published, in crown 8vo, price 5s.,

EXEGETICAL STUDIES.

By PATON J. GLOAG, D.D.

'Careful and valuable pieces of work.'—*Spectator.*
'A very interesting volume.'—*Literary Churchman.*
'Dr. Gloag handles his subjects very ably, displaying everywhere accurate and extensive scholarship, and a fine appreciation of the lines of thought in those passages with which he deals.'—*Baptist.*
'Candid, truth-loving, devout-minded men will be both instructed and pleased by studies so scholarly, frank, and practical.'—*Baptist Magazine.*

T. and T. Clark's Publications.

CREMER'S LEXICON.

Just published, in demy 4to, price 14s.,

SUPPLEMENT
TO
BIBLICO-THEOLOGICAL LEXICON
OF
NEW TESTAMENT GREEK.

BY

HERMANN CREMER, D.D.

Translated and Arranged from the latest German Edition

BY

WILLIAM URWICK, M.A.

The Complete Work, including Supplement, is now issued at 38s.

GRIMM'S LEXICON.

Will shortly be published, in demy 4to,

A GREEK-ENGLISH LEXICON
OF THE
NEW TESTAMENT.

BEING GRIMM'S 'WILKE'S CLAVIS NOVI TESTAMENTI.'

Translated, Revised, and Enlarged

BY

JOSEPH HENRY THAYER, D.D.,

BUSSEY PROFESSOR OF NEW TESTAMENT CRITICISM AND INTERPRETATION
IN THE DIVINITY SCHOOL OF HARVARD UNIVERSITY.

T. and T. Clark's Publications.

Just published, in demy 8vo, price 12s.,

AN INTRODUCTION TO THEOLOGY:
ITS PRINCIPLES, ITS BRANCHES, ITS RESULTS, AND ITS LITERATURE.

By ALFRED CAVE, B.A.,
PRINCIPAL, AND PROFESSOR OF THEOLOGY, OF HACKNEY COLLEGE, LONDON.

'We can most heartily recommend this work to students of every degree of attainment, and not only to those who will have the opportunity of utilizing its aid in the most sacred of the professions, but to all who desire to encourage and systematize their knowledge and clarify their views of Divine things.'—*Nonconformist and English Independent.*

Just published, in crown 8vo, price 4s. 6d.,

THE BIBLE
AN OUTGROWTH OF THEOCRATIC LIFE.

By D. W. SIMON,
PRINCIPAL OF THE CONGREGATIONAL COLLEGE, EDINBURGH.

'A book of absorbing interest, and well worthy of study.'—*Methodist New Connexion Magazine.*

Just published, in crown 8vo, price 3s. 6d.,

THE RELIGIOUS HISTORY OF ISRAEL.
A DISCUSSION OF THE CHIEF PROBLEMS IN OLD TESTAMENT HISTORY, AS OPPOSED TO THE DEVELOPMENT THEORISTS.

By Dr. FRIEDRICH EDUARD KÖNIG,
THE UNIVERSITY, LEIPZIG.

TRANSLATED BY REV. ALEXANDER J. CAMPBELL, M.A.

'An admirable little volume. . . . By sincere and earnest-minded students it will be cordially welcomed.'—*Freeman.*
'Every page of the book deserves study.'—*Church Bells.*

Just published, in crown 8vo, price 6s.,

NEW TESTAMENT TEACHING IN PASTORAL THEOLOGY.

By J. T. BECK, D.D.,
PROF. ORD. THEOL., TÜBINGEN.

EDITED BY PROFESSOR B. RIGGENBACH.

TRANSLATED BY REV. JAS. M'CLYMONT, B.D., AND REV. THOS. NICOL, B.D.

'The volume contains much which any thoughtful and earnest Christian minister will find helpful and suggestive to him for the wise and efficient discharge of his sacred functions.'—*Literary World.*

T. and T. Clark's Publications.

PROFESSOR GODET'S WORKS.

In Three Volumes, 8vo, price 31s. 6d.,

A COMMENTARY ON THE GOSPEL OF ST. JOHN.

By F. GODET, D.D.,
PROFESSOR OF THEOLOGY, NEUCHATEL.

'This work forms one of the battle-fields of modern inquiry, and is itself so rich in spiritual truth, that it is impossible to examine it too closely; and we welcome this treatise from the pen of Dr. Godet. We have no more competent exegete; and this new volume shows all the learning and vivacity for which the author is distinguished.'—*Freeman.*

In Two Volumes, 8vo, price 21s.,

A COMMENTARY ON THE GOSPEL OF ST. LUKE.

TRANSLATED FROM THE SECOND FRENCH EDITION.

'Marked by clearness and good sense, it will be found to possess value and interest as one of the most recent and copious works specially designed to illustrate this Gospel.'—*Guardian.*

In Two Volumes, 8vo, price 21s.,

A COMMENTARY ON ST. PAUL'S EPISTLE TO THE ROMANS.

'We prefer this commentary to any other we have seen on the subject. . . . We have great pleasure in recommending it as not only rendering invaluable aid in the critical study of the text, but affording practical and deeply suggestive assistance in the exposition of the doctrine.'—*British and Foreign Evangelical Review.*

'Here indeed we have rare spiritual insight and sanctified scholarship.'—*Weekly Review.*

Just published, in crown 8vo, price 6s.,

DEFENCE OF THE CHRISTIAN FAITH.

TRANSLATED BY THE HON. AND REV. CANON LYTTELTON, M.A., RECTOR OF HAGLEY.

'There is trenchant argument and resistless logic in these lectures; but withal, there is cultured imagination and felicitous eloquence, which carry home the appeals to the heart as well as the head.'—*Sword and Trowel.*

LOTZE'S MICROCOSMUS.

Just published, in Two Vols., 8vo (1450 pages), price 36s.,

MICROCOSMUS:
CONCERNING MAN AND HIS RELATION TO THE WORLD.
By HERMANN LOTZE.

CONTENTS:—Book I. The Body. II. The Soul. III. Life. IV. Man. V. Mind. VI. The Microcosmic Order; or, The Course of Human Life. VII. History. VIII. Progress. IX. The Unity of Things.

'These are indeed two masterly volumes, vigorous in intellectual power, and translated with rare ability. . . . This work will doubtless find a place on the shelves of all the foremost thinkers and students of modern times.'—*Evangelical Magazine.*

Just published, in ex. 8vo, price 9s.,

THE OLDEST CHURCH MANUAL
CALLED THE
Teaching of the Twelve Apostles.

The Didachè and Kindred Documents in the Original, with Translations and Discussions of Post-Apostolic Teaching, Baptism, Worship, and Discipline, and with Illustrations and Fac-Similes of the Jerusalem Manuscript.

By PHILIP SCHAFF, D.D., LL.D.

'This is *par excellence* the edition to possess.'—*Freeman.*

'This is by far the most complete *apparatus criticus* for the study of that interesting and important document.'—*British Quarterly Review.*

Just published, in One Vol., 8vo (640 pp.), price 15s.,

HISTORY OF THE SACRED SCRIPTURES OF THE NEW TESTAMENT.

By Professor E. REUSS, D.D.

Translated from the Fifth Revised and Enlarged Edition.

'One of the most valuable of Messrs. Clark's valuable publications. . . . Its usefulness is attested by undiminished vitality. . . . His method is admirable, and he unites German exhaustiveness with French lucidity and brilliancy of expression. . . . The sketch of the great exegetic epochs, their chief characteristics, and the critical estimates of the most eminent writers, is given by the author with a compression and a mastery that have never been surpassed.'—Archdeacon FARRAR.

T. and T. Clark's Publications.

HISTORY OF THE CHRISTIAN CHURCH.

By PHILIP SCHAFF, D.D., LL.D.

A New Edition thoroughly Revised and Enlarged.

Now Ready,

APOSTOLIC CHRISTIANITY, A.D. 1-100. In Two Vols. ex. demy 8vo, price 21s.

ANTE-NICENE CHRISTIANITY, A.D. 100–311. In Two Vols. ex. demy 8vo, price 21s.

NICENE AND POST-NICENE CHRISTIANITY, A.D. 311–600. In Two Vols. ex. demy 8vo, price 21s.

MEDIÆVAL CHRISTIANITY, A.D. 590–1073. In Two Vols. ex. 8vo, price 21s.

'For a genuine healthy Christian criticism, which boldly faces difficulties, and examines them with equal candour and learning, we commend this work to all who are interested in investigating the early growth of the Christian Church.'—*Church Quarterly Review.*

'These volumes cannot fail to prove welcome to all students.'—*Freeman.*

'No student, and indeed no critic, can with fairness overlook a work like the present, written with such evident candour, and, at the same time, with so thorough a knowledge of the sources of early Christian history.'—*Scotsman.*

In Three Volumes, demy 8vo, price 12s. each,

A HISTORY OF THE COUNCILS OF THE CHURCH.

FROM THE ORIGINAL DOCUMENTS.

TRANSLATED FROM THE GERMAN OF

C. J. HEFELE, D.D., BISHOP OF ROTTENBURG.

VOL. I. (*Second Edition*) TO A.D. 325.
BY REV. PREBENDARY CLARK.

VOL. II. A.D. 326 TO 429.
BY H. N. OXENHAM, M.A.

VOL. III. A.D. 429 TO THE CLOSE OF THE COUNCIL OF CHALCEDON.

'This careful translation of Hefele's Councils.'—Dr. PUSEY.

'A thorough and fair compendium, put in a most accessible and intelligent form.'—*Guardian.*

'A work of profound erudition, and written in a most candid spirit. The book will be a standard work on the subject.'—*Spectator.*

'The most learned historian of the Councils.'—*Père Gratry.*

'We cordially commend Hefele's Councils to the English student.'—*John Bull.*

T. and T. Clark's Publications.

In crown 8vo, price 6s.,

THE INCARNATE SAVIOUR:
A LIFE OF JESUS CHRIST.

BY REV. W. R. NICOLL, M.A.

'It commands my warm sympathy and admiration. I rejoice in the circulation of such a book, which I trust will be the widest possible.'—Canon LIDDON.

'There was quite room for such a volume. It contains a great deal of thought, often penetrating and always delicate, and pleasingly expressed. The subject has been very carefully studied, and the treatment will, I believe, furnish much suggestive matter both to readers and preachers.'—Rev. Principal SANDAY.

In crown 8vo, Eighth Edition, price 7s. 6d.,

THE SUFFERING SAVIOUR;
OR, MEDITATIONS ON THE LAST DAYS OF THE SUFFERINGS OF CHRIST.

BY F. W. KRUMMACHER, D.D.

'The work bears throughout the stamp of an enlightened intellect under the teaching of the Holy Spirit, and of a profound study of the Word of God.'—*Record*.

'The reflections are of a pointed and practical character, and are eminently calculated to inform the mind and improve the heart. To the devout and earnest Christian the volume will be a treasure indeed.'—*Wesleyan Times*.

BY THE SAME AUTHOR.

In crown 8vo, Second Edition, price 7s. 6d.,

DAVID, THE KING OF ISRAEL:
A PORTRAIT DRAWN FROM BIBLE HISTORY AND THE BOOK OF PSALMS.

At the close of two articles reviewing this work, the *Christian Observer* says: 'Our space will not permit us to consider more at large this very interesting work, but we cannot do less than cordially commend it to the attention of our readers. It affords such an insight into King David's character as is nowhere else to be met with; it is therefore most instructive.'

In demy 8vo, price 7s. 6d.,

SERMONS TO THE NATURAL MAN.

BY WILLIAM G. T. SHEDD, D.D.,
AUTHOR OF 'A HISTORY OF CHRISTIAN DOCTRINE,' ETC.

'Characterized by profound knowledge of divine truth, and presenting the truth in a chaste and attractive style, the sermons carry in their tone the accents of the solemn feeling of responsibility to which they owe their origin.'—*Weekly Review*.

T. and T. Clark's Publications.

In crown 8vo, price 6s.,

SERMONS FOR THE CHRISTIAN YEAR.
ADVENT—TRINITY.
By Professor ROTHE.

'The volume is rich in noble thoughts and wholesome lessons.'—*Watchman.*

'The sermons before us are wonderfully simple in construction and expression, and at the same time remarkably fresh and suggestive. . . . It is a mind of real keenness, singularly pure and gentle, and of lofty spirituality, that expresses itself in these discourses.'—*Weekly Review.*

In Two Volumes, large crown 8vo, price 7s. 6d. each,

THE YEAR OF SALVATION:
WORDS OF LIFE FOR EVERY DAY.
A BOOK OF HOUSEHOLD DEVOTION.
By J. J. van OOSTERZEE, D.D.

'This charming and practical book of household devotion will be welcomed on account of its rare intrinsic value, as one of the most practical devotional books ever published.'—*Standard.*

BY THE SAME AUTHOR.
In crown 8vo, price 6s.,

MOSES: A BIBLICAL STUDY.

'Our author has seized, as with the instinct of a master, the great salient points in the life and work of Moses, and portrayed the various elements of his character with vividness and skill. . . . The work will at once take its place among our ablest and most valuable expository and practical discourses.'—*Baptist Magazine.*

In crown 8vo, price 4s. 6d.,

THE WORLD OF PRAYER;
OR, PRAYER IN RELATION TO PERSONAL RELIGION.
By Bishop MONRAD.

'English readers are greatly indebted to Mr. Banks for his translation of this work: he has rendered available to them a book of devotional reading which admirably combines the truest Christian mysticism with the soundest and healthiest practical teaching.'—*London Quarterly Review.*

'One of the richest devotional books that we have read.'—*Primitive Methodist Magazine.*

In One Volume, crown 8vo, price 5s., Third Edition,

LIGHT FROM THE CROSS:
SERMONS ON THE PASSION OF OUR LORD.
Translated from the German of A. THOLUCK, D.D.,
Professor of Theology in the University of Halle.

'With no ordinary confidence and pleasure, we commend these most noble, solemnizing, and touching discourses.'—*British and Foreign Evangelical Review.*

T. and T. Clark's Publications.

In demy 8vo, price 9s.,

A POPULAR INTRODUCTION
TO THE
HISTORY OF CHRISTIAN DOCTRINE.
By Rev. T. G. CRIPPEN.

'In every respect excellent. . . . The information is so clear in statement that the volume cannot fail to be acceptable and useful in no ordinary degree.'—*British and Foreign Evangelical Review.*

'The essence of a whole library is included in Mr. Crippen's work. . . . It is a scholarly work, and must have entailed an incalculable amount of research and discrimination.'—*Clergyman's Magazine.*

'If this book can be made known widely, we feel satisfied that it will be as widely used and valued. It is easy for reference, and the Appendices contain most valuable summaries of exceedingly important matters. The whole scope of Christian doctrine is more or less covered by this compendious history.'—*Christian World.*

In crown 8vo, price 6s.,

STUDIES IN THE CHRISTIAN EVIDENCES.
By ALEXANDER MAIR, D.D.

'Dr. Mair writes as one who has fully assimilated the various elements which enter into the category of Christian Evidences; and he has presented them in these pages with an order and accuracy, and a clearness, rising at times into a sober and chastened eloquence, which will make the work one of the highest value to the student.'—*Literary Churchman.*

'An admirable popular introduction to the study of the evidences.'—*Baptist.*

'Dr. Mair's work is one of the most useful for its purpose of any we have seen.'—*Church Bells.*

'One of the very best works we have perused on the subjects therein treated.'—*Evangelical Magazine.*

In demy 8vo, price 10s. 6d.,

THE LORD'S PRAYER:
A PRACTICAL MEDITATION.
By NEWMAN HALL, LL.B.

'A new volume of theological literature by the Rev. Newman Hall is sure to be eagerly welcomed, and we can promise its readers that they will not be disappointed. . . . A very able and suggestive volume.'—*Nonconformist.*

'This work will prove a help to many. Its devotional element is robust and practical.'—*Churchman.*

'Mr. Hall's thoughts are sharply cut, and are like crystals in their clearness. . . . Short, crisp sentences, absolute in form and lucid in thought, convey the author's meaning and carry on his exposition.'—*British Quarterly Review.*

'We heartily commend this able as well as earnest, exegetical as well as spiritual, volume to all our readers.'—*Evangelical Magazine.*

Just published, in crown 8vo, price 6s.,

OLD AND NEW THEOLOGY:
A CONSTRUCTIVE CRITIQUE.

By Rev. J. B. HEARD, M.A.

'We can promise all real students of Holy Scripture who have found their way out of some of the worst of the scholastic byelanes and ruts, and are striving to reach the broad and firm high road that leads to the Eternal City, a real treat from the perusal of these pages. Progressive theologians, who desire to find "the old in the new, and the new in the old," will be deeply grateful to Mr. Heard for this courageous and able work.'—*Christian World.*

'Among the many excellent theological works, whether English or German, published by Messrs. Clark, there are few that deserve more careful study than this book. . . . It cannot fail to charm by its grace of style, and to supply food for solid thought.'—*Dublin Express.*

BY THE SAME AUTHOR.

Fifth Edition, in crown 8vo, price 6s.,

THE TRIPARTITE NATURE OF MAN:
SPIRIT, SOUL, AND BODY.

Applied to Illustrate and Explain the Doctrines of Original Sin, the New Birth, the Disembodied State, and the Spiritual Body.

'The author has got a striking and consistent theory. Whether agreeing or disagreeing with that theory, it is a book which any student of the Bible may read with pleasure.'—*Guardian.*

'An elaborate, ingenious, and very able book.'—*London Quarterly Review.*

Just published, in demy 8vo, price 9s.,

THE DOCTRINE OF THE HOLY SPIRIT.
(The Ninth Series of the Cunningham Lectures.)

By GEORGE SMEATON, D.D.,
Professor of Exegetical Theology, New College, Edinburgh.

'The theological student will be benefited by a careful perusal of this survey, and that not for the moment, but through all his future life.'—*Watchman.*

'Very cordially do we commend these able and timely lectures to the notice of our readers. Every theological student should master them.'—*Baptist Magazine.*

'It is a pleasure to meet with a work like this. . . . Our brief account, we trust, will induce the desire to study this work.'—*Dickinson's Theological Quarterly.*

www.ingramcontent.com/pod-product-compliance
Lightning Source LLC
Chambersburg PA
CBHW030817230426
43667CB00008B/1261